Lions of the Faith

Lions of the Faith

Saints, Blesseds, and Heroes of the Catholic Faith in the Struggle with Islam

Andrew Bieszad
Lux Orbis Press
2013

Lions of the Faith © by Lux Orbis Press. 2013.

ISBN-13: 978-0-9888768-0-4

All rights reserved. No portion of this book may be published, reprinted, or altered in any form without the publisher's consent.

There are places where this book may be difficult to access. In the spirit of promoting knowledge, persons interested in seeking to reprint with permission at cost or freely distribute this book are asked to contact Lux Orbis Press in order to seek a waiver to do so. In all cases, neither the author nor the publisher accept responsibility for any consequences that may directly or indirectly arise from reprinting with permission or distributing this book in any form and in any place.

Lux Orbis Press
inquiries@luxorbispress.com
http://www.lionsofthefaith.com

Cover Artwork assembled by author. Lion image provided by Sodacan, and was created on April 13th, 2009. Jerusalem Cross provided by Odejea, and was created on April 21st, 2008. Both images are respectively licensed under the Creative Commons Attribution-Share Alike 3.0 Unported License and 2.5 Unported License as uploaded on and sourced from http://www.wikipedia.com under the articles Lion (heraldry) and Jerusalem cross.

Table of Contents

Acknowledgments i

Dedication iii

A Note About Organization v

Preface vii

Introduction 1

Section I: The Rise of Islam 3
    The Years that Changed History 5
    The Islamic Invasion of Europe 21
    The Church in the Muslim World 33
    The Troubled 9th and 10th Centuries 49
    The Eve of the Crusades 71

Section II: The Crusades 79
    The Crusades Begin 81
    First Crusade 83
    Second Crusade 91

Table of Contents, continued

    The Military Orders of the Crusades 109

    Third Crusade 125

    Later Crusades 135

Section III: The Expansion 175

    The Expansion Begins 177

    The Rise of the Ottomans 179

    Generations of Fame and Infamy 195

    Chivalric Orders of the Period 215

    Endings and Beginnings 219

Section IV: Modern Times 261

    A Church Between Worlds 263

    Nothing has Changed 283

A Final Thought 291

Works Cited 293

Appendices 363

    Appendix A: List of Feast Days 365

    Appendix B: The Pact of 'Umar 385

    Appendix C: The Treaty of Tudmir 391

Table of Contents, continued

Appendix D: 395

Appendix E: 1504 Fatwa to the Moriscos 403

Appendix F: Sultan Murad III's Letter 407

Index 415

Endnotes 427

Acknowledgments

I would like to thank my wife, family, and friends for their help and support. Their contributions in time, resources, and patience were invaluable.

My appreciation also extends to the many libraries and organizations in collaboration with Google® books who invested time and efforts to make rare books available to the public online. Thanks are in particular order to the ones I visited in person and in which I spent considerable time doing research. They are the Hartford Seminary Library, the Holy Apostles College and Seminary Library, the Olin Library at Wesleyan University, the Paul E. Raether Library at Trinity College, and the Divinity and Sterling Memorial Libraries at Yale University.

Thanks are also due to the many persons whose photographs went into the text with their permission. Their work and licensing information has been acknowledged in the footnotes.

I would also like to thank the saints of this book. Their intercessory prayers and assistance were equally important in all aspects of producing Lions of the Faith.

I lastly thank the Holy Trinity- Father, Son, and Holy Spirit- for His help, inspiration, motivation, and research. For without such aid, this book would not exist.

For Caritas
January 4th, 2012
Rest in Peace

A Note About Organization

The main text for <u>Lions of the Faith</u> is divided into four sections. The first section covers the rise of Islam to the Crusades. The second section covers the period of the Crusades up until the destruction of the Knights Templar. The third section covers the expansion of Europe's empires globally as well as the growth of the Ottoman Empire until the Treaty of Karlowitz. The fourth section covers the Ottoman Empire's decline up to the current time.

Each section is further subdivided into various headers based upon the historical events of each time. Each one is prefaced by essays which give context to the conditions under which the various persons of the book lived.

With the exception of the last header of the last section, there is a final division within each header that classifies the book's persons into one of four categories:

Martyrs
Saints and beatified persons who
were killed by Muslims in zeal for Islam.

Contenders
Saints and beatified persons who
contended for the Catholic Faith among Muslims.

Inspirers
Saints and beatified persons who inspired, interceded for,
and motivated the Church to continue the struggle with Islam.

Notable Mention
Non-saints and non-beatified persons who modeled Catholic
piety, charity, and zeal while working with Islam and Muslims.

There are several saints included who are not Catholic, but were canonized by the Eastern Orthodox Churches. They have been clearly noted in the text. They were included because their lives were in some way formally recognized by either the Holy Father or one of the Catholic religious orders. If a person was in one of the areas dominated by the Eastern Churches before Schism of 1054, he is included as a Catholic. There are also several people who are neither saints nor beatified persons, but have been listed among the former three categories because their lives and deeds were recognized by the Holy Father. They have also been clearly noted. All of the saints within their respective categories have been generally arranged by death date.

Preface

Lions of the Faith was born out of research that began while I was pursuing my master's degree in Islamic Studies at Hartford Seminary. During this time, I was exposed to a large amount of classical Islamic texts. While most of these works pertained to matters of Islamic history, theology, and law for Muslims, I was interested in the documentation and portrayal of Christians.

For one assignment, we were asked to research and document a particular historical event in Shiite Islamic history of our choosing. Given that I was able to speak Arabic and with my interests in Christian-Muslim relations, I began to look through the classical sources for something of interest.

I wrote about the Fatimid Caliph Al-Mu'izz Li-Din Ilahi. This Caliph threatened to massacre Egypt's Coptic Orthodox population if they could not move a mountain by their faith. While the Coptic Pope Abraham prayed about what to do, the Blessed Virgin appeared to him. She told him to have the Coptic Church pray and fast for three days, and to find and follow the lead of a holy man named Simon. After three days and following her instructions, in the presence of the Caliph and the entire Coptic community, St. Simon the Tanner with Pope Abraham prayed and raised Mt. Moqattam by their faith from the earth.

When the Caliph saw this, he renounced Islam and became a Christian. He was baptized in the Church of St. Mercurius, and the font which he ordered constructed for his baptism still exists. He became a patron of the Coptic Orthodox Church, and died a holy man. The Coptic Orthodox Church added three additional days of fasting prior to the Advent fast as a perpetual remembrance of this miracle.[*]

---

[*] For the story, see Ibn Al-Muqaffa', Severus. History of the Patriarchs of the Egyptian Church: Known as a History of the Holy Church. Khaël

As I delved further into my own research about the Eastern Orthodox Church in Muslim areas, I found that there was a noticeable amount of research about Eastern Orthodox saints who interacted in some way with Islam. However, I did not find such available data about the Catholic Faith.

I slowly began to research Catholic as well as Islamic sources for information about Catholic saints who interacted in some way with Islam. With the exceptions of Spain and Portugal, Western and Central Europe did not experience the same intense domination and persecution under Islam as did Christians in the Middle East. But after uncovering the stories of not a few saints, beatified persons, as well as many great holy and heroic men and women, it was clear that it was time for the history of the Catholic Church's saints with Islam to be told.

The inspiration for the title Lions of the Faith comes from the medieval Islamic biographical work Usd Al-Ghaba, which translates as "Lions of the Forest." It was written by Abu Al-Hasan Ali Ibn Al-Athir, who was a Kurd that prior to his becoming a historian and author was a member of Saladin's army. It was likely that he was not only present during Saladin's infamous massacre of the Crusaders at Hattin in 1187, but also fought against many other persons written about in this book. These include King Richard the Lionheart, Mercedarian martyr St. Serapion, Knight Hospitaller Bl. Gerard Mecatti of Villamagna, and Templar Knight and martyr St. Nicasius of Sicily.

It is my hope that Lions of the Faith will tell the story of the Catholic Church's saints, beatified persons, and heroes in their interactions with Islam.

III – Shenouti II (880 – 1066). Trans. O.H.E. Burmester. L'Institut Français d'Archéologie Orientale. 1948. Vol II. Part II. Pages 128-153.

Introduction

The situation of the Church with Islam has become one of the major issues of the third millennium. However, the reality is that there are no new issues with Islam and the Church that have not been faced before. Times and places have changed, but the basic problems, differences, and resolutions have not.

There are many differences between Islam and the Catholic Faith, and they have been extensively discussed by many persons. However, Islam is unique among world religions because it is the only religion whose theology specifically denounces and calls for the destruction of Christianity as a whole and regardless of form. This is motivated by its antipathy toward Jesus' divinity. Islamic theology teaches that belief in the divinity of Christ is the worst sin a man can commit. This has been unanimously noted by every orthodox Islamic theologian going back to Islam's founder Muhammad.[1] Since professing Islam means renouncing Jesus' divinity and being a Christian means embracing Jesus' divinity, there is an unbridgeable divide between the two religions. This belief is the reason why Islam has actively worked to convert, suppress, and exterminate Christianity and Christians in Islamic society for the past fourteen centuries.

Catholics are mandated to witness to people of all religions in the context of each man's particular vocation. Muslims are no exception. It is not hateful to disagree with or criticize Islam, for if a man believes in the Catholic Faith, he likewise testifies against Islam and Muhammad's claims. Muslims are, as the Catholic Faith teaches with all men, made in the image and likeness of God,[2] and thus possess the same intrinsic human dignity that is inherent to all men.[3] The Church's criticism and rejection of Islam speaks to Islam's theology, and not the Muslim people. Likewise the Muslim people, as with all men, possess the same conscience and ability to choose good or evil of their own free wills.

It is an unfortunate but undeniable fact that Islamic theology teaches its followers to destroy Christianity and the Church. Catholics have a responsibility to appropriately respond to Islam when Muslims attempt to fulfill these teachings. The Catholic Faith has a great collection of saints, beatified persons, and heroes who, despite coming from a wide range of times, cultures, and backgrounds, demonstrate examples for engaging Islam and the Muslims. These men and women were the inspiration for Lions of the Faith.

These are their stories. It is for the Church to derive inspiration from their examples, and seek their prayerful intercession and guidance in her dealings with Islam and Muslims.

Section I: The Rise of Islam

The Years that Changed History:

632 – 711

During the early 7th century, the Middle East was divided between three great empires. The Byzantines controlled Anatolia, northern Egypt, the Holy Land, and the Levant. The Persians controlled the eastern parts of the Middle East and northern Arabia. The Aksumites controlled southern Egypt through the horn of Africa and the southern Arabian Peninsula.

Christianity had penetrated deeply into all these areas through centuries of missionary work. Catholics constituted the majority of Christians in the Byzantine territories. The Oriental Orthodox constituted the majority of Christians in Egypt, Ethiopia, and Armenia. The Assyrian Church of the East stretched from northern Syria throughout what is today known as Iran, Central Asia and western China. There were also many heretical Christian groups that existed in small numbers, in addition to a considerable number of pagans.[1]

On the eve of Muhammad's death in 632, Islam exercised considerable influence over the western Arabian Peninsula. However, it was Islam's sweeping military expansions that followed over the next century which forever inverted the religious, social, and political order of the Middle East and the world. In spite of Muhammad's claims, the Byzantines, Persians, and Aksumites initially perceived Islam to be a quasi-barbarian invasion. However, the invaders' religious zeal was soon evident, as Christians were discriminated against regardless of sect. Many persons, particularly those who resisted the invasions, were given the choice of conversion to Islam or death, following in the example of Muhammad.[2]

The Islamic government, known as the Caliphate,[3] was established by Muhammad in Medina in 622. The Caliphate was moved by Caliph Mu'awiya ibn Abu Sufyan to Damascus when he assumed power in 661. Mu'awiya established the Umayyad dynasty, named after the patriarch of the ancient Umayya tribe in Arabia. Most of Islam's expansions happened under the Umayyads. By the time of the Umayyads' fall in 750, an Islamic empire stretched from Portugal to Western China.

Early Islamic literature claims that the Middle East's Christian peoples mass converted to Islam. This is not entirely accurate, as Islamization happened gradually in the centuries after the conquests. This usually came about by one of two ways. The first was the marriage of a Muslim man to a non-Muslim woman, since non-Muslim men cannot marry Muslim women in Islam. The second was out of a desire to improve one's socioeconomic status, since under Islamic law non-Muslims are legally forbidden from holding positions of authority over Muslims. Christians converted in order to rise into positions of prominence within Islamic societies.

It is true that at times, Christians did live well in Islamic societies. However, this was subject to the time, place, and disposition of the particular Muslim ruler in power towards Christianity. It does not change the well-documented historical record that Islam has of violence and destruction towards Christians and Christianity as whole and wherever it spreads. As the fifteenth century Spanish Muslim historiographer Ibn Khaldun poignantly noted about Christianity and Judaism:

We do not think that we should blacken the pages of this book with discussion of (the Christians and Jews) dogmas of unbelief. In general, they are well known. All of them are unbelief. This is clearly stated in the noble Quran. To discuss or argue those things with them is not for us. It is for them to choose between conversion to Islam, payment of the poll tax, or death.[4]

The Church found itself in a situation it had never experienced. As much as "the blood of martyrs is the seed of the Church,"[5] Islam's militant hatred of Christianity forced the Church to fight back against the jihads[6] if she was to survive. However, she also had to assimilate into Islamic society to survive in situations where she could not militarily resist. This dichotomy established a pattern which characterized the Church's relationship with Islam for centuries to come.

The Umayyad Mosque of Damascus, Syria. This was once the Church of St. John the Baptist, but it was captured during the Fall of Damascus in the early years of Islam's spread and was formally converted into a mosque by the Umayyad Caliphate. Many churches across the Middle East suffered this fate.[7]

Martyrs

Sts. Florian, Calcanicus, and the 56 Martyrs of Eleutheropolis
Feast Day: December 17th

The Martyrs of Eleutheropolis were among the first Catholic martyrs killed in zeal for Islam. Eleutheropolis was a city south of Jerusalem, north of Yarmuk,[8] and on the main road between both locations. It was an important center of Christianity and was the home of St. Epiphanus. It was one of the first major cities attacked by Islamic armies during the early conquests, and was besieged by the Caliph 'Umar in 637.

'Umar was a rough man with sadistic tendencies. Prior to his conversion to Islam from paganism, 'Umar used to harass and intimidate Muhammad. After his conversion he became one of Muhammad's closest confidants, and subsequently directed his anger towards non-Muslims who he felt criticized or insulted Muhammad.

'Umar was attempting to conquer Eleutheropolis because of its location as a central crossing point along the ancient Silk Road. The city resisted and when Islamic armies broke through, they demanded that those who fought in the resistance either convert to Islam or be executed. Sts. Florian and Calcanicus were part of this resistance that, along with 56 other soldiers, refused to abandon the Catholic Faith, and were beheaded.

Sts. Torcatus and Twenty-Seven Martyrs
Feast Day: February 26th

St. Torcatus, also known as Torcato Felix, was the Archbishop of Guimarães, Portugal. He lived during the invasion of the Iberian Peninsula in the early 8th century under Muslim General Tariq ibn Ziyad. When St. Torcatus received word that the Muslims were approaching Guimarães in 715, he called upon the Catholics to stand up and fight the invaders. Unfortunately, it is said that only twenty-seven people responded to St. Torcatus' call. The group was terribly outnumbered when the Muslims arrived. Tariq had crossed into Spain four years earlier in 711, and was already well on his way to conquering all of what is today Spain and Portugal.

St. Torcatus addressed the invaders and implored them to embrace the Catholic Faith. When he finished, one of the Muslims took his sword and swiftly cut off St. Torcatus' head. The other twenty-seven were subsequently beheaded as well.

While St. Torcatus' call to arms was not heeded by his own community, it was being independently answered by the Spaniard Pelagius of Asturias. His resistance began the 781 year-long struggle to liberate Spain and Portugal from Islamic rule, known as the Reconquista.

Contenders

St. Sophronius
Feast Day: March 11th

St. Sophronius was the Patriarch of Jerusalem during the time of the Islamic invasions of the Middle East. Prior to this, he was deeply involved in discourses against the Monothelites[9] across the Byzantine Empire and was a champion of Catholic orthodoxy.

St. Sophronius personally witnessed the fall of Jerusalem to Islamic armies. It is likely he also witnessed the mass slaughter and the conversion of many Christians to Islam in order to avoid execution. His knowledge about Islam is not fully known, but he did recognize that something had to be done in order to stop or mitigate the damage that Islam caused to the Catholic Faith as it spread. When Jerusalem fell in 637, the Caliph 'Umar and St. Sophronius met to discuss the future of Jerusalem and her Christian inhabitants. The specific details of what happened at the meeting are not fully known, but there were three major outcomes.

First, was that the Christian inhabitants would be spared execution or forced conversion. This was crucial because even in the early days of Islam, Christians were experiencing severe persecution as Islam's armies advanced into their lands.

Second, was that the Church of the Holy Sepulcher would be spared conversion into a mosque. This came about because St. Sophronius, as a gesture of good will, invited 'Umar to pray inside the church. However, 'Umar declined to because it is said he told St. Sophronius he did not want Muslims laying future claims to it. As such, St. Sophronius entrusted the keys to the church with Muslim custodians as a token of mutual good will. The church's custody has remained with the Muslims since this day.[10]

Third, and most unfortunately, was the Pact of 'Umar.[11] The Pact of 'Umar was a treaty drawn up between 'Umar and St. Sophronius which imposed discriminatory conditions upon Christians that if it was followed, permitted for their continued existence under Islamic rule. The status given to Christians as well as Jews was the title of "dhimmi." This comes from the Arabic word "dhimma," meaning "pact," and it signifies that such people are "protected" by the Pact of 'Umar.

The Pact of 'Umar might be regarded as an act of treachery on St. Sophronius' part, but this is not so. The Pact must be viewed through the long-term effects it has had on Christian-Muslim relations. Though the Pact was written almost fourteen centuries ago, it is still regarded as a standard by Muslims for relations with Christians. While the Pact neither grants nor guarantees anything and is very repressive, it emphasizes the permissibility for Christianity to exist alongside Islam. This is a crucial point, since it has often acted as a buffer to prevent or lessen the persecution of Christians in zeal for Islam within Islamic societies.

It can be said that St. Sophronius was the first person to engage in Catholic-Muslim dialogue. He managed to save what remained of Jerusalem's Christian community following the city's invasion by Islamic armies. Nevertheless, he was so heartbroken at Jerusalem's destruction that it affected his physical health, and he died the following year on March 11th, 638.

Our Lady of Covadonga, Pelagius of Asturias, and Oppas the Bishop of Seville
Feast Day[12] of Our Lady of Covadonga: September 8th

Islamic armies took control over North Africa in the early 8th century and were looking for a chance to invade Europe. An opportunity for this came following the death of the King Wittiza in what is now Spain and his throne's usurpation by King Roderic in 710. Political tensions were high because of conflict between various factions vying for power. Within society, the Christian community was composed primarily of Visigoths who mixed with the Iberian people. There was also a large Jewish community, and relations between the Jews and the Catholics were mutually disagreeable at this point.

The story told by both Islamic and Christian sources say that King Roderic raped Florinda, the daughter of a Count Julian from the island of Ceuta off the southern Iberian coast by Morocco.[13] It is said that Julian was so enraged that he sought revenge upon King Roderic by dispossessing him from his throne. Since he could not do this himself, Julian met in secret with Musa ibn Nusayr, Commander of the Islamic armies in North Africa. Julian pledged to provide military intelligence and raise an army in exchange for protection for himself, his family, and a portion of the spoils that would be available after the conquest. He was appointed a spy named Tarif ibn Malluk who helped him to chart the Iberian coastline. Julian built an army to assist the Islamic forces by exploiting the religious and political divisions that existed between the Catholics and the Jews.

When the time was ready, Musa commissioned the North African Berber Muslim General Tariq ibn Ziyad to lead the invasion. On April 29th, 711, Tariq and his army secretly crossed from Africa to Europe and landed at a mountainside coast in Spain near Ceuta. The mountain where he landed was given the name "Jabal Tariq", meaning "Tariq's mountain," and was latinized as "Gibraltar."

Tariq began a reign of terror against the Catholic inhabitants of what is now southern Spain to bring about submission to his army's demands. King Roderic took immediate notice and responded militarily. On July 19th, 711, he met and engaged Tariq at the Battle of Guadalete. However, the attack was a rout because of the material and military support that Julian provided to the Muslims before to the invasion. King Roderic was killed, and his kingdom was now under Islamic control.

The Muslims dealt with the conquered Spanish people according to the way they assisted the Islamic invasion. Most Catholics were subjugated under conditions based upon the Pact of 'Umar in what became known as the Pact of Tudmir.[14] Many Catholics converted to Islam in order to avoid having to live under these laws. The Jews did not convert, but were thanked by being entrusted with custody of the cities of Córdoba and Seville. However, the favorable treatment initially shown the Jews was but temporary. Eventually, they became as persecuted as the Catholics were.[15]

Most of King Roderic's family was killed at Guadalete. His wife, Egliona, was taken prisoner by 'Abd Al-'Aziz, Musa ibn Nusayr's son. 'Abd Al-Aziz married her and Egliona converted to Islam, taking the name Umm 'Asima. Count Julian was thanked and given the spoils promised to him. However, his betrayal cost him his friends and made him a social outcast. He died filled with guilt on account of his treachery. Islamic Spain was renamed "Al-Andalus," or "Andalusia", named after the colloquial latinized term "Vandalusia," or "Land of the Vandals," in reference to Spain's past.[16]

One of the few members of the old Visigoth royalty who escaped was King Roderic's bodyguard, Pelagius of Asturias, known as Pelayo.[17] He was accompanied by several military regiments that survived Guadalete and were committed to fight for Spain's liberation. Among the men was Oppas, who was both the Bishop of Seville and King Roderic's uncle. Pelagius and his men fled to the mountain caves in the Asturias region of Spain near Covadonga. It was here that the Reconquista was born.

Over a decade passed since Guadalete, and by this time Pelagius and his men were well-prepared to confront the Muslims. Nearly all of Spain was subjugated to Islam, and Islam's armies were now crossing into France. News of the nascent Reconquista reached Munuza, the Islamic Governor of Asturias. He and his officer Al-Qama prepared an invasion to crush Pelagius and his men. In response, Pelagius placed a statue of Our Lady at Covadonga where they trained and petitioned his men to seek her intercession for victory.

The Muslims arrived at Covadonga in 722 and swiftly attempted to crush Pelagius' force. While he was gravely outnumbered and undersupplied, Pelagius' men managed to obliterate the attacking Muslims as well as kill both Munuza and Al-Qama. The Muslims retreated, and Pelagius had dealt the Muslims their first ever major loss with Our Lady's intercession. His army gained repute, and Catholics from Spain and France flocked to Asturias to support him. Pelagius' army grew in numbers and supplies, and the Reconquista was able to continue.

Pelagius thanked Our Lady for her intercession and with the later help of King Alfonso the Catholic, built a shrine to Our Lady of Covadonga. Queen Isabella and King Ferdinand sought Our Lady's help in the final stages of the Reconquista nearly eight centuries later. In the centuries between, Spanish

Catholics sought out Our Lady's inspiration and help in contending for the Faith against Islam and in bringing the Faith to the Muslims.

Pelagius continued to lead the Reconquista until his death in 737. His son, Favila, took over after his death, but died soon after in 739. The Reconquista was then continued by the Kingdom of Asturias and later, the Spanish people for the next seven centuries.

The current statue of Our Lady of Covadonga at the caves where the Reconquista's first victory was won. The original statue placed by Pelagius of Asturias was destroyed in a fire. This statue was donated by the Cathedral of Oviedo in 1778.[18]

Inspirers

St. James the Greater
Feast Day: July 25th

St. James the Greater was one of Jesus' disciples and is Spain's patron saint. There are various stories about St. James and his affiliation with Spain. Traditionally, it is believed that he visited Zaragoza around the year 40 before he traveled back to Judaea and was executed. Other accounts say that he was intending to go to Spain but was beheaded by King Herod Agrippa I in 44 before he could.

In the year 813, a hermit saw a bright star in the sky. He followed the star, which pointed him to an area of thick vegetation under which there was a tomb with St. James' relics in it. He reported his findings to the local bishop, Theodemir of Ira. After an investigation, the bishop ordered the immediate construction of a church dedicated to St. James. Since the relics were found in Compostela, the church would be known as the Shrine of St. James at Compostela or Santiago de Compostela. The Shrine became a popular site for pilgrimage as well as a gathering point for the Reconquista.

St. James' intercession was often sought before going into battle. Sometimes people claimed to have visions of St. James leading the Catholics as they fought the Muslims, such as at the Battle of Simancas in 939. For this reason, he is also known as "Matamoros" in Spanish, meaning "Muslim killer." He is sometimes portrayed on horseback with a sword drawn in one hand and a dead Muslim trampled underneath his horse's hooves.

St. Emilian of Cogolla
Feast Day: November 12th

St. Emilian of Cogolla, who is also known also as St. Millán, was a 5th and 6th century saint from the region of La Rioja, Spain. He died 138 years before the Islamic invasion. He was both a priest and Benedictine monk who was well-loved by many. He is the patron saint of the Spanish Kingdom of Castile and with St. James is invoked as a co-patron saint of Spain. Similarly, his intercession was frequently sought during the Reconquista. He is often portrayed as a Benedictine monk, holding a sword and sometimes on a horse leading the Catholics into battle with the Muslims.

A mural from St. Mary's Cathedral in Valencia of St. James the Muslim killer, or Matamoros.[19]

Notable Mention

Jabalah ibn Al-Aiham

Jabalah was from the ruling Christian Ghassan family in Syria and was the last of the Ghassanid kings before the coming of Islamic rule under the Umayyad Caliphate. He served as the commander of a small army of Christian Arabs that joined with the Byzantines in fighting against Islamic armies at the pivotal Battle of Yarmuk in August 636. The Battle of Yarmuk pitted a large Byzantine force with its Arab allies against the smaller Islamic armies of the south. The hit-and-run tactics of the Muslims combined with better leadership routed the Byzantines and opened up the way for Islam's invasion.

Jabalah along with his relatives converted to Islam two years after Yarmuk in 638. He most likely did this in order to save himself from execution. However, he soon left Islam and fled to the Assyrian and Armenian Christian enclaves along the modern Syro-Turkish border, where he died in 645. While little more is known about Jabalah, the fact that he returned to the Faith and died as a believer is worthy of recognition.

Sts. 'Abd Al-Masih and Barbar

St. 'Abd Al-Masih means "Slave of the Messiah." He was allegedly a man named Qays ibn Rabi'a Al-Ghassani, from the famous Christian Ghassan tribe that ruled Syria and later converted to Islam after the Islamic conquest of Syria. 'Abd Al-Masih is said to have converted to Islam but later returned to the Faith and became a monk at the monastery of St. Sabas. After the Muslims discovered his conversion, he was confronted by them. When he refused to apostatize from the Faith, he was executed in the late 7th century.

St. Barbar is said to have been a Muslim from North Africa. He converted to the Faith and then went on to evangelize his entire tribe before proceeding to resist Islam's armies. There is little to no additional data to corroborate his story. His martyrdom date is unknown.

Whether Sts. 'Abd Al-Masih and Barbar are real people or not, their experiences at the very least reflect those of many Middle Eastern Christians who lived, fought, and died for the Catholic Faith.

The statue of Pelagius of Asturias that stands at Covadonga. Known as Pelayo, he began the heroic resistance against the Muslim invaders in 711 which birthed the Reconquista.[20]

The Islamic Invasion of Europe

The Byzantine Empire managed to repel the Umayyads as they rapidly expanded during the 8th century. Western Europe, on the other hand, was still politically and socially weak following the collapse of the Roman Empire in 476. Infighting between various barbarian tribes plagued Western Europe. This subsequently assisted Islam's expansion into Spain and France.

Fortunately, the Church's tireless missionary work ultimately saved Europe from Islamization. One of the most powerful tribes who converted to the Catholic Faith was the Franks. The Franks grew over the next two centuries and eventually became the French people. It was the Franks under their leader, Charles Martel, who conclusively defeated the yet largest Islamic army in history at the Battle of Poitiers in 732.

Although Islam was only a recent arrival, the Muslims made numerous attempts to seize control of the Mediterranean coastline in order to better attack mainland Europe. The most common attacks took the form of piracy. Muslim pirates set up bases of operation across the North African coastline in major port cities such as Algiers, Oran, and Tunis. Pirate attacks were done for material wealth, but the primary target was human cargo. The people captured in these raids were then sold as slaves in North Africa and across the Islamic world.

The Catholics quickly realized all that was happening, and set to immediate work defending their European homeland and the Church. Yet unbeknownst to the Church, it was the beginning of a struggle that lasted nearly a thousand years.

St. Eurosia
Feast Day: June 25th

She is also known as St. Orosia. There are two versions of St. Eurosia's story. The most likely one is that she was born in Bayonne, France and for unknown reasons came to the region of Huesca in the Spanish Kingdom of Aragón. During the Islamic invasions, she was killed at the city of Jaca in 714, and later was named as the city's patron saint.

The other account says that St. Eurosia was a Czech orphan adopted by Czech duke Borivoj and his wife St. Ludmila around 880. At the age of 16, she was brought to Spain to be married to King Fortún of Pamplona. However, she was captured by Muslims during a raid and was dismembered when she would not convert to Islam. This account is likely a legend that became confused with the real story of King Fortún's daughter, Iñiga[21] Fortúnez. She was captured by Muslim soldiers, converted to Islam, and married to Spanish Umayyad Caliph 'Abdullah ibn Muhammad, the son of Muhammad I, who was instrumental in executing the Martyrs of Córdoba. Iñiga later reverted to the Catholic Faith, escaped to Pamplona, and married the Catholic nobleman Aznar Sánchez de Larón. In either case, St. Eurosia's memory lives on as a martyr for the Catholic Faith in the struggle with Islam.

St. Fructus and his brothers
Feast Day: October 25th

St. Fructus and his two brothers Valentine and Engratia were hermits prior to the Islamic invasion of Spain. They lived in the forest of what is now the Hoces del Río Duratón Natural Park outside of Segovia.

St. Fructus' brothers were martyred in 715 by the invading Islamic armies. It is said that after their deaths, the Muslims attempted to kill St. Fructus. When they reached him, he drew a line in the ground and told them not to cross it. When they did, the earth was rent asunder and swallowed up his attackers.

St. Fructus died naturally several months later. His memory lives on as the patron saint of Segovia.

St. Eusebia and Companions
Feast Day: September 20th

St. Eusebia was the abbess of the monastery of St. Victor in Marseille. She and 40 other nuns were killed in an attack by Islamic armies in 731, and the monastery was destroyed.

St. Porcarius and Companions
Feast Day: August 12th

St. Porcarius was a Benedictine monk who died in 732 along with many other monks during a Muslim pirate raid on the abbey of St. Lérins, located on the island of St. Honorat. It is said that at the time the monastery housed 500 monks, postulates, and students.

St. Porcarius was informed by an angel in a dream about the Muslims' coming. He ordered all of the students, postulants, and younger monks evacuated in advance so that none were killed or sold into slavery. By the time the Muslims arrived, only the older monks were left.

The Muslims' action was quick and ruthless. After pillaging the monastery for valuables, they killed all but four of the monks, who were later sold as slaves in North Africa. St. Porcarius was one of those who perished.

St. Theofrid of Orange
Feast Day: November 18th[22]

St. Theofrid of Orange or Carmery was the abbot of the monastery of Le Monastier-Sur-Gazeille, in Le Puy-en-Venlay, France. Little is known about his life, but he is remembered for giving his life to save fellow monks from Muslim attack.

A month or two after the Battle of Poitiers, word came that Islamic armies were heading towards the monastery. St. Theofrid dismissed the monks and ordered them to hide in the woods. However, he stayed behind, noting:

> *"It is not right that in a time of persecution that the shepherd should flee."*

When the Muslims came, all they found was St. Theofrid in prayer. They seized him, savagely beat him, and when he would not renounce the Faith, they began to stone him. It is said that as St. Theofrid prayed, a great storm quickly formed that poured out divine wrath upon his persecutors in the forms of thunder, lightning, and hail which dispersed them.

The monastery and the monks were saved, but a wound incurred by one of the stones which hit St. Theofrid in the head brought about his demise. He died a week after the attack on November 18th, 732.

Contenders

St. Ebbo
Feast Day: August 27th

Little is known about St. Ebbo's life. Prior to his becoming an Archbishop, he was the abbot of the Benedictine monastery of St. Pierre le Vif in what is today Sens, France. After he became Archbishop, Islamic armies started pushing into France with the goal of conquering Europe. While the main body of the Islamic army moved on a slow path across the French countryside, the Muslims sent out smaller armies to conduct raids and prepare the way for a larger invasion. One of these armies headed to the city of Sens in 725. It was an important city, since its location provided a direct route to Paris by means of the Yonne River leading to the Seine. Additionally, its capture would open to invasion by Islamic armies the areas of what are today Belgium, Holland, Germany, and England.

St. Ebbo received word of the encroaching army, and he ordered the city barricaded in preparation for a siege. For several days the Muslims besieged Sens, but they were unable to take it. Since the Muslims could not overrun Sens, they attempted to burn the city down. They cut down trees, dragged them around the city's walls, and set them on fire in hope this would end St. Ebbo's resistance.

St. Ebbo rallied the people of Sens, and they prayed for the strength to survive as well as to be victorious. After a time, St. Ebbo and his men rushed out from the city's burning walls and charged the Muslim army. The Muslims were completely taken by surprise and panicked as they tried to retreat. St. Ebbo and his men did not just overrun the entire army, but they chased it across the French countryside for thirty-six miles until the last remnants were destroyed at Seignelay. Were it not for

St. Ebbo's brave actions, Charles Martel may not have been able to effectively repel the main Islamic army that he would eventually confront and defeat in 732 at the Battle of Poitiers. St. Ebbo died in 740.

St. Urbicius
Feast Day: December 15th

Little is known about St. Urbicius, who is also called St. Urbez. He was born in Bordeaux around 718. His father was killed at the Battle of Poitiers and he and his mother, Asteria, were captured and sold into slavery in Muslim Spain. His mother died during her slavery, and during this time St. Urbicius became devoted to the two child martyrs of Sts. Justus and Pastor, who were killed during the Diocletian persecutions of the early 4th century. St. Urbicius had a vision of them, and by their intercession, he was freed from his slavery.

Following his escape, St. Urbicius had another vision of Sts. Justus and Pastor. They indicated to him the location of their relics, which were in a church that had been destroyed by the Muslims. St. Urbicius rescued their relics and restored them to their rightful place. He became a Benedictine monk, and lived out the rest of his life in prayer, fasting, and mortification. He died in 802, and his body remained incorrupt until it was destroyed in the 20th century during the Spanish Civil War.

St. William of Gellone
Feast Day: May 28th

St. William of Gellone was born in 755 and was Charles Martel's grandson. He confronted and stopped Emir of Córdoba Hisham bin 'Abd Ar-Rahman Ad-Dakhil from conquering Languedoc and Narbonne in 793. His victory routed the Caliph and drove his army back into Spain.

However, St. William did not stop here. In 801 with his cousin Louis the Pious, he invaded Spain and captured the city of Barcelona. In the following centuries, Barcelona would be the last major city in the West before crossing into the Islamic world. He died in 812.

A drawing of Charles Martel during the Battle of Poitiers (also called Tours) in which he routed Caliph 'Abd Ar-Rahman Al-Ghafiqi's army and prevented the Islamization of Europe.[23]

Inspirers

St. Beatus of Liébana
Feast Day: February 19th

St. Beatus of Liébana was a monk and scholar from Asturias. His fame comes from his <u>Commentary on the Apocalypse</u>, in which he equated Islam with the religion and rule of the Antichrist. This found an audience among many Spanish Catholics, since their Faith and community were continually suppressed and under attack in zeal for Islam.

St. Beatus' commentary served for centuries as an inspiration for the Catholic faithful to continue the Reconquista to its successful completion. He died in 800.

The Battle of Poitiers (or Tours) took place outside of what is today the hamlet of Moussais, France. This is a picture of the official historical landmark. The large, chessboard-like square in the central-left part of the picture tells the story of the attack as it was carried out by the Caliph and Charles.[24]

Notable Mention

Charles Martel
d. 741

Charles Martel was born in 686 as the illegitimate son of Duke Pepin of Herstal. He began a series of wars aimed at consolidating power over the Germanic tribes that settled across France, Belgium, Holland and northern Italy in 715.

Spanish Muslim General 'Abd Ar-Rahman Al-Ghafiqi crossed the Pyrénées and began raiding the French Province of Aquitaine in 725. Due to a conflict between Charles Martel and the ruler of Aquitaine, Odo the Great, Odo was forced to fight against both the Muslims and Charles Martel at the same time. Charles Martel eventually sacked Aquitaine in 731. This action weakened the area so much that Islamic armies conquered it the following year.

Aquitaine's fall expedited 'Abd Ar-Rahman's invasion, and Islamic armies quickly moved into France. Not only was Martel's empire in danger, but so was all of Europe. After putting political differences aside, he and Odo the Great formed an alliance to stop the Muslims at the city of Poitiers. However, their army was undersupplied and outnumbered at least two-to-one. There was also a great deal of fear among the army because of the widespread destruction the Muslims caused as they conquered the French countryside.

Martel established his defense strategy in the forested hillsides around Poitiers. He assumed that since he could not engage in a direct attack, he could exploit the Muslims' greed to force a siege and draw them out. Martel knew that it was theoretically possible for the Muslims to bypass Poitiers and move directly towards Paris. However, if he could engage them at Poitiers, there was a chance they could be defeated. When the army arrived, 'Abd Ar-Rahman chose to lay siege, which was exactly what Martel hoped for.

The Muslims relied on their heavy cavalry for most of the battle. Yet despite repeated charges, Martel's soldiers held their positions and they could not break his defensive line. It was said that:

"The northern peoples remained as immobile as a wall, holding together like a glacier in the cold regions. In the blink of an eye, they annihilated the Arabs with the sword."[25]

In addition, Martel sent scouts into 'Abd Ar-Rahman's camp to free slaves and start fires. He ordered arrows fired at the Muslims by day and night so they could not rest. When the Muslims tried to retreat, they were weighted down by the treasures they had stolen from churches and monasteries on the way to Poitiers. In their greed to protect their ill-gotten gains, their battle stratagems were thrown into disarray.

After a week-long siege and a three-day battle, 'Abd Ar-Rahman was killed by a stray arrow. This caused the entire Islamic army to fall apart, and Martel's forces chased the Muslims back over the Pyrénées. Charles spent the rest of his military career running the Muslims out of southern France. He continued to be a great patron of the Church until his death in 741.

Odo the Great
d. 740

Odo the Great shared a critical role alongside Charles Martel in helping to defend Europe against the Muslim invasions of his time. If it were not for his staunch defense of

Aquitaine, 'Abd Ar-Rahman's armies may have overrun Europe much earlier. Odo and Charles Martel initially were enemies, but after Aquitaine's fall to the Muslims, the two leaders reconciled and worked together at the Battle of Poitiers in 732.

While Odo's kingdom was restored to him, three years after Poitiers he abdicated his throne and became a Benedictine monk. He died in 740.

Tariq's mountain. In Arabic it is pronounced *Jabal Tariq*, and is the origin of the area's current name, Gibraltar. It was here that Muslim General Tariq ibn Ziyad with the help of his spy Tarif ibn Malluk and Julian, Count of Ceuta, landed in 711 and began the Islamic occupation of Spain for the next 781 years.[26]

The Church in the Muslim World

Within Islamic society, merely preserving the Church's public presence was a formidable challenge. As evidenced by the Pact of 'Umar, the Church's existence was a conditional permission that could be revoked at any time. The Church lived in a daily tension of hope for a better future with the looming fear of its extermination in zeal for Islam. This same basic situation has persisted to this day across the Muslim world.

Many martyrs and heroes were produced in the initial centuries following the Islamic invasions of the Middle East. The stories from this period inspired future generations of Catholics to continue their defense of the Church.

A 10th century patch worn in Egypt by Coptic Orthodox Christians as mandated under the Pact of 'Umar. The Jews were also required to wear similar attire.[27]

Martyrs

St. Peter of Damascus
Feast Day: October 4th

St. Peter of Damascus was the Metropolitan of Damascus. He was martyred in 743 for publicly preaching against Islam and evangelizing Muslims. He was tortured to death by having his eyes ripped out, tongue cut off, hands and feet cut off on opposite sides, was crucified, and finally beheaded.[28] His execution follows the instructions Muhammad gave in the Quran for punishing Muslim apostates and anybody who preaches against Islam:

The punishment of those who wage war against Allah, his messenger, and who make mischief in the land is execution, crucifixion, the cutting of the hands and feet from opposite sides, expulsion, and this is their part in this life and a terrible punishment awaits them in the hereafter.[29]

St. Peter Mavimenus
Feast Day: February 21st

St. Peter Mavimenus, also known as St. Peter the Scribe, was originally from Gaza, where he was called the "scribe of Majuma."[30] What brought about St. Peter's move to Damascus is not known. It is possible that he was working for Caliph Al-Walid I, as the Umayyads often hired educated Christians to work as bureaucrats. However, St. Peter Mavimenus remained in unwavering commitment to the Catholic Faith, and this is what eventually brought about his martyrdom.

One day St. Peter became sick with an unspecified illness, and several Muslims went to visit him. The full context of the conversation he had with them is not known, but it is likely they tried to convert him to Islam. In response, St. Peter said:

> "Whoever does not embrace the Catholic Christian Faith is lost, like your false prophet Muhammad."

At this, the visitors seized St. Peter and killed him.

Sts. Constantine and David, Princes of Georgia
Feast Day: October 15th

Sts. Constantine and David were brothers and princes who fought against the Islamic invasions of Georgia. However, they were eventually captured and told to convert to Islam or die. Choosing death rather than apostasy, the brothers were tortured and drowned in the Rioni River in 740.

St. Elias of Heliopolis
Feast Day: February 1st

St. Elias of Heliopolis was born in Heliopolis, which corresponds with the city of Baalbek, Lebanon, around 760 to an Arab family. When he was 12, he father apprenticed him to a Muslim carpenter who was also an apostate Christian. Since the carpenter had a degree of authority over St. Elias, he attempted to convert him to Islam, but was unable to do so.

One day, this same carpenter asked St. Elias to attend a Muslim feast where there was much dancing and eating. As was stipulated in the Pact of 'Umar, Christians were required to wear certain articles of clothing in order to distinguish them from the Muslims. One of these was the zunar, which was a brightly-colored belt. Publicly removing this belt was regarded during this time as a sign of conversion to Islam, since only Muslims did not have to wear it.[31] The carpenter, who was still trying to convert St. Elias to Islam, told him that he should remove his belt because it would loosen his clothes so he could dance better. This was done with the secret intention of saying that the boy removed it because he converted to Islam. Because St. Elias was still a boy and did not understand this devious trick, he removed the belt. When he tried to put it back on later, he accused him of converting to Islam by its removal and then apostatizing from Islam, which carries the death penalty.

After a long argument, the carpenter released St. Elias to his family and promised not to press charges of apostasy. For eight years, St. Elias worked in his hometown of Baalbek until one day, his former employer wanted to re-hire him, at which he kindly refused. The enraged employer then went to the local authorities and accused him of apostasy based on the incident which happened eight years earlier and sought to have him punished in revenge. Despite his claims that he never apostatized and was tricked into removing his zunar, he was arrested and sent before a judge who would determine his fate.

The judge presiding over the case was Layth ibn Sa'd ibn 'Abd Ar-Rahman.[32] Before St. Elias was brought to trial, he had a vision of the martyrdom he would suffer. He later recounted this vision to Layth when he was told to convert to Islam or die, saying that:

"I saw all these things of which you speak in a night vision. Truly, I was decapitated, and crucified, and burned, and I have prepared myself to suffer all this willingly so that I might sit in the bridal chamber and the chambers may be interwoven with flowers and that I may be crowned with unsullied wreaths. Therefore, do what you command and begin whence you will."[33]

Layth condemned St. Elias to death, where he suffered the terrible passion he saw in his vision. He was severely beaten by a mob of enraged Muslims that stepped, kicked, and spat upon him. In prison he was beaten daily and became sick with dysentery. Finally, since St. Elias would not give up his Catholic Faith, Layth ordered his head cut off and his corpse crucified and put on public display. After a time, Layth ordered the corpse taken down, chopped into pieces, and catapulted into the Chebar River in order that, as Layth said, "So that there will be no remembrance of you on the Earth!" However, the opposite happened. People were able to recover parts of St. Elias' body, and many miracles were attributed to his intercession.

St. Abu of Tbilisi
Feast Day: January 8th

St. Abu of Tbilisi's real name is not known, as the name "Abu" in Arabic means "Father." He was likely a Muslim mercenary soldier who served under the Georgian Christian ruler Nerses of Iberia.

This was a time of great turmoil, as the Islamic 'Abbasid Caliphate[34] was aggressively pushing into Georgia. Eventually, Georgia was forced to become an 'Abbasid vassal kingdom. Nerses fled with St. Abu of Tbilisi to Khazaria, an empire set up between the Black and Caspian Seas by Turkic migrants from Central Asia. It was during his time in Khazaran, an outlying city near Atil, the capitol of Khazaria, when St. Abu converted to the Catholic Faith.

Soon after St. Abu's baptism in 782, he returned to Tbilisi. For the next three years, he professed his conversion and proceed to evangelize Muslims. This continued until agents from the 'Abbasid Caliphate arrested him and demanded that he re-convert to Islam. When he refused, he was convicted of apostasy from Islam and was beheaded.

St. Archil of Kakheti
Feast Day: July 4th

St. Archil of Kakheti was a Georgian prince who was captured in battle against the 'Abbasids in 786. He was promised to be released from prison if he converted to Islam. He refused, and was beheaded in 787.

St. Bacchus Dahhat
Feast Day: December 15th

St. Bacchus Dahhat was born to a Palestinian Arab family. He eventually became a monk at the monastery of St. Sabas. One day, his family unbeknownst to him converted to Islam. When he returned home and found what happened, he immediately began to evangelize his brothers. All of them returned to the Catholic Faith except for one, who reported him to the authorities. St. Bacchus was then arrested and beheaded around the year 787.

St. Anthony Ruwah
Feast Day: December 25th

St. Anthony Ruwah was born Rawh Al-Qurayshi.[35] He was related to the Quraysh tribe, which was the same tribe Muhammad descended from. It is said he fought in the jihads waged against the Assyrians, Armenians, and Georgians, and used to enjoy destroying churches.

One day St. Anthony went to the Church of St. Theodore in Syria[36] intending to desecrate it. Upon seeing an Icon of St. Theodore in the church, he fired an arrow at it. But to his great surprise, the arrow returned and hit him in the hand. Following this event, he later attended Mass at the Church and saw an image of a lamb surrounded by a white light upon the Eucharist during the consecration. That night, St. Theodore appeared to him and spoke with him, upon which he was immediately converted and sought baptism. Rawh Al-Qurayshi was baptized with the help of two monks in the Jordan River, and he took the name Anthony.

When St. Anthony returned to Damascus, he reported his conversion to his family. They had him arrested, and he was brought before 'Abbasid Caliph Harun Ar-Rashid.[37] He was offered both money and threats of imprisonment with hard labor, yet he refused to apostatize. Finally, the Caliph ordered St. Anthony's execution on Christmas Day in 799. It was said that prior to his death, he made many converts to Christianity from Islam.

St. Ashot I of Iberia
Feast Day: January 29th

St. Ashot of Iberia was born in 786 and became King of Georgia in 809. He led a series of wars against the 'Abbasid Caliphate and its vassal emirs in the Caucasus region. He was assassinated on January 29th, 830.

Forty-two Martyrs of Amorion
Feast Day: March 6th

The Forty-two Martyrs of Amorion perished under the reigns of Byzantine Emperor Theophilus and 'Abbasid Caliph Al-Mu'tasim.

Byzantine Emperor Theophilus had begun an aggressive campaign against the 'Abbasid Caliphate's presence in eastern Anatolia. Internal spiritual and political divisions had preoccupied Al-Mu'tasim's ventures, but with the help of Turkish and Persian mercenaries he began a long march against the Byzantines in 838.

One of the key cities of the Byzantine Empire was Amorion. At the time, it was both the largest city in central Anatolia as well as the Emperor's home. During the march to Amorion, Al-Mu'tasim ordered the words "Amorion" painted on his soldiers' shields as a warning to the Emperor and a sign of his confidence.

On the way to Amorion, Al-Mu'tasim ambushed the Byzantines at Anzen and wiped them out. Al-Mu'tasim's armies then marched unopposed to the city. With the Emperor's army weakened and the assistance of a Byzantine traitor named Baditses who knew about weaknesses in Amorion's walls, the city fell after a five-week siege. It was estimated that only half of Amorion's 70,000 people survived, and they were only to be imprisoned and sold away as slaves.

Among the men captured were forty-two military officers of the Byzantine Empire. They were marched to the 'Abbasid capitol of Samarra in Iraq where they met with Caliph Al-Mu'tasim. He offered to grant them freedom if they converted to Islam. They refused, and so they were kept as prisoners for seven years.

On March 6th, 845, the men were asked one last time to apostatize. When they refused, they were beheaded.

Al-Mu'eiyyad and St. Theodore of Edessa
St. Theodore of Edessa Feast Day: July 9th

'Abbasid Caliph Al-Mutawakkil executed a series of persecutions directed at the Christians of Homs, Syria, as well as issued an intensified version of the Pact of 'Umar[38] beginning in 854. St. Theodore of Edessa was a teacher and monk who went to visit Al-Mutawakkil's court to address the violence and persecution against the Church.

While addressing these concerns, St. Theodore visited with Al-Mutawakkil's family. One of his sons, Al-Mu'eiyyad, was very sick. St. Theodore prayed in secret with Al-Mu'eiyyad, and he was miraculously healed. Al-Mu'eiyyad became friends with St. Theodore, and decided to become Catholic along with three of his friends. He was baptized with the name of John. Al-Mu'eiyyad kept his Catholic Faith a secret for this entire time. They remained friends until St. Theodore's death on July 9th, 857.

Al-Mutawakkil died on December 11th, 861. As with the previous Caliphs, he passed rule to his four sons in order of age after his death. Al-Muntasir was the eldest but reigned for only one year, and died in 862. Since at the time Turkish warlords wielded tremendous influence in the 'Abbasid Caliphate, they requested a vote for a new Caliph and chose Al-Musta'in, a nephew of Al-Mutawakkil. However, as the Caliphate was traditionally passed from father to son in order of birth,[39] Al-Mu'eiyyad was the legitimate Caliph.

Al-Mu'eiyyad's brother Al-Mu'tazz, desirous of the Caliphate, went to war against both Al-Musta'in and Al-Mu'eiyyad in an attempt to seize power with the help of his brother Abu Ahmad. Al-Mu'tazz first killed Al-Musta'in, and then he murdered Abu Ahmad before turning his attention to Al-Mu'eiyyad.

During this time, St. Theodore appeared to Al-Mu'eiyyad and warned him of his coming execution. Finally, on August 8th, 866, Al-Mu'eiyyad was executed by Al-Mu'tazz.[40]

The monastery of St. Sabas, known as Mar Saba.[41]

Contenders

St. John Damascene
Feast Day: December 4th

St. John Damascene was born Mansur ibn Sarjun At-Taghlabi into a noble Christian family in Damascus around 676. The Taghlabi tribe maintained the Catholic Faith for several generations until it mass converted to Islam.

St. John Damascene's father served as a tax collector for the Umayyad Empire. It is possible his father was conscripted into military service under the Umayyad Caliph Yazid I. The name "Mansur," which means "victorious" in Arabic, might be an indication that his father was a great warrior.

In addition to St. John receiving an education from the Muslims, his Christian education happened in an unexpected manner. One day while he and his father were in the local market, they saw a group of slaves for sale that had been just brought back from a Muslim slave raid against Italy.[42] One of those captured in this raid was an Italian monk named Cosmas. St. John's father bought and freed Cosmas, and soon it was found that Cosmas was a highly-learned man. He became St. John's close friend, confidant, teacher, and superior in the years to come.

St. John Damascene worked under the reign of two Caliphs- Abu Malik ibn Marwan and Al-Walid. Marwan was a more relaxed, lenient man in dealing with Christians and other non-Muslims. Al-Walid was not, and he worked to forcibly arabize the Christian populations with the goal of eventual Islamization. While St. John served in the Umayyad Caliphate, he was also a staunch voice for orthodoxy among Christians in the Middle East, which was still plagued by heresy.

St. John's orthodoxy eventually got him into trouble with Caliph Al-Walid. In the years leading up to the Iconoclast controversy,[43] St. John engaged in dialogue by letter against the Byzantine Emperor Leo the Issaurian, who was pro-Iconoclast. Leo became so enraged by St. John's arguments that he forged and sent a letter in St. John's name to Al-Walid in order to give the impression St. John was encouraging a Byzantine military invasion. Al-Walid believed the fake letter, so he called St. John before him and had his right hand chopped off and hung by a string in public. The night after this happened, St. John prayed to Our Lady and she appeared to him. During this time, she reattached his severed hand. The next day he went to Al-Walid and showed him his healed hand, at which Al-Walid was stunned and believed his innocence. However, the actions of Al-Walid motivated St. John's decision to retire to the monastery of St. Sabas in Jerusalem.[44] He lived out the rest of his days praying, reading, and writing against heresies until his death in 749.

St. John's writings about Islam can be found in his monumental book, <u>On Heresies</u>, in which he addresses various Christian sects and their claims. In this book there is a section dedicated to the "heresy of the Ishmaelites," which concerns Islam. In this writing, he asserts that the black rock in the Ka'ba[45] is not the cornerstone of a building built by the Biblical Patriarch Abraham as Muhammad claimed. Rather, he writes that it was actually the head of an old statue of the Greek goddess Aphrodite, and that he cannot understand why the Muslims pay such homage to it.[46]

Inspirers

St. Peter of Mt. Athos
Feast Day: June 12th

In eastern Christianity, Mt. Athos is regarded as a very holy site. Many great saints and mystics in the past and through modern times have had a connection to this holy place. One of these is St. Peter of Mt. Athos.[47]

When St. Peter was a young man and a soldier serving in the Byzantine Army, he was captured by Muslim pirates. He was taken to prison in Samarra, located in what is now known as Iraq in 767. He fell to his knees, prayed that he might be able to escape, and if so, he would become a monk. After fasting and prayer, he sought St. Nicholas' intercession, who answered his prayers and told him to offer them to St. Simeon, the holy man who saw Jesus and prophesized his deeds and death in the New Testament.[48] By the miraculous intercession of St. Simeon, he was granted the gift of invisibility and was able to escape the pirates. Upon returning to Greece, he went to meet the Pope, who said that St. Nicholas told him of his coming to him in a dream.

Following his escape, St. Peter became a monk. The Blessed Virgin later appeared to him, and upon her request he went to Mt. Athos, where he spent the rest of his life. He died later in the 8th century.

Notable Mention

The Conversion of the Banu Habib

The story of the Banu Habib begins with the Banu Taghlabi tribe. For many centuries, the Banu Taghlabi was Catholic. One of the tribe's most famous members was St. John of Damascus. However, in the following centuries, the Banu Taghlib tribe converted to Sunni Islam.

One man from the Banu Taghlib separated after he converted to Shiite Islam. He founded the tribe of the Banu Hamdan in what is today southeastern Turkey and northern Iraq. One tribe which grew out of the Banu Hamdan was the Banu Habib. It is not to be confused with the Banu Habib tribe of Yemen and Oman, which had existed since the first century.

When the 'Abbasids took power, they gave the Banu Habib and the Banu Hamdan control over much of what is now southeastern Turkey and northern Iraq. Eventually, the Banu Habib began migrating into the outer territories of the Byzantine Empire on the modern Syrian-Turkish border. Most of the people in these areas belonged to either the Catholic Church or the Assyrian Church of the East.

Interestingly, the Banu Habib mass converted back to the Catholic Faith in 935. Details are not specific as to how the conversion happened, but it likely was assisted by Byzantine missionaries. The Banu Habib settled and mixed among the area's Christian population, which remained Christian until the Armenian Genocide in 1917.

The Troubled 9th and 10th Centuries

The Church in both east and west faced considerable persecution in zeal for Islam during the 9th and 10th centuries. This had been taking place since the 7th century, but by this time Islam had deeply rooted itself into the invaded cultures and peoples. Muslims were no longer the descendants of the Arab conquerors, but were the children of converts to Islam from the conquered peoples. The struggle was no longer with a foreign enemy, but with one's own family, friends, and neighbors.

The most notable event for the Church in the 9th century is that of the Martyrs of Córdoba. They were a group of 54 people martyred for criticizing Islam or apostatizing from it from 822 to 864 during the reigns of Caliphs 'Abd Ar-Rahman II and Muhammad I. Each martyrdom inspired new martyrdoms in different years. The 10th century likewise had many martyrs in the West, thus continuing the long chain of suffering that the Church endured.

However, there were also many good developments. The Reconquista had been going strong for a century, and now had developed into a full-fledged movement. The Church in Spain adapted to the Islamic culture by integrating the Arabic language and cultural customs into the Catholic Mass, creating the Mozarabic Rite.[49] This helped to expedite a great number of conversions from Islam to the Faith. But most importantly, the Catholic faithful remained steadfast with the Church, which guided them during these difficult times.

Martyrs of Córdoba
822 - 864

Sts. Adulphus and John
Feast Day: September 27th (822)

Sts. Adulphus and John were brothers who were born to a Catholic mother and a Muslim father. Both sons were raised as Muslims, but apostatized from Islam and were beheaded when they refused to reconvert.

St. Perfectus
Feast Day: April 18th (850)

St. Perfectus was a priest in the Church of St. Acislus in Córdoba whose execution was set up by two Muslim men looking to entrap him. The men came to him and asked him to say if Jesus or Muhammad was greater. To say Jesus was greater meant death, as it would be regarded as an attack upon Islam. However, neither could he say that Muhammad was greater because that would contradict his Catholic Faith. St. Perfectus told the men that Jesus was the true prophet and Muhammad was a false prophet because he seduced and married his dead son's widow.[50]

The Muslim men originally said they would not report him for blasphemy, but a few days later they did. St. Perfectus was arrested, convicted, and sentenced to be beheaded. As his last words, he cursed Muhammad and the Quran before giving thanks to God for his martyrdom on account of the Faith.

St. Isaac of Córdoba
Feast Day: June 3rd (851)

St. Isaac of Córdoba was only 27 when he was martyred. He was a Mozarab Catholic who was a secretary for a judge in Caliph 'Abd Ar-Rahman II's government. He later left his work to become a monk at the monastery of Tábanos.[51] During a visit to his former place of employment, he and the judge he worked with were talking about religion, and St. Isaac criticized Islam. That same judge immediately arrested St. Isaac and when he would not retract his statement, the judge had him tortured, decapitated, and his corpse hung on display before being burned and thrown into the Guadalquivir River.

St. Sancho the Soldier
Feast Day: June 5th

Two days after St. Isaac of Córdoba's death, St. Sancho the Soldier was executed. He was originally a Frenchman who was captured as a boy and was conscripted to fight for the Caliph. However, he never lost his Catholic Faith. It is said that he criticized Muhammad, and when he refused to retract his criticism, he was publicly impaled.

Sts. Habenitus, Jeremiah, Peter, Sabinian, Walabonsus, and Wistremundus
Feast Day: June 7th

Less than a week after St. Sancho was killed, another series of martyrs were made yet again. St. Habenitus, a monk of St. Christopher's monastery, St. Jeremiah a monk from the monastery of Tábanos in Córdoba, St. Peter, a priest, St. Sabinian, a monk from St. Zoilus' Church, St. Walabonsus, a deacon, and St. Wistremundus, a companion of St. Sabinian, publicly criticized Muhammad and were executed by beheading. The only exception was St. Jeremiah, who was flogged to death.

Before their deaths, they were given the chance to save themselves by converting to Islam. In response, they said:

"We abide by the same confession, O Judge, that our most holy brothers Isaac and Sancho possessed. Now hand down the sentence, multiply your cruelty, and be kindled with complete fury in vengeance for your prophet. We profess Christ to be truly God and your prophet to be a precursor of the Antichrist and other profane doctrine."[52]

St. Sisenandus
Feast Day: July 16th

St. Sisenandus was also stationed at St. Acislus' Church in Córdoba, where St. Perfectus was martyred a year earlier. For reasons not exactly clear, he was imprisoned by the Muslims. When he would not abandon his Catholic Faith, he was beaten and beheaded.

St. Paul of St. Zoilus
Feast Day: July 20th

St. Paul was a deacon from St. Zoilus' Church who was known for his work in helping Catholics who were imprisoned by Muslims. After having a vision of Sts. Peter and Walabonsus, he likewise publicly criticized Muhammad, and was beheaded.

St. Theodemir
Feast Day: July 25th

St. Theodemir, inspired by St. Paul of St. Zoilus' example, likewise followed in publicly criticizing Muhammad, and was beheaded.

Sts. Alodia and Nunilo
Feast Day: October 22nd

Sts. Alodia and Nunilo were sisters born of a Catholic mother and a Muslim father. Their father insisted upon raising the girls as Muslims and did so publicly, but their mother secretly raised them as Catholics. When the girls were nine, their father died and their mother married another Muslim. He was abusive to them and tried to force the girls to abandon their Catholic Faith and convert to Islam. When they would not convert, they were given over to local authorities who first placed them in a brothel to try and shame them into becoming Muslims. When they refused to surrender neither their dignity nor their Catholic Faith, they were beheaded as apostates.

Sts. Flora and Maria
Feast Day: November 24th

Like Sts. Alodia and Nunilo, Sts. Flora and Maria were born of a Muslim father and a Catholic mother. The girls were the sisters of St. Walabonsus, who was executed five months earlier on June 7th for criticizing Muhammad and Islam. When their father died, the girls announced they were Catholics. They were arrested for apostasy because all children born of a Muslim father and a non-Muslim woman are automatically regarded as Muslims. When questioned in court, they both denounced Islam and Muhammad. First they were flogged, and then they and were beheaded for apostasy.

Sts. Gumesindus and Servus-Dei
Feast Day: January 13th (852)

St. Gumesindus was originally from Toledo and was studying for the priesthood. Servus-Dei was an unnamed monk who accompanied St. Gumesindus. Both of them were beheaded for denouncing Muhammad before the Islamic authorities.

Sts. Aurelius, Felix, George, Liliosa, and Natalia[53]
Feast Day: July 27th

St. Aurelius was born of a Muslim father and Catholic mother. He married St. Liliosa, a Catholic. St. Aurelius' cousin St. Felix was born Catholic, became a Muslim, and then reverted back to the Faith and married a Catholic named Natalia. Both couples were considered Muslims by law, and they kept their Faith a secret. However, after St. Aurelius witnessed a Catholic merchant being beaten by a Muslim for the Faith, he decided that he must witness publicly for the Faith. The four criticized Islam publicly and were arrested, convicted of apostasy, and put in prison to await their executions. Another person would yet come to join them, and that was St. George.

St. George was a monk from the monastery of St. Sabas in Jerusalem. He was traveling and working on collecting donations for monasteries in North Africa when he went to Spain. While visiting the monastery of Tábanos, he was arrested and imprisoned along with the four. When the Muslim authorities offered them a chance to save themselves by converting to Islam, the five answered:

"Any cult which denies the divinity of Christ, does not profess the existence of the Holy Trinity, refutes baptism, defames Christians, and derogates the priesthood, we consider to be damned."[54]

All five were executed by beheading.

Sts. Christopher and Leoviglid
Feast Day: August 20th

St. Christopher was from the monastery of St. Martín en la Rojana, and St. Leoviglid was from the monastery of Sts. Justus and Pastor. They were both imprisoned for independently gone to the Islamic authorities and denounced Islam after hearing about the stories of the other martyrs. They met in prison, became friends, and were executed together.

Relics of the Martyrs of Córdoba
From St. Peter's Church in Córdoba[55]

Sts. Emilias and Jeremiah
Feast Day: September 15th

Sts. Emilias and Jeremiah were childhood friends. Following the example of the previous martyrs, they went to the Islamic authorities and denounced Muhammad and Islam in Caliph 'Abd Ar-Rahman II's presence. Since the Caliph was dying, as part of his last orders he had the two saints executed.

Sts. Rogelius and Servus-Dei
Feast Day: September 16th

Muhammad I ascended to the Caliphate on September 16th, one day after the death of 'Abd Ar-Rahman II and the martyrdom of Sts. Emilias and Jeremiah. As one of his first orders, he executed Sts. Rogelius and Servus-Dei for evangelizing Muslims and denouncing Islam. He had their hands and feet cut from opposite sides, as the Quran instructs, before beheading them.

St. Fandilas
Feast Day: June 13th (853)

St. Fandilas was a priest at the monastery of St. Salvador en Pinna Mellaría in Guadix. He criticized Islam before Caliph Muhammad I and was beheaded.

Sts. Anastasius, Digna, and Felix
Feast Day: June 14th

St. Anastasius was a priest from St. Acislus' church, St. Digna a nun from the monastery of Tábanos, and St. Felix a Berber Muslim who converted to the Faith and became a monk while in northern Spain. All followed the example of St. Fandilas, and were beheaded.

St. Benildus
Feast Day: June 15th

St. Benildus was a pious woman who likewise confessed the Faith and denounced Islam before Caliph Muhammad I and was beheaded.

St. Columba
Feast Day: September 17th

Because so many martyrs had come from the monastery of Tábanos, Caliph Muhammad I sought to close it. St. Columba was a nun at the time it was closed. Following its closing, she publicly criticized Muhammad and was beheaded.

St. Pomposa
Feast Day: September 19th

St. Pomposa was connected to St. Fandilas' monastery, the monastery of St. Salvador en Pinna Mellaría. She likewise followed St. Columba's example, and was beheaded.

St. Abundius
Feast Day: July 11th (854)

St. Abundius was a priest accused of insulting Muhammad and was brought before the Caliph, but he did not argue his criticism. He was beheaded and his corpse was chopped up and fed to stray dogs.

Sts. Amator, Louis, and Peter
Feast Day: April 30th (855)

St. Amator was a priest, St. Louis was St. Paul of St. Zoilus' brother, and St. Peter was a monk. They were accused of blasphemy against Islam and were beheaded.

St. Sandilia
Feast Day: September 3rd

St. Sandilia was a deacon who was beheaded for criticizing Islam.

Sts. Elias, Isidore, and Paul
Feast Day: April 17th (856)

St. Elias was a priest from Córdoba, and Sts. Isidore and Paul were monks and students of St. Elias. All were beheaded for criticizing Islam.

St. Witesindus
Feast Day: May 15th

St. Witesindus was a Catholic who converted to Islam but later reverted to the Faith. When he would not re-convert to Islam, he was beheaded.

St. Argymirus
Feast Day: June 28th

St. Argymirus worked in Caliph Muhammad's government and was falsely accused by Muslims of having insulted Muhammad and Islam. Caliph Muhammad extended him a chance to redeem himself by converting to Islam, but he refused. St. Argymirus was placed in a gibbet for several days, and then was beheaded.

St. Aurea
Feast Day: July 19th

St. Aurea was a nun and the younger sister of Sts. Adulphus and John, who were the first of the martyrs of Córdoba killed 36 years earlier for apostasy under Caliph 'Abd Ar-Rahman II. Her mother was Catholic and had also become a nun, and the two resided quietly together in a monastery. Many of their relatives had already converted to Islam, but this was not known to them. St. Aurea's family pressured her to convert to Islam, which she did publicly, but continued to secretly practice the Faith. When this was discovered, she proclaimed that she had always been a Catholic and never was a Muslim. Because she would not re-convert to Islam, she was beheaded.

Sts. Roderick and Salomon
Feast Day: March 13th (857)

St. Roderick was born in a Catholic family as one of three brothers, and eventually he became a priest. One of his brothers converted to Islam, and the other did not practice any religion. One day, St. Roderick went to break up a fight between his brothers and in the process he was knocked out. When he awoke, he found that his Muslim brother had told the local authorities that he had converted to Islam. He fled to the countryside, but was discovered by his Muslim brother and the authorities arrested him. St. Roderick maintained that he was always a Catholic and that his brother was lying, but he was told to convert to Islam or be executed. While in prison, he met St.

Salomon, a Catholic who converted to Islam but returned to the Faith and was awaiting his death for apostasy. The two were beheaded together.

St. Eulogius of Córdoba
Feast Day: March 11th (859)

St. Eulogius was a priest and scholar from Córdoba. He was stationed for a time at the monastery of St. Zoilus and was educated along with the Mozarab theologian Alvarus Paulus by the famed Spanish Catholic scholar Speraindeo. He was the first Catholic to translate part of the Quran from Arabic into Latin. Additionally, he secretly converted Muslims to the Faith as well as protected apostates from Islam against the wrath of the Caliphate. He also wrote the Memoriale Sanctorum, which chronicled the lives of the Martyrs of Córdoba.

One day an apostate from Islam, St. Leocrita, came to him seeking his protection and help. He was able to help her for a while, but when his actions were discovered, he was arrested and beheaded. Interestingly, it was Alvarus Paulus who wrote St. Eulogius' biography after his death.

St. Leocritia
Feast Day: March 15th

St. Leocritia was born to Muslim parents but converted to Catholicism after learning about it secretly from a relative. When her parents discovered this, they were enraged and wanted to kill her. She sought protection with St. Eulogius from her family. Her discovery with him also precipitated St. Eulogius' own execution, and she was beheaded four days after he was.

St. Laura
Feast Day: October 19th (864)

St. Laura is considered the last of the Córdoban Martyrs. She was a nun who denounced Islam and was arrested by the Islamic authorities. When she refused to convert to Islam, she was boiled to death in a vat of molten lead.[56]

St. Eulogius' martyrdom[57]

Martyrs

St. Bernulf
Feast Day: March 24th

Little is known of St. Bernulf other than that he was the Bishop of Asti, Italy. In 825, Muslim pirates began launching attacks against Italy from their base at Fraxinetum. During an attack on the city of Asti in 836, St. Bernulf led the city's successful defense against the pirates. However, he was martyred during the attack.

St. Victor of Cerezo
Feast Day: August 26th

St. Victor of Cerezo was born in Burgos, Spain in 800. He was a priest for many years and later became a hermit.

In 850, St. Victor had a vision from an angel to preach to a group of Muslims who were besieging his hometown of Cerezo del Río Turón. His preaching was very successful, and he made many converts to the Catholic Faith. He is also said to have cured diseases, including that of an unnamed man who was probably a local Muslim leader.

During St. Victor's preaching, he was captured by the Muslims and taken to the countryside where he was tortured for three days and eventually beheaded. However, to the Muslims' amazement, his decapitated body picked up his head and carried it back to the siege. When they saw him, they panicked and ended the siege, thus saving Cerezo del Río Turón from conquest.

In commemoration of St. Victor's death and this particular miracle, statues of him show his decapitated body standing and carrying his head in his hands.

St. Daniel of Arles
Feast Day: September 1st

St. Daniel of Arles was said to have been from Armenia, but it is more likely he was a Frenchman. It is said that while he was on pilgrimage in Arles, France, he was captured by Muslims in a raid in 888. When he refused convert to Islam, he was beheaded.

St. Lambert of Saragossa
Feast Day: April 16th

St. Lambert was a farmer and a slave owned by a Muslim master in the city of Zaragoza. He was beaten to death for refusing to convert to Islam in 900.

Sts. Andrew, Anthony, John, and Peter
Feast Day: September 23rd

Sts. Andrew, Anthony, John, and Peter were Sicilians captured in a slave raid by Muslims in 900 and taken to North Africa. When they refused to convert to Islam, they were tortured to death.

Sts. Pelagius the Boy Martyr of Córdoba and Hermogius
Feast Day: June 26th

One of the hotly-contested areas of the Reconquista during the 10th century was the city of Tuy. It was the scene of a great battle in 926 that is known as the Battle of Valdejunquera in which the Muslims were routed. However, two prisoners were taken, and both of them were bishops. The first was Dulcidio, Bishop of Braga in what is today Portugal. The other was St. Hermogius, Bishop of Tuy, also known as Ermogio.

Dulcidio was ransomed by the Castilian King Ordoño I, but St. Hermogius was not. Therefore, St. Hermogius' nephew, St. Pelagius, offered to take his place in prison. St. Hermogius returned to the city of Tuy and some years later built a church dedicated to St. Christopher in nearby Labruge, Portugal.[58]

St. Pelagius was only a young teenager at the time. He was brought to Córdoba and presented to Caliph 'Abd Ar-Rahman III. 'Abd Ar-Rahman was bisexual, and he had harems of both men and women. He took an immediate liking to St. Pelagius, and he offered him a position as his preferred homosexual sex slave.[59] St. Pelagius responded to this perverse offer by saying, in the words of the 10th century nun and poetess Hrotsvitha:

"It is not meant that a man cleansed in the baptism of Christ submit his chaste neck to a barbarous embrace, nor should a worshipper of Christ who has been anointed with the sacred Chrism court the kiss of a led-slave of the demon. Therefore do thou, with heart unrestrained, embrace those ignorant men who with thee attempt to appease stupid gods of clay; let those be thy companions, who are servants of an idol."[60]

'Abd Ar-Rahman was furious at St. Pelagius, and he ordered his execution. There are two accounts of his death. One story states that St. Pelagius was slowly cut or ripped apart alive over the course of several hours. Another is that he was catapulted to his death, upon which the body was retrieved before being impaled and dismembered. Nevertheless, St. Pelagius the Boy Martyr was killed in 926, and his uncle St. Hermogius continued his episcopal work and died in 942. Both of them are commemorated on June 26th.

Martyrs of Cardeña
Feast Day: August 6th

San Pedro de Cardeña is a large monastery in Burgos, Spain. On August 6th, 953 the monastery was attacked by Muslims, who captured and beheaded 200 of the monks after they refused to convert to Islam.

A rendition of St. Victor of Cerezo.[61]

Contenders

Sts. Atilan and Froilan
Feast Day: October 5th

St. Atilan was a Mozarab Catholic priest in the city of Tarazona. St. Froilan was born in Lugo, Spain in 833. He became a priest as a young man and later, a hermit. At the age of 29 he heard about the martyrdom of St. Eulogius, which compelled him to leave hermetic life and begin his work with Islam. Upon returning from the wilderness, he met St. Atilan. The two became lifelong friends.

St. Atilan eventually became the Bishop of Zamora, and St. Froilan the Bishop of León. The two built monasteries as well as spread the Catholic Faith among the Muslims. Thanks to their influence, many Muslims converted to the Faith. They were also both great proponents of the Reconquista, and their preaching inspired the Church in Spain to continue her struggle.

St. Froilan died in 905, five years after becoming a bishop. St. Atilan died in 916.

St. Emilian of Cogolla's hermitage.
It was converted to a Mozarab Catholic church by monks during the 10th century.[62]

Inspirers

St. Olivia[63]
Feast Day: June 10th

St. Olivia lived during the 9th century. There is little information available about her life. She was said to have been born into a noble family in Palermo. One day, she was captured as a young woman by Muslim pirates and brought to Tunis. It is said that when she arrived in Tunis, she stunned her captors with her physical beauty. They released her and permitted her to live as a hermitess in a cave.

It is said that eventually St. Olivia began to come out from her cave to pray with local sick people. Many people were healed, and some even converted to the Catholic Faith. This enraged some of the other Muslims, who demanded her execution. They tied her up and threw her into a fire, but the flames did not harm her. It was at this point that one of them decapitated her.

St. Theoctiste of Lesbos
Feast Day: November 10th

Little is known of St. Theoctiste except that she was born on the isle of Lesbos during the 9th century. When she was 18, she was captured by Muslim pirates. They took her to the island of Paros, where she escaped and lived as an anchorite for the next 30 years dedicated to the Virgin Mary. It is said that a hunter named Simeon found her one day, and she asked him to take her to a church where she could receive the Eucharist. Upon doing so, she passed away naturally. [64]

Sts. Arsenius, Pelagius and Silva of Arlanza
Feast Day: August 30th

Sts. Arsenius, Pelagius, and Silva of Arlanza were three hermits and friends who founded the monastery of San Pedro de Arlanza. It is said that the three met with Count Ferdinand González of Castile in 912, but this is unlikely as Ferdinand does not seem to have become count until at least 930.

The three saints had a vision of the Catholics led by Count Ferdinand winning a great battle over the Muslims. This was the Battle of Simancas in 939, in which Count Ferdinand along with Kings García Sánchez I of Pamplona and Ramiro II of León led an army to victory against the Muslim Governor of Zaragoza, Abu Yahya. The Battle of Simancas did not stop the Muslim expansions, but it ensured the continued long-term survival of the Catholic kingdoms, which were limited to Spain's northernmost regions. This was also where the Catholics had visions of St. James leading the soldiers into battle against the Muslims.[65] The three men continued their work at the monastery, and they all died peacefully around 950.

A picture of a small Arabian-style boat, known as a dhow. Large dhows were used by Muslim pirates for over a millennium to conduct slave raids in Europe and Africa as well as to transport their human cargo to the slave markets.[66]

St. Majolus
Feast Day: May 11th

St. Majolus was a Benedictine monk from Cluny, France who played a critical role in the Clunaic reforms which transformed western monasticism. He is one of the great holy men of Medieval Europe. He also played an unintended role in destroying a major Muslim pirate base.

Fraxinetum, which is located in southern France, was well-established during St. Majolus' time as a major center of Muslim piracy. For decades, the pirates had launched many slave raids against France and Italy. They were hated by the people, but nobody had done anything to conclusively stop them. This changed when one day in 973, St. Majolus was walking back to his abbey in Cluny. While going through St. Bernard's Pass in France, he was captured by Muslim pirates from Fraxinetum.

When the abbey of Cluny found out about his capture, they gladly paid the one-thousand pounds of silver ransom the pirates demanded. However, the fact that St. Majolus was captured deeply angered the French and Italians alike because he was so loved by the people. William I, Count of Provence, France, allied local lords and peasants to confront the pirates. Through a series of skirmishes that culminated in the Battle of Tourtour, the entire pirate base at Fraxinetum was destroyed and most of the pirates were killed. A few pirates fled to Spain and never returned, and William's actions earned him the title of "The Liberator."

St. Majolus continued his work until his death in 994. While he was not directly involved in the expulsion of the Muslims from France, were it not for his capture and ransom, neither would Fraxinetum have been liberated.

The Eve of the Crusades

The 11th century was a major turning point in the Church's history with Islam.

In the West, the "Golden Age" of Islamic Spain was coming to a fast end as internal division fractured Muslim rule. The Church suffered more severe persecutions, but at the same time penetrated further into Muslim areas. Islamic Spain eventually broke apart into a series of small kingdoms, known as ta'ifa states. The Catholic kingdoms of northern Spain were able to quickly conquer many of the ta'ifa states, and for a time it seemed that Islam might be driven out of Spain. However, in 1086 a Muslim named Yusuf ibn Tashfin led a massive invasion from Rabat, Morocco that reversed many of the Reconquista's gains and ushered in the Almoravid Dynasty.[67] While even in the best of times relations between the Church and Islam were tenuous, they steadily declined from this point forward as the Almoravids aggressively worked to eliminate the Church's presence.

In the East, the Byzantines initially made headway fighting against the 'Abbasid Caliphate. However, following the Great Schism with the Church in 1054, the Byzantine Empire fell into massive decline by losing successive battles with the Muslims. The greatest loss was in 1071 at the Battle of Manzikert in Armenia. This resulted in the loss of most Byzantine gains and from which the Byzantine Empire never recovered. The Seljuk Turks, who were migrating from Central Asia to the Middle East to serve as mercenary soldiers for the 'Abbasid Caliphate, were rising in power. Many of them converted from Paganism to Islam and continued Islam's wars of expansion.

The rise of the Almoravids and the Seljuks in the West and East respectively were not unnoticed by the Church. These movements set the background for Pope Bl. Urban II's call for a crusade in 1092.

St. Bernard's Pass, where St. Majolus was captured by Muslim pirates from Fraxinetum.[68]

Martyrs

Sts. Calixte and Mercurial of Osca
Feast days:
St. Calixte: October 15th
St. Mercurial: August 26th

Sts. Calixte and Mercurial were cousins from Huesca, Spain who traveled to the Spanish-French border near the village of Cazaux to fight invading Islamic armies that were attempting to cross the Pyrénées. It is most likely they battled against the forces of Abu 'Amir Muhammad ibn 'Abdullah ibn 'Amir Al-Hajib Al-Mansur, better known as Almanzor. Under the rule of Caliph Hisham II, Almanzor expanded Islamic Spain's territory back into the Pyrénées and southern France.

In 1003, Sts. Calixte and Mercurial were both killed in separate skirmishes with the Muslims. The Church of St. Calixte in Cazaux stands in memory of the former.

Sts. Argentea and Vulfura
Feast Day: March 13th

St. Argentea was Muslim apostate and Catholic warrior 'Umar ibn Hafsun's daughter. She converted with her father and siblings to the Catholic Faith. She lived a life of penance, mortification, and prayer as an anchorite. She was arrested and imprisoned for her apostasy by Caliph 'Abd Ar-Rahman III. During this time she met St. Vulfura, who was another convert to the Catholic Faith from Islam. The two women were tortured to death for refusing to apostatize in 931.

Contenders

St. John of Gorze
Feast Day: February 27th

St. John of Gorze was a Frenchman born into an upper-class family in 900. His father intended for him to enter into civil service, but St. John chose to renounce his inheritance in 933 and become a Benedictine monk. He was soon appointed abbot of Gorze Abbey in Metz in northeastern France near Germany where he began a series of strict applications of the Benedictine Rule similar to the Clunaic reforms.

In 954 he was appointed ambassador for King Otto II to Caliph 'Abd Ar-Rahman III of Córdoba. St. John's main objective was to negotiate a settlement to stop the Muslim pirate attacks from Fraxinetum, which the Caliph supported.

St. John also met with Bishop Recemundus of Córdoba. He gave several Arabic texts to St. John, who in turn brought them back to his home of Lorraine, France to study. This inspired an interest in Islam from the Church's missionaries, which eventually developed into the beginning of Islamic Studies in the West.

St. John did reach a diplomatic agreement with the Caliph to stop the Fraxinetum pirate attacks in 956. However, this agreement was short-lived, and was broken with the capture of St. Majolus in 973.

He died on March 7th, 974.

St. Rudesind
Feast Day: March 1ˢᵗ

St. Rudesind was born in Galicia, Spain in 907. He was appointed Bishop of Montodeno at age 18, and lived amidst an age of unparalleled chaos.

In 956, there was a Muslim uprising in Galicia supported by Caliph 'Abd Ar-Rahman III. Since St. Rudesind was also appointed governor of the area by King Ordoño III, he successfully led the Catholics in battle against 'Abd Ar-Rahman. Later, he also defended his homeland from attacks by Vikings as well as his own power-hungry brother Sisenand.

St. Rudesind was known for working miracles, and many people who came to him were cured of illnesses. He died in 977 in Celanova.

St. Madruina of Barcelona[69]
Feast Day: September 5ᵗʰ

St. Madruina was abbess of the monastery of St. Peter in Barcelona. In 985, the Muslim General Almanzor invaded and destroyed the monastery. Most of the nuns were killed, and the surviving nuns were sold into slavery, including St. Madruina.

St. Madruina was eventually sold to a Muslim slave dealer on the island of Majorca in 992. However, this was a blessing, as a merchant recognized her from Barcelona. He purchased her and promised to bring her home. In order to do this, he hid her in a sack of cotton being shipped to Spain.

Upon returning to Barcelona, she went to the monastery and was warmly received. She spent the rest of her days helping restore order to the monastery, but was no longer its abbess. She died in 999.

St. Dominic of Silos
Feast Day: December 20th

St. Dominic of Silos was born in La Rioja, Spain to a peasant family in 1000. He became a Benedictine monk at the monastery of St. Emilian of Cogolla, but was forced to flee due to a conflict with King García Sánchez III of Navarre.

King Ferdinand I of León granted St. Dominic protection and allowed him to take possession of the monastery of St. Sebastian of Silos. At the time, the monastery had only six monks and was literally falling apart from physical, spiritual, and fiscal decay. St. Dominic renewed the monastery into a center of Spanish Catholic culture. It became a grand promoter of the Mozarabic Rite, and was the first monastery that systematically ransomed Catholics who were enslaved by Muslims. The monastery also researched and preserved the old Visigoth language and writings that existed prior to Islam. Even after the Mozarabic Rite fell out of use in later centuries, the monastery continued to preserve the Rite and has one of the largest collections of Mozarabic texts in the world.

St. Dominic of Silos died in 1073. The St. Dominic who founded the Dominican Order was named after St. Dominic of Silos. His mother, Bl. Joan of Aza, made pilgrimage to his tomb asking for another son, at which St. Dominic of Silos appeared to her.

St. Casilda
Feast Day: April 9th

St. Casilda was the daughter of the Berber Muslim Yahya ibn Isma'il Al-Ma'mun, ruler of the ta'ifa state of Toledo. She was known for her great kindness and love, since she secretly smuggled bread to starving Catholic prisoners that her father's armies captured in the Reconquista's battles.

St. Casilda is often portrayed in artwork holding roses. This is because one day her father stopped her and asked what she was holding under her dress. She told him it was a bucket of roses when in reality it was a bucket of bread. When he demanded that she show him the bucket, the contents had miraculously changed into roses.

Though St. Casilda was a Muslim, she learned about the Catholic Faith from the prisoners she assisted. One day, she became very sick with an unspecified blood-flow sickness. Despite her best efforts and those of the doctors that attended to her, she remained ill. At the suggestion of the prisoners she secretly cared for, she went to the Shrine of St. Vincent in Oviedo. She bathed in the streams by the Shrine, and upon doing so she was healed of her sickness by the intercession of St. Vincent.

Having become convinced of the Catholic Faith, St. Casilda renounced Islam, abandoned her family, and sought baptism. She was baptized at the Cathedral in Burgos and lived out the rest of her life as a hermitess, praying and doing penance until her death around 1050. Her relics can be found in both the Cathedral of Burgos where she was baptized and the Cathedral in her home city of Toledo.

Notable Mention

'Umar ibn Hafsun
d. 918

'Umar ibn Hafsun was a Córdoban Muslim born in Málaga in 850. Although he was a Muslim, he was also a criminal, and he attracted the wrath of Caliph 'Abd Ar-Rahman III. He eventually built a castle known as Bobastro, which served as his main base of operation. In 899, he renounced Islam and became a Catholic, taking the name Samuel. His sons 'Abd Ar-Rahman, Hafs, Sulayman, and daughter St. Argentea also converted. His resistance against the Caliph combined with his patronage of the Church made him a hero for many of the Mozarab Catholics.

Caliph 'Abd Ar-Rahman III dedicated his efforts to Samuel's extermination. In 917, Samuel was killed in battle with the Caliph's forces. His sons 'Abd Ar-Rahman and Sulayman were also eventually killed, and Hafs surrendered Bobastro in 928. The bodies of 'Abd Ar-Rahman, Samuel, and Sulayman were buried but the Caliph ordered the corpses exhumed and crucified at the Great Mosque of Córdoba. St. Argentea was martyred with her companion, St. Vulfura, in 931.

The Cathedral of Burgos, and home of St. Casilda's relics.[70]

Section II: The Crusades

The Crusades Begin

Catholic Europe and the Muslim world had been deadlocked against each other for over 450 years by the mid-11th century. The Church worked hard to strengthen her people in spite of external attacks by Muslim armies and internal turmoil. However, between the advances of the Almoravids in the West and the rise of the Seljuk Turks in the East, the Church recognized something more had to be done.

After a careful analysis of the situation as well as communication with the Patriarch of Constantinople, Pope Bl. Urban II called for an armed pilgrimage to the Middle East to assist the Christians living in Byzantine territories and the Holy Land.[1] The pilgrimage involved defending them against Muslim attacks and asserting claim to Christian holy places. In the West, it meant making pilgrimage to the Shrine of Santiago de Compostela and assisting the Reconquista.[2] For the next 200 years, people sewed small crosses onto their clothes to "take up Christ's cross" before making the pilgrimage. This lasted from 1091 to 1291 and became known as the Crusades.

The majority of Crusaders knew very little about Islam outside of second-hand accounts. But the Crusaders were not fools as they are sometimes portrayed. There were many peasants who went, but they often did so under the leadership of a wealthy and well-educated knight or nobleman. The Crusaders were architects, and they built castles and military reinforcements that have lasted for centuries. They learned from what was available to them in the Middle East, which they brought back to Europe. There were missionaries and charity workers who not only converted many Muslims but also earned their respect and admiration.[3]

The greatest problem that the Crusades to the Holy Land faced was that most Crusaders returned to Europe after completing the pilgrimage. This was exacerbated by the fact that the Crusader State rulers were European nobles, and they transferred their territorial struggles in Europe to the Holy Land. As time progressed, their ability to govern became hampered by their personal interests.

Another major problem was that the Crusader leaders lacked knowledge about Islam. This resulted in well-meaning, pious Catholics making poor decisions that caused long-term damage. For instance, the Crusaders focused many efforts on attacking Egypt. However, they did not consider or fully understand the military, political or religious realities of such an attack. It was this pattern of poor choices following a lack of planning that helped facilitate the Crusader States' ultimate demise.

Ultimately, the greatest success of the Crusades was the Reconquista in Spain and Portugal. While there were corrosive political struggles between noblemen, the Crusaders who went to both nations usually stayed. They married Spanish or Portuguese women, and as the Turks did when they conquered Anatolia, the knights built themselves into the local populations.[4] This facilitated not only the long-term struggle, but gave them important knowledge about Islam which they used to aid the Reconquista.

While there were Crusaders who strayed from the pilgrimage's original purpose, there were far more honest and pious men who participated. Their actions must not be forgotten on account of a few. The Crusaders were only a brief note in history, but their actions long out lived their presence in Spain, Portugal, and the Holy Land.[5]

First Crusade

Pope Bl. Urban II called for the First Crusade following correspondence with the Patriarch of Constantinople and meeting with various European noblemen. He made the call in a speech at Clermont, France on November 27th, 1095, and the reception was overwhelmingly positive. The news quickly spread across Europe, and while people were excited, it was not clear how to execute the pilgrimage. Unfortunately, the European nobility almost immediately began to squabble over how to manage the affair. This was a problem that plagued the Crusades.

The earliest informal attempts at organizing a Crusade were disastrous. The worst was the Peasant's Crusade in 1095 when a large number of peasants traveled across Europe into Seljuk-controlled Anatolia and were massacred. With Pope Bl. Urban II's assistance, the First Crusade happened under the leadership of three European noblemen: Godfrey of Bullion, Tancred, and Stephen of Blois. The Pope originally appointed the French Bishop Adhemar of Puy to lead the Crusade, but he served as a spiritual rather than military leader. The first group of Crusaders numbered around 35,000 people from all across Europe. After several months of travel, the ragged army arrived at Constantinople in June 1097. They rested for a short while, but they soon left again, this time for the long and dangerous march to the Holy Land.

The First Crusade took two years to reach Jerusalem. Every step of the way was filled with vicious life-or-death battles against an unknown enemy with completely different military tactics and cultural idioms. It is easy to criticize or mock the Crusaders, but to think about the trials they endured is astonishing. Many of them never came home as they died of hunger, thirst, or disease on the way. Others were captured and sold into slavery by the Muslims, and others were killed in battle. They were isolated from their families, and all they had to rely upon was their Catholic Faith and their equally unprepared leaders. The suffering, fear, and concern families and children had for those who went on the Crusade cannot be forgotten. The Crusaders were not fools, but great men of faith and valor. They loved God and sought to serve him wholeheartedly, even in what they knew was a venture from which they likely would not return home.

Each Muslim-controlled city along the Mediterranean coast to Jerusalem fell as the Crusader army advanced. However, the army dwindled as disease and death consumed them. Finally, a small but ragged army clinging to their Faith and life made it to the massive city of Jerusalem. Reminiscent of Joshua's attack on Jericho from the Old Testament, the Crusaders walked barefoot around the city and prayed for victory. With their Faith and swords ready, they scaled the walls of Jerusalem and took the city on July 3rd, 1099, establishing the Crusader States.

The First Crusade was overall a great success, and it was the most successful of all the Crusades to the Middle East. With the Crusader States firmly established, the stories of their faith, valor, and heroism shaped the Middle East for the next two centuries and influenced European society for untold generations.

The Jerusalem Cross, which was carried
by many Crusaders as they marched to the Holy Land.[6]

Martyrs

St. Matthew of Beauvais
Feast Day: March 27th

St. Matthew of Beauvais was from Beauvais, France and was a knight of the First Crusade. He was captured by Muslims while in route to Jerusalem somewhere between the time of the Battle of Dorylaeum (July 1st, 1097) and the Siege of Antioch (October 21st, 1097). He was imprisoned and when he refused to convert to Islam, he was beheaded in 1098.

St. Thiemo
Feast Day: September 28th

St. Thiemo was Bishop of Salzburg, Austria. He took part in the Minor Crusade of 1101 following the victory of the First Crusade. After arriving in the Holy Land, St. Thiemo ministered to the Catholic Crusaders and eastern Christians. He evangelized many Muslims, and was present at many skirmishes. Eventually, he was captured at the Battle of Ramla on May 17th, 1102.[7] Ramla was a terrible loss, as almost all the Catholic soldiers who took part in the battle were killed, including First Crusade leader Stephen of Blois. The rest were imprisoned at the city of Askalon near what is today Gaza.

St. Thiemo was offered freedom if he converted to Islam, but he refused and was tortured. This process continued over the next several months. Finally, the Muslims became so angry with his refusal to abandon the Faith and convert to Islam that they stabbed him in the stomach and while he was still alive, tied his intestines to a spool, and ripped them out of his body by winding them onto the spindle. He was martyred on September 28th, 1102.

Contenders

St. Aleaunie
Feast Day: January 30th

St. Aleaunie, sometimes known as St. Adelelmus, was born in Poitou, France to a wealthy family and entered into the Benedictine Order as a young man. He worked at the monastery of St. John the Baptist in Burgos, Spain, helping pilgrims make safe passage to the Shrine of Santiago de Compostela. When the Almoravids invaded in 1084, St. Aleaunie led military expeditions against the Muslims and participated in battle himself. He died at the monastery in 1097, and he is the patron saint of Burgos.

Bl. Gerard Thom
Feast Day: September 3rd

Bl. Gerard Thom was the founder of the Knights Hospitaller.[8] Born around 1040 in Italy, Bl. Gerard helped to provide safe passage and lodging for European pilgrims to the Holy Land as well as was one of the primary forces for the Catholic Faith's military struggle with Islam. Bl. Girard died in September 1120.

St. Adjutor
Feast Day: April 30th

St. Adjutor was born in 1070 in Vernon, Normandy, France. He was the subject of many miracles, but two stand out in particular with his relationship to Islam. The first was that while traveling to the Holy Land during the First Crusade, he and his company of 200 men were attacked by 1500 Muslims, which they miraculously were able to fight off.

The second miracle was that around 1116, almost two decades after St. Adjutor arrived in the Holy Land, he was captured and imprisoned by Muslims. The most common account was that while he was in his cell, the prison gates miraculously opened up during the night and he ran out. He continued running until he reached the Mediterranean. Having heard a voice from God telling him to swim, he jumped into the water and swam all night.[9] When he reached dry land by morning, he realized that he was nowhere else but in his hometown of Vernon, having made the journey from the Middle East back to France in only one night. He built a chapel in the nearby town of Pressagny, became a monk, and lived out the rest of his life in prayer, contemplation, and performing miracles until his death in 1131.

Bl. Raymond du Puy
Feast Day: November 12th

Bl. Raymond du Puy was born in 1083 in France and was the first Grand Master of the Knights Hospitaller. He was responsible for developing the Knights' military character and signature cross. He died in 1160.

Cross of the Knights Hospitaller.[10]

Inspirers

Our Lady of Almudeña
Feast Day: November 9th

Our Lady of Almudeña is the patroness of Madrid, Spain. Her story begins with St. James the Apostle, who is said to have brought a statue of Our Lady to Spain during his visit. The statue was housed in the Church of St. Mary in Madrid for centuries. During the Islamic conquest of Spain in 711, the church was desecrated and turned into a mosque by the Muslims. However, the statue could not be found, and for several centuries it was assumed to be lost or destroyed.

When King Alfonso VII of Castile re-captured Madrid in 1085, the statue was found hidden underneath a granary in the city known as "Al-Mudin." King Alfonso destroyed the mosque, rebuilt the church, and renamed the statue after the place where it was hidden.

Pope Bl. Urban II
Feast Day: July 29th

Pope Bl. Urban II was the most important early figure of the Crusades, because it was by his influence that the Crusades began.

Pope Bl. Urban II understood the threat which Islam posed to Europe, having seen its advances in Spain and the Byzantine Empire. After he assessed the situation in both locations, on November 27th, 1095, Pope Bl. Urban II gave a monumental speech that called for the pilgrimage which became the Crusades.

There are four known transcriptions of Bl. Urban's speech which exist, and all widely differ from each other.[11] However, a persistent theme was that the Church ought to send an armed pilgrimage to aid the defense of the Holy Land's Christians that are suffering under the yoke of Islam. Bl. Urban granted remission of all sins to anybody who went on the Crusade. The response was enormous but disorganized, and Pope Bl. Urban II directed his efforts into organizing the nascent movement and appropriately channeling its actions.

Pope Bl. Urban II died peacefully two weeks after the Crusaders successfully conquered Jerusalem on July 29th, 1099.

Our Lady of Almudeña.
Note that she is standing on the crescent moon, which has been used since Muhammad's lifetime as a symbol of Islam and can also be seen in Our Lady of Guadalupe's image.[12]

Second Crusade

After the First Crusade's success, the leaders established a series of states and began to assert their presence in the Holy Land. Unfortunately, these leaders were the same ones who had long wars and territorial disputes with each other in Europe. These problems did not disappear with the Crusades, but were transferred to the Holy Land. Thus the Crusader States' rulers at times conflicted with each other as much as they did with the Muslims.

When they were united, the Crusader States focused much of their military efforts against the Shia Muslim Fatimid Caliphate in Egypt, which was in terminal decline at this point. However, this prevented the Crusaders from seeing a real danger rising in what is now northern Iraq.

This danger was the ruler Zengi, Emir of Mosul. He was a powerful military leader with strong connections to the Kurdish people. After securing his rule, he proclaimed a jihad against the Crusaders and he dedicated his reign to their destruction and the revival of Islam in the Holy Land. Zengi began his jihad by attacking the city of Edessa, which is the modern city of Şanlıurfa, Turkey. On Christmas Eve, 1144, Zengi's army took the city and executed all European Catholic Crusaders. Eastern Catholics and Orthodox Christians were permitted to live. These actions led Muslims to call Zengi the "Defender of Islam."

Zengi was assassinated in 1146 and succeeded by his son Nur Ad-Din, whose name means "light of religion." Nur Ad-Din was as zealous and aggressive as his father in his intentions to eradicate the Catholics. His first major move was to force an alliance with Damascus, which was ruled by the Seljuk Turkish leader Mu'in Ad-Din Unur Al-Atabeği in 1147. Mu'in accepted Nur Ad-Din's offer, but did so because he sought to prevent himself from being attacked and deposed from power by Nur Ad-Din. At the time, Damascus was already allied with the Crusaders. Mu'in did not like the Crusaders, but he preferred an alliance with them because they were his best help in keeping Nur Ad-Din away from him. Unfortunately, many of the Crusader leaders failed to realize that Mu'in was compelled to accept Nur Ad-Din's offer, and that Nur Ad-Din was a common enemy. Instead of working with Mu'in in secret to undercut Nur Ad-Din's moves, the Crusader leaders turned against Mu'in. This was exactly what Nur Ad-Din was hoping for.

When news of Edessa's fall reached Pope Bl. Eugene III, he issued the bull <u>Quantum Praedecessores,</u> calling for the Second Crusade. He commissioned his friend, St. Bernard of Clairvaux, to preach the Crusade. While many people went on the Crusade, the poor judgment by the Crusader States' leaders about Mu'in turned what should have been an attack on Nur Ad-Din into an assault on Damascus in 1148. As Nur Ad-Din hoped, this forced Damascus to ally closer with him, and caused Damascus to distrust the Crusaders in the future. To make matters worse, the Crusader leaders bickered with each other during the siege. After much infighting, the Crusaders were forced to withdraw the siege from Damascus. St. Bernard was gravely embarrassed, and in a letter to Pope Bl. Eugene III he correctly noted that the Crusade failed on account of the sins of the Crusaders and their leaders.

Meanwhile in Europe, the Spanish and Portuguese Reconquistas were raging. A half-century of war had expelled the Almoravids. However, they were soon replaced by the "Al-Muwahhidun,"[13] latinized as "Almohads," beginning in 1146. They were founded by Abu 'Abdullah Muhammad ibn Tumart and were even more zealous in their desire to exterminate the Faith than the Almoravids. The Almohads were so successful in their attacks that they penetrated deep into the Catholic kingdoms of northern Spain so much that they were nearly conquered.

In spite of the Almohad invasion, the saving grace of the Second Crusade was the great victories in Portugal. The Portuguese Kingdom was fighting hard for the Faith and its political sovereignty. A mass influx of new knights from England, France, the Low Countries, and Germany gave the struggling King Alfonso of Portugal the boost he needed to capture Lisbon and solidify the Portuguese Reconquista. Thus it was through the Second Crusade that the modern country of Portugal was born and the Reconquista able to continue.

Portuguese King Alfonso I.
Portugal was born out of the events of the Second Crusade.[14]

Martyrs

St. Cosmas of Aphrodisia
Feast Day: September 10th

St. Cosmas was the Bishop of Aphrodisia in Sicily. He was killed by the Almohads in 1160.

St. Ernest
Feast Day: November 7th

St. Ernest was originally from Stüsslingen, Switzerland. He grew up in a pious Catholic family and entered the Benedictine monastery in Zwiefalen, Germany as a young man. He was known for his work against corruption in Europe, which he did until he went to the Holy Land. While in the Holy Land, he evangelized many Muslims. He was present during the Christmas Eve massacre at Edessa in 1144 by the Muslim ruler Zengi. Following this incident he began calling for the Second Crusade, and he was one of its organizers in the Holy Land.

In November of 1148, he was captured by Muslims along with thirty-four other priests and missionaries. The thirty-five men were taken to the Islamic holy city of Mecca where he was scalped, stabbed, and finally flayed to death along with twenty-three of his companions. An Armenian priest named Marsilius and ten other men were spared and traveled back to the Crusader States.

Sts. Bernard, Grace, and Maria of Alcira
Feast Day: August 21st

Sts. Bernard, Grace, and Maria were born Ahmed, Zaida, and Zoraya to the ta'ifa governor of the city of Carlet near Valencia, Spain. St. Bernard was born in the year 1135 as the second of four children. The birthdates of his two younger sisters are not known.

When Ahmed was 21 years old in 1156, he was sent as ambassador to try and secure the release of a group of Muslim war prisoners. He failed in his mission, and while returning home, he stopped at the Cistercian monastery of St. Mary of Poblet. While at the monastery, he had a miraculous conversion and decided not to return home. He renounced Islam and became a Cistercian monk, taking the name Bernard.

St. Bernard stayed at the monastery for 25 years until 1181, when he decided to visit his siblings. While visiting, he converted his sisters Zaida and Zoraya to the Catholic Faith, and had them baptized with the names Grace and Maria. However his elder brother, Mansur, became angry with him and had his brother and sisters arrested for apostasy. When the three refused to apostatize from the Faith, they were executed.

Contenders

St. Olegarius
Feast Day: March 6th

St. Olegarius was born in 1060 to nobility from Barcelona and became an Augustinian monk. He was a well-known reformer in Church affairs, participated in the council of Clermont, and was a great promulgator of Catholic orthodoxy. He later became the Archbishop of Tarragona.

St. Olegarius' set out on a Crusade in 1124 but returned home after arriving at Antioch due to concern for Tarragona. The area was recently reconquered from the Almoravids, and he was charged with rebuilding and evangelizing the city following the damage done to it. He also brought the Knights Templar to Tarragona to help aid the Reconquista. He died in 1137.

St. Raymond of Roda
Feast Day: June 21st

St. Raymond of Roda was born in 1067 and became Bishop of Barbastro, Spain in 1104. He was involved in many of the church-state conflicts between various bishops and King Alfonso I of Aragón. He accompanied King Alfonso on his failed southward expedition to conquer the city of Granada from the Almoravids in 1125. It is possible he may have done this in response to allegations that he did not support the Crusades, which seems to have been a rumor spread by other bishops in order to gain favor with King Alfonso over St. Raymond.

St. Raymond became sick during a failed expedition to capture Granada, and he died in 1126.

St. Raymond of Fitero
Feast Day: March 15th

St. Raymond of Fitero was a Cistercian monk and abbot of the monastery of Fitero in Navarre, Spain. In 1157, Castilian King Sancho III conquered the city of Calatrava as part of the Reconquista. However, he was unable to defend it. As such, he commissioned him to build an army and defend the city beginning in 1158, which was the beginning of the Order of Calatrava. St. Raymond died in 1163.

St. Julian of Cuenca
Feast Day: January 28th

St. Julian of Cuenca was born in 1127. He became a priest and worked as a traveling preacher across what was then Almohad Spain. He was very brave, as he preached and evangelized Muslims in the Almohad strongholds of Toledo and Córdoba. He was also known for his care of the poor- Catholic, Jew, and Muslim alike. He died in 1208.

A representation of a flag used by the Almohads. They overthrew the Almoravids in 1148. The Almohads nearly overtook all Spain during the course of their invasions.[15]

Inspirers

Pope Bl. Eugene III
Feast Day: July 8th

    Pope Bl. Eugene III was born in Pisa of unknown origins, but entered the Church as a deacon around 1115. He eventually entered the Cistercian Order, which was then recently founded by St. Bernard of Clairvaux. The two became friends, and his reputation rose in the Church until he was elected Pope in February 1145. When he learned about the fall of Edessa to Zengi, he issued the bull <u>Quantum Praedecessores</u> calling for the Second Crusade, which he entrusted St. Bernard to preach. While the Second Crusade was a failure due the personal and political intrigue of the Crusaders' leaders, Pope Bl. Eugene III nevertheless continued to support the Crusades. He died in 1153.

St. Bernard of Clairvaux
Feast Day: August 20th

    St. Bernard was born into a noble family in 1090 and received an extensive secular education before becoming a monk at age 19. When he was 23, St. Bernard founded the Cistercian Order at Clairvaux, France. The Order grew rapidly and soon attracted the attention of Pope Callixtus II. The Cistercians, known as the "White Robes,"[16] sought for a strict, literal application of St. Benedict's rule. This was because he felt that many Benedictines, and specifically the Benedictines of Cluny, France who made the famous Clunaic reforms of the 10th century, had become lackadaisical.

St. Bernard of Clairvaux was famous for his conflict with Bl. Peter the Venerable of Montbossier. This likely was due to his perceptions of the monastery at Cluny before Bl. Peter's arrival, as Bl. Peter cleaned up many of the problems there after taking charge of the monastery. The conflict between St. Bernard and Bl. Peter only intensified after Bl. Peter defended the theologian Peter Abélard against St. Bernard's charges of heresy against him for taking a rationalistic view of the Holy Trinity.[17] Nevertheless, the two were eventually reconciled.

When the Order of the Knights Templar emerged, St. Bernard greatly admired and praised them in a book entitled <u>On the New Knighthood</u>, which gave the Templars support and recognition from the Church. As the official preacher for the Second Crusade, he executed his commission with great success. When the Second Crusade failed, he likewise correctly noted in a letter to the Pope that it was the Crusaders' sinful intrigues, particularly those of their leaders, which caused the Crusade's failure.[18]

St. Bernard of Clairvaux lived a full life as a theologian and preacher. He died on August 20th, 1153 and was buried in the abbey he founded. Eight hundred years later, Pope Pius XII called him the "Last of the Fathers," and gave him the title of Doctor Mellifluus.[19]

St. Bernard of Clairvaux[20]

Bl. Peter the Venerable of Montbossier
Feast Day: Dec 25th

Bl. Peter the Venerable of Montbossier was a Frenchman born in 1092 who became a Benedictine monk at the monastery of Cluny when he was 17. He was known from an early age for emphasizing the union of Faith and reason.

Following a visit to Spain in 1139, Bl. Peter began intensive research on Islam. With the assistance of the Benedictine Order, the Archbishop of Toledo, and the Catholic King Alfonso X of Castile, he started the Toledo School of Translators in Toledo. The school's purpose was to identify and translate Arabic manuscripts of religious and scientific importance into Latin for study.

Among the texts Bl. Peter's school translated were the first full translation from Arabic into Latin of the Quran, known as The Words of the False Prophet Muhammad and the Apology of Al-Kindi, which is a polemic between a Muslim and a Christian. He also produced the first known European Catholic intellectual writings criticizing Islam, entitled The Summary of All the Saracen's Heresies and A Refutation of the Saracen's Sect or Heresy. Both texts explain Islam to be a Christian heresy influenced by Paganism. Bl. Peter's work became so influential that the entire Benedictine Order mandated that any priest commissioned to preach a Crusade would have to read the Quran so as to correctly criticize Islam before preaching.

Bl. Peter the Venerable of Montbossier died on Christmas Day, 1156. He is sometimes regarded as one of the founders of Islamic Studies. Pope Benedict XVI mentioned him in an address on October 14th, 2009 at St. Peter's Square as a model for Islamic Studies and the Church today.

Our Lady of Fatima
and the tale of Sir Gonçalo Hermigues and Princess Fatima
Feast Day: May 13th (1917 apparitions)

The story of Our Lady of Fatima as is known to many Catholics began in 1917 when the Blessed Virgin appeared to three Portuguese children- Francisco Marto, Jacinta Marto, and Lúcia dos Santos. The Blessed Mother warned them about great chastisements coming upon man. She said that many souls would be damned if they refused to repent of their sins and convert their lives. Fatima remains the most important revelation of Our Lady in modern times, and one of the most important in Catholic history. What is less known is that Our Lady of Fatima is connected to the Portuguese Reconquista during the Second Crusade.

It is no secret in Islam that Muhammad, Islam's founder, engaged in misogyny of the worst kinds. A brief reading of Islamic sacred scripture in the Quran and Islamic sacred tradition in the Hadith immediately exposes this, and is verified by 14 centuries of Islamic theological exegesis and historical example. But in spite of Muhammad's teachings and actions, he always showed great care for his beloved daughter Fatima. The name Fatima means "the weaned one," and suggests that she may have been a small or sickly child when born. Muhammad loved her, never abused her, and always sought to protect her.

In Islamic tradition, Fatima is associated with purity. Muslims have often made comparisons between the Blessed Virgin Mary[21] and Fatima. Mary and Fatima are the only two women in Islam whose names command extraordinary respect.

During the Second Crusade in Portugal, King Alfonso I launched an aggressive military campaign beginning in 1147 after the capture of Lisbon from the Muslims. One major target was the city of Alcácer Do Sal, which sat on a contested border region and was in the territory of the Catholic Count Gonçalo Hermigues.

King Alfonso I worked secretly with Count Hermigues and the Knights of St. James of the Sword to plan an attack on Alcácer Do Sal. On June 24th, 1158, the feast day of St. John the Baptist's nativity, they launched a stealth attack upon the city and swiftly wrested it from Muslim control. In the process, Count Hermigues captured the Muslim governor's daughter, who was named Fatima, and stole away with her to the surrounding Serra de Aire Mountains.

However, the hostage situation quickly changed, as the Count and the Princess fell in love with each other. Princess Fatima converted to Catholicism, taking the name Oureana, and the two married. Count Hermigues renamed the region around Alcácer Do Sal with the title "Ourém" after his wife. Likewise, the village of Fatima within Ourém was named after her. When she died, Count Hermigues became a Cistercian monk in the monastery at Alcobaça, being heartbroken at the loss of his beloved.

The Castle at Alcácer do Sal taken in 1158.[22]

It was in the village of Fatima that the three children had their vision in 1917 of the Blessed Virgin. It is fitting that the Blessed Virgin should appear at Fatima, as the name conveys honor among Muslims and the actual woman for whom the place is named was a convert from Islam to the Catholic Faith. The connection Islam makes between Fatima as Muhammad's daughter and the Blessed Virgin Mary is an even more crucial point, especially in the history and story of Our Lady of Fatima. As Venerable Bishop Fulton Sheen has pointed out, Our Lady of Fatima is a great hope for the conversion of the Muslims because Mary always points the way to Christ:

Missionaries in the future will increasingly see that their apostolate among the Muslims will be successful in the measure that they preach Our Lady of Fatima. Because the Muslims have a devotion to Mary, our missionaries should be satisfied merely to expand and develop that devotion with the full realization that Our Blessed Lady will carry the Muslims the rest of the way to her Divine Son. As those who lose devotion to her lose belief in the Divinity of Christ, so those who intensify devotion to her gradually acquire that belief.[23]

The Shrine of Our Lady of Fatima[24]

St. Bertold
Feast Day: March 29th

St. Bertold was a priest and knight from Limoges, France. Little information is available about his life, but an experience he had during the Second Crusade brought about his personal conversion and led to the establishment of the Carmelite Order.

After the Crusader siege against Damascus in 1148 failed miserably, Nur Ad-Din resumed his aggressions. He had already captured Aleppo, and Antioch was next on his list of places to overtake. On June 29th, 1149 he laid siege to Antioch. To make matters worse, he wiped out Antioch's entire army at the Battle of 'Inab as the siege began. Antioch's military leader, Raymond of Antioch, was killed in the conflict. The situation was disastrous, and it looked as though Antioch would fall to the Muslims.

St. Bertold was at Antioch during the siege. Fortunately, he did not forget that no matter how bad a situation can be, God is always in control. Turning to God, St. Bertold prayed for the salvation of the city and its people, for he knew that if Nur Ad-Din won, it meant certain death for everyone. By a miracle, Nur Ad-Din was not only unable to take Antioch, but a Crusader army from Jerusalem arrived that drove away Nur Ad-Din's army and ended the siege.

After this incident, St. Bertold exchanged military life for monastic life. He founded a community at Mt. Carmel, which was the beginning of the Carmelite Order. St. Brocard carried on his work after his death in 1195.

St. Brocard
Feast Day: September 2nd

St. Brocard was a Carmelite monk in the Middle East and the prior of the Carmelite Order after St. Bertold. He was loved and respected by Muslims for his humility. He died in 1231.

The Castle of Calatrava.
Here the Order of Calatrava led its defense of the Kingdom of Castile against the Almohads beginning in 1158.[25]

Notable Mention

Martim Moniz
d. 1147

Martim Moniz was a Portuguese soldier who took part in the Second Crusade in Portugal. His fame comes from his actions in taking the Castle of St. George in 1147.[26] According to tradition, the Muslims attempted to close the castle doors to prevent the Crusaders from coming in. In an act of selfless bravery, Martim threw himself between the doors to prevent them from closing. His body opened a gap that was just large enough for the Crusaders to successfully pry the doors open in order to rush in and take the castle.

Martim died during the siege, as his body was crushed by the doors. Nevertheless, his memory lives as a great Catholic knight who gave his life to liberate Portugal for God and country.

Gerald the Fearless
d. 1173

Gerald the Fearless is to Portugal as El Cid is to Spain. But unlike El Cid,[27] Gerald the Fearless was an ardent Catholic who saw alliances with the Muslims as an end to aiding the Reconquista. Certainly he desired and did carve out his own kingdom, but he was shrewd and meticulous in the way he went about doing so. He was a popular Catholic folk hero, and he was called "the dog" by the Muslims because of his great successes against them.

Little is known about his early life, although it is believed he came from a peasant family. From 1162 to 1173 he waged an aggressive war against the Muslim provincial strongholds of Alentejo in Portugal and Extremadura in Spain. He is credited with taking the cities of Beja,[28] Cáceres, Évora, Juromenha, Montánchez, Monfragüe, Serpa, Trujillo, and Urenha. His particular method of capturing cities was what made him infamous. When attacking a city, Gerald and his men gave no advance notice, but scaled the city's walls by night and killed the guards. They would then open the city's gates and slip his army in as the city still slept. By the time morning came, Gerald had already taken control and it would be too late to rally any efforts to oppose him.

Gerald's bravery and boldness eventually found him trouble by when he impinged on territory belonging to the Spanish Kingdom of León. In order to keep peace between Portugal and León, Gerald surrendered his cities, fled to Morocco, and pledged his support to the Almohad Caliphate. In exchange, he was made governor of the Province of Sous in northern Morocco. However, his support was a farce, because all the time he was secretly working with the Portuguese in preparations to attack Morocco. Before Gerald had a chance to realize his plans, the Almohads discovered them, and he was arrested and beheaded for treason.

Many of the cities which Gerald liberated later fell back under Muslim control. These cities were not finally liberated until King St. Ferdinand III of Castile's reign in the 13th century.

Gerald the Fearless is a notable example of Catholic chivalry, bravery, and intelligence in the struggle with Islam. His sacrifices were remembered by Catholics throughout the Reconquista, and a great debt of gratitude is owed to his efforts.

The Military Orders of the Crusades

Most of the Catholic Military Orders emerged in the 12th century and were inspired by the heroic deeds of the Knights Templar in the Holy Land. By combining the virtues of faith, hope, and charity with chivalry and the force of arms, they enabled Catholics to channel their Faith into actions that served God, the Church, and their fellow man.

The Military Orders of the Crusades are roughly separated into two classes- those who fought in Spain and Portugal, and those who fought in the Crusader States. There were fewer orders founded in the Crusader States, but they long outlasted the Crusades. Some of them continue to exist today, such as the Knights of Malta. In Spain and Portugal more orders were founded, but they were often dissolved following the end of the Reconquista.

The Military Orders developed for two major reasons. The first reason was that Catholic pilgrims needed to be protected while on pilgrimage or living in areas with sizeable Muslim populations. The second reason was that the Church needed men who would invest themselves into establishing a long-term presence in Muslim-dominated areas. The Military Orders were ideal for this, and did both with great success. Many of the knights which comprised them were monks, priests, or other religious, and they often committed themselves to the crusader cause for life.

But the Military Orders had missions that encompassed far more than just fighting Islam. They were often the sole providers for the Church in services such as care for the sick, the dying, and the mentally ill. They also served as highly-respected mediators between Catholics and Muslims when non-military disputes arose.

The Military Orders were critical to executing the Church's mission. In a militant sense, they successfully undertook great works in the temporal struggles with Islam. In society as a whole they helped and cared for all people, Catholic and Muslim alike, who came to them for assistance. While no group is perfect, the Military Orders represented some of the best lived witnesses of faith, hope, and charity of the Middle Ages and Church history.

Godfrey of Bouillon, First Crusade leader and ancestor of St. Anthony of Padua. His successes with the victors of the First Crusade helped inspire the later Catholic Military Orders.[29]

Orders of Spain and Portugal

While St. Bernard of Clairvaux was preaching the Second Crusade in 1147, the Almoravids fell from control in Muslim Spain. However, they were only to be replaced with the even more violent Almohads. The persecutions which the Almohads wrought combined with the successes of the Knights Templar in the Holy Land inspired many Catholics to establish similar orders of knighthood in Spain and Portugal. As the Reconquista pressed on, the Military Orders exemplified the spirit of the Catholic Faith and her struggle with Islam.

Order of Avíz

The Order of Avíz was originally founded in 1128 by Benedictine monks as a copy of the Knights Templar in Portugal and with the financial backing of Theresa, Countess of Portugal. King Alfonso I of Portugal gave the Order the city of Évora upon its capture, after which the Order was also known as the Order of Évora. The Order of Avíz worked closely with the Spanish Order of Calatrava. In certain respects, the Order of Avíz came to be regarded as a branch of the Order of Calatrava. However, it retained its autonomy.

The Order of Avíz participated in various excursions during the 15th century, notably in attacks against Ceuta and Tangiers. The Order declined after the end of the Reconquista, and was formally secularized by the Church in 1789.

Order of Calatrava

The Order of Calatrava was the first order to come from Castile, Spain and was one of the strongest forces of the Reconquista. The group was originally formed of knights who were Cistercian monks and lived in community under strict application of the Benedictine Rule.

Calatrava is the Spanish name of the Arabic "Qala'ah Rabbah," meaning "the citadel of Rabbah."[30] King Alfonso VII of Castile originally conquered Calatrava in 1157, but did not have the ability to easily defend it. As such, he entrusted the care of Calatrava to St. Raymond of Fitero and several other Cistercian monks. It was out of this action that the Order of Calatrava was born.

For nearly 40 years, the Order of Calatrava managed to hold back the Muslims from the Kingdom of Castile. In 1195, the Order took part in the disastrous Battle of Alarcos, which almost resulted in the fall of Calatrava as well as the Islamic conquest of Castile. The Order regrouped at Salvaterra in Castile and managed to defend the fortress for 14 more years until it fell in 1209. As the Almohads continued their advance, it appeared that the Order of Calatrava might be destroyed along with the Kingdom of Castile.

Pope Innocent III took notice of what happened, and he called for the Church to aid the Spanish against the Almohads. Catholics across all of Western Europe responded by going on Crusade to Spain in order to assist the Spanish. With an influx of new members, the Order of Calatrava and the Kingdom of Castile were refreshed. The Order went on to play a critical role in the pivotal Battle of Las Navas de Tolosa in 1212, which began the formal decline and fall of Islamic Spain.

The Order of Calatrava continued to grow over the next three centuries. It reached its apex of influence with the Fall of Granada in 1492 that ended Islamic rule in Spain. It continued to survive until it was formally secularized and dissolved in 1838.

Order of St. James of the Sword
(also called the Order of Santiago)

The Order of St. James of the Sword came into existence in 1171. It was based at the Shrine of St. James of Compostela and was composed of both Spanish and Portuguese knights. Its goal was to protect pilgrims going to the Shrine from Muslim attacks, but it quickly emerged as a formidable force in the Reconquista by taking the town of Cáceres in Extremadura Province, Spain in 1177. The Order participated in many battles of the Reconquista, including Las Navas de Tolosa in 1212 and the Fall of Granada in 1492. Eventually, the Order was separated into Spanish and Portuguese branches with the emergence of the two separate kingdoms.

Order of Alcántara

The Order of Alcántara was formed in the city of Alcántara, Extremadura Province, Spain in 1176. Since Extremadura Province was a hotly contested area between the Catholic kings and the Muslims, the city of Alcántara repeatedly changed possession until 1214 when it was definitively transferred to Catholic hands. The Order was recognized by the Papacy in 1177, and there existed a long-standing conflict between it and the Order of Calatrava due to property and political disputes. Nevertheless, the Order of Alcántara remained a prominent force in the Reconquista, and is known for having the most stringent requirements for membership in that one would have to prove he was of pure Spanish nobility.[31]

Order of Mountjoy

Known also as the Order of Trufac, the Order of Mountjoy was established in 1180 by Spanish Count Rodrigo Álvarez while on Crusade in the Holy Land. The name is a reference to Jerusalem, described as the "mountain of joy." The Order participated in many battles in the Holy Land, and often fought alongside the Knights Templar. Certain members of the Order wanted to merge with the Templars, but others dissented and founded the rival Order of Monfragüe in Spain. In any case, the Order was uniquely Spanish in character and based on the Cistercian Rule. The Order of Mountjoy, like the Order of Monfragüe, was merged by King St. Ferdinand III of Castile into the Order of Calatrava in 1221.

Order of Monfragüe

The Order of Monfragüe was founded in Monfragüe, Extremadura Province, Spain in 1196 by knights from the Order of Mountjoy who did not want to fully merge with the Knights Templar. It existed as early as 1187 and was commanded by a Gonzalo Padilla. However, there seems to have been more internal conflict within the Order than external action taken. The Order fought alongside the Order of Calatrava at Las Navas de Tolosa in 1212, and was merged into the Order of Calatrava in 1221 by King St. Ferdinand III of Castile.

Order of the Knights of St. George

The Order of the Knights of St. George was formed in Cataluña in 1201 by King Pedro II of Aragón. It was also known as the Knights of St. George of Alfama and it participated in the wars against Islamic Spain. However, it was short-lived and was merged into the Order of Montesa[32] by the Pope in 1363.

A view of Extremadura Province, Spain. While not all parts of Extremadura look like this, it was in these lands that many of the Reconquista's battles took place, particularly involving the Catholic Military Orders.[33]

Orders of the Crusader States

There were four notable Orders of the Crusader States. They were the Knights Templar, the Knights Hospitaller, the Teutonic Knights, and the Knights of St. Lazarus. The Knights of St. Lazarus was the only order that did not survive beyond the Crusades in its previous form. The Knights Templar was forcibly dissolved by the Pope owing to Church-State conflicts of the early 14th century, but has been re-established since 1979 by the Vatican as a private association of the faithful. The Knights of Malta and Teutonic Knights continue to exist today, albeit as humanitarian orders. However, both retained their military character and involvement for centuries after the Crusades in conflicts with the Muslims and inter-European affairs.

The Orders of the Crusader States were the most critical to the development of the later Catholic Military Orders. However, the most important of all these was unquestionably the Knights Templar. Almost all other orders were modeled after them, and their repute has been maintained throughout the centuries.

Knights Templar

The Knights Templar is the most lauded Military Order in Catholic history. It was born after a group of French Knights led by Hugh de Payens petitioned King Baldwin II of Jerusalem in 1118 to form a group to help protect Catholic pilgrims as well as fight for the Faith. They adopted the name "Poor Knights of the Temple," in reference to the city of Jerusalem, where they took perpetual vows of chastity, poverty, and obedience. The Order was not formally approved until 1128 at the Council of Troyes. The Knights' greatest supporter was St. Bernard of Clairvaux, who lauded them in his work <u>On the New Knighthood</u>.[34]

The Knights Templar was unique because it functioned with almost complete autonomy within the Church. Though it was governed by the Church, it was subject solely to the Pope's authority and was exempt from Church taxes or property management. This enabled it to amass great wealth and power, which facilitated its ability to successfully combat attacks by Islamic armies.

The Knights Templar had a fierce dedication to the Church, and they spent their nights in prayer before going into battle. Their policy in battle was to fight even to their deaths, and it was understood that no Templars would be ransomed by the order because Muslims often attempted to convert or use prisoners as tools of ransom. It was guaranteed that any Knight who was captured by the Muslims would be executed, and many Knights were. However, this also grew their fame because they refused to convert to Islam in order to save their lives.

The Order of the Knights Templar was known for its bravery. This was particularly shown during the Second Crusade at the Siege of Askalon in 1153. Its reputation continued at the disaster of Hattin in 1187, and the Third Crusade's Siege of Acre and Battle of Arsuf in 1191. The Knights Templar also took part in the Fall of Acre in 1291 to the Mamluks, as well as the Siege of Ru'ad Island in 1302 that formally ended the Crusades in the Holy Land.

Yet in spite of the ferocity of the Knights Templar, it was also highly respectful of the Muslims. Many Muslims sought the order's help for resolving disputes as well as against the occasional band of marauding Crusaders. The Knights integrated into the Holy Land, learning about Islam, the local culture, and the Arabic language. While its members had no sympathy for Islam and were ardently dedicated to defending and propagating the Catholic Faith, they knew the Middle East and the Muslim people. This enabled the Knights to effectively protect and grow their interests and those of the Church while honoring the dignity and humanity of the Muslims.

The Templars declined as fewer and less-dedicated members joined than those of the past. As the Order became richer, it shifted focus from military activity into banking. This alarmed many European princes, as they correctly saw the Templar's monetary holdings and it ability to offer loans as developing a second government within their own kingdoms. While the Knights Templar had not formally caused revolutions, its autonomy and financial power was a real threat. This was worsened by the fact that based on the Templar's example, other Military Orders formally petitioned to have their own temporal domains in Europe.

While these conflicts with the Knights Templar were happening, King Philip IV of France, also known as "Philip the Fair," was destroying the French treasury to feed his spending habits. When the Pope ordered the Knights Templar suppressed, King Philip saw this as an opportunity to seize its assets. Since many of the Knights were French, he arrested them and forced them to confess under torture to the sins of blasphemy, sodomy, and worshipping "Baphomet".[35] Philip's tyrannical behavior caused much tension between France and the Church, but there was little the Pope could do to stop Philip's behavior. King Philip mass executed the remaining Templar knights, and the order was destroyed by 1314. However, the Pope officially pardoned each knight in so far as proclaiming that the charges brought against them by King Philip were false and they had never left the Church.

In later years, organizations such as the Freemasons and other anti-Catholic groups sought to use the memory of the Templars to support fanciful claims to so-called "esoteric" secrets. None of these are true and are merely distractions and insults against what was a great Catholic Military Order.

There were two successors to the Knights Templar. The Order of Montesa succeeded the Templars in Spain in 1312 and until 1319 operated independently, having been given the Cistercian Rule by Pope John XXII in 1317. However, in 1319 it was folded into the Order of Calatrava.

The Order of Christ was the Portuguese successor to the Knights Templar, founded in 1319 and was stationed at Santarém, where it supported the Portuguese Reconquista. After the Reconquista, the Order of Christ followed the Portuguese navy across Africa and the Far East where it evangelized the people it encountered, including many Muslims. It eventually declined and was secularized in later centuries.

As mentioned earlier, the Knights Templar was revived in 1979 as the *Militia Templi*. However, it is only a private association of the faithful with an emphasis on Catholic traditionalism.

Seal of the Knights Templar[36]

Knights Hospitaller

The origins of the Knights Hospitaller stem from 600, and their purpose was to care for Christian pilgrims on their way to the Holy Land. The beginning of the Crusades, however, transformed the Knights Hospitaller into a formal Military Order. This can be traced to the Benedictine monk Bl. Gerard Thom, who began the order's transformation in 1099 following the conquest of Jerusalem. Pope Paschal II approved the Order in 1113, and they spread quickly across the Holy Land. The Knights Hospitaller was unique because like the Knights Templar, it operated with near complete autonomy within the Church. It was exempt from Church taxes, owned its own religious buildings, and was answerable solely to the Pope.

As in the past, the Knights Hospitaller continued to operate hospitals and provide lodging for pilgrims in addition to their military character. The Knights played pivotal roles in many battles, such as the success at the Siege of Askalon in 1153 and the disastrous failure at Hattin in 1187. Because the Knights Hospitaller operated in the Holy Land full-time and was not constituted of people who would return to Europe any time soon, its members were able to fully immerse themselves in Middle Eastern culture. While they remained ardent Catholics, they became intimately familiar with Islam and the Muslims. This perspective enabled the Knights to make strategic decisions that many of the Crusaders and their rulers failed to do on account of their connections with the European monarchies.

The Knights Hospitaller ultimately separated into two orders. One of these eventually became known as the Knights of Malta, and the other developed into the Order of St. Lazarus. The latter was disbanded when the Crusades in the Holy Land ended. The former and larger branch of the Hospitallers fled to the island of Cyprus, where they took refuge and continue to engage in battle against the Mamluks and later the Ottomans.

This continued until 1309, when they took the island of Rhodes in the Aegean Sea. The order transferred its operations to Rhodes and changed its name to the "Knights of Rhodes." However, the Ottomans ousted the Knights in 1522. The Knights finally took refuge on the Mediterranean island nation of Malta, from which they have since been called the "Knights of Malta." It continued for many following centuries to fight against the Ottomans until the early 19th century. The order continues to exist today, albeit as a humanitarian order.

Teutonic Knights
or the German order of St. Mary in Jerusalem

The Order of the Teutonic Knights originally began in 1192[37] and was modeled on the Knights Hospitaller. It took special efforts to establish hospices for the care of German-speaking pilgrims to the Holy Land. The order was based on the Rule of St. Augustine, and played military roles in every later Crusade up until the Fall of Acre in 1291. After the Crusades in the Holy Land ended, the order returned to Europe and participated in the inter-European Crusades against the Slavic and Baltic peoples.

The Protestant movement caused many divisions within the Teutonic Knights, as it was a uniquely German order. Eventually the order's military character was abandoned, and it became a humanitarian organization which survives to this day.

The Order of St. Lazarus

The Order of St. Lazarus took its name from the leper under the rich man's table[38] in the New Testament, as it was founded in 1098 to care for lepers. However, since many members also belonged to the Knights Hospitaller, it developed a military character and emerged as a separate order. The Order was vital in the Holy Land as both a source of caring for the sick and fighting for the defense of the Catholic Faith.

The Order was gradually destroyed with the losses incurred in the later Crusades during the 13th century. By the Fall of Acre in 1291, the Order was so weak that it was formally dissolved.

A Templar Knight (left) and Knight Hospitaller (right).[39]

Third Crusade

The Crusader States continued to hold their territories in the north against Nur Ad-Din while they focused the majority of their conquest efforts on the Fatimid Dynasty in Egypt. The last two Fatimid rulers, Al-Fa'iz Bi-Din Allah (1149 – 1160) and Al-'Adid Li-Din Allah Abu Muhammad 'Abdullah bin Yusuf Al-Hafiz Li-Din Allah (1160 – 1171) were both children who were titular more than actual rulers. Most of the ruling in Egypt was done by Nur Ad-Din's empire through his viziers that he sent to Egypt, as the Fatimids formed an alliance with Nur Ad-Din on account of the Crusaders' attacks.

The most important of the Egyptian viziers was Asad Ad-Din Shirkuh bin Shadhi, known as Shirkuh. He was sent to Egypt in 1164 to resolve a conflict with the reigning vizier, Shawar bin Mujayr As-Sa'di. In order to prevent Shirkuh's ascent to power, Shawar allied with the Crusaders against Shirkuh. After a period of skirmishing, Shirkuh eventually overtook Shawar and executed him.[40] However, he died after only two months in power, and was replaced by his nephew Salah Ad-Din Yusuf Al-Ayyubi, known better by his latinized name, Saladin.

Saladin had already spent considerable time in Egypt before Shirkuh's ascent to power. While in Egypt, he had a religious conversion that brought him to strict practice of Islam. Beginning in 1169 he started a series of wars that drove the Crusaders from their territories near Egypt and consolidated his power before expanding outward. In 1174, Nur Ad-Din died of poisoning. It is suspected that Saladin was complicit in this. Immediately after his death, Saladin sent a letter to Nur Ad-Din's 11-year old son, As-Salih Ismail bin Nur Ad-Din Mahmoud bin 'Ammad Ad-Din bin Aq Sanqar, the reigning ruler, promising to avenge his father's death. Saladin then married Nur Ad-Din's widow, 'Isma Ad-Din Khatun, and by this action took control over all of Nur Ad-Din's former empire.

Saladin was now free to focus on his goal of waging jihad against the Crusaders. The reigning Crusader King of Jerusalem, Baldwin IV, was merely a teenager at the time of Saladin's ascent. He was a sickly young man already overwhelmed with trying to survive the mess of the entangling alliances on account of the European nobility's territorial conflicts. The leadership vacuum and incessant bickering among the Crusader leaders directly aided Saladin's ascent to power and the destruction of the Crusader States.

From 1174 until 1187, there were a series of small to mid-range battles fought between the Crusaders and Saladin. The greatest Crusader victories were the routing of Saladin's forces at the Battle of Montisgard in 1177, the holding of the Castle of Belvoir in 1182, and the Siege of Kerak in Jordan in 1183. Credit for these victories, however, does not go to the Crusader States' leadership but to the Catholic Military Orders, since they did the majority of the difficult fighting. Saladin also had several victories, including the Crusader rout at Marjayoun in southern Lebanon in 1179, the Battle of Al-Ful in 1183, and the Battle of Cresson in 1187. However, the most infamous Crusader loss and greatest victory of Saladin was the massacre at Hattin on July 4th, 1187.

Hattin is a small village in northern Israel near an extinct volcano that forms a hillside with a plateaued indenture in middle and the sides protruding upwards, creating a horn-like shape. It was at the "Horns of Hattin" where Crusader leader Raynald of Châtillon marched with an army of about 20,000 soldiers in an attempt to confront Saladin. This was what Saladin hoped for. He drew out the Crusader army and once they were at Hattin, he cut off the water and escape routes to leave them stranded in the hot desert sun. Saladin also demoralized the Crusaders by having soldiers shoot arrows and start fires around the camp. The Crusaders attempted to charge their way through Saladin's army, but it was impossible due to their positioning and the sheer volume of Saladin's forces.

Out of the 20,000 Crusaders who participated, it is estimated that approximately 10% survived, and they were taken prisoner. All members of the Catholic Military Orders were executed. Raynald was beheaded personally by Saladin because of Saladin's anger at him for violating a treaty they brokered in 1184. However Guy de Lusignan, who led the failed attack at Hattin with Raynald, was spared and later ransomed.

Saladin has been portrayed positively in European art and literature, often as a cross between a folk hero, gentleman, and warrior. It is true that Saladin was favorably documented by his biographer, Baha' Ad-Din. But the zeal of Saladin's charity and faith was the spread of Islam through waging jihad against the Crusaders and supporting institutions to build up Islam's presence in the Middle East to the detriment of Christianity and the Catholic Faith.

Pope Urban III died of grief upon receiving the news about Hattin. The day after his death, Pope Gregory VIII was elected and called immediately for a Third Crusade. The great hero of the Third Crusade was the English King Richard Plantagenet, also known as Richard the Lionheart. Richard was so dedicated that he even enacted a special "Saladin Tax" in 1188 in England to help pay for his expedition, and he spent more time overseas than ruling his own kingdom. Other European monarchs offered to go on the Crusade, and thus the Third Crusade is also known as the "King's Crusade."

King Richard's presence was short but immensely helpful, and he gave Saladin the greatest disgrace of his life. This was the acceptance of a three-year armistice that ultimately incapacitated Saladin, who died in 1193 and thus failed in his goal to exterminate the Crusader States. King Richard returned home to England to re-assert territorial claims between various warring nobles and his power-hungry brother John.

Overall, the Third Crusade was successful in its mission. It prevented but did not stave off the eventual decline and fall of the Crusader States.

A famous statue of Saladin in Damascus, Syria. On the other side the Third Crusade leader Raynald of Châtillon can be seen in chains as Saladin's prisoner. Saladin later beheaded Raynald.[41]

Martyrs

St. Nicasius of Sicily
Feast Day: July 1st

St. Nicasius was a knight from Palermo, Sicily who traveled to the Holy Land for the Third Crusade. He was a Knight Hospitaller and was captured at the disastrous Battle of Hattin in 1187. As with all knights of the Catholic Military Orders, they were brought before Saladin and he promised to spare their lives if they converted to Islam. St. Nicasius refused to leave the Catholic Faith, and he was beheaded.

Raynald of Châtillon, continued from the previous image.[42]

Contenders

Bl. Gerard Mecatti of Villamagna
Feast Day: May 13th[43]

Bl. Gerard Mecatti of Villamagna was born in 1174 to a poor Tuscan family. His parents died when he was 12, but the feudal lords his parents worked for took him in and gave him an education. Shortly thereafter, the family left for the Third Crusade. While in the Holy Land, they were imprisoned by the Muslims but later were ransomed and returned to Italy. However, Bl. Gerard went back to the Holy Land, joined the Knights Hospitaller, and distinguished himself as a valiant warrior. Upon returning home, he became a Third Order Franciscan and hermit, and he lived out the rest of his days in prayer, fasting, and service to others until his death in 1242.[44]

Bl. Gerard was beloved for his heroism and humility. His reputation was well-known during his life and continued after his death, particularly in his hometown of Villamagna. His name christens the Oratory of Bl. Gerard in Villamagna, which was constructed over his grave from funds raised by those who loved him.

Hattin in 1934. The "horns" between which the Crusaders took up position is visible in the background from this angle.[45]

Notable Mention

Richard the Lionheart
d. 1193

Richard the Lionheart was to the Catholics as Saladin was to the Muslims. He was born Richard Plantagenet in 1157 and although he was King of England, he served more time on Crusade and abroad than in his kingdom. Like Charles Martel, King Richard often represented both the best and worst in Christendom, as he was known for acts of both great devotion and savagery. Nevertheless, he was a pious Catholic who went to Mass daily and persistently strove to live the Faith in both public and private life, including imposing public penance upon his person at least three times after committing serious sin.[46]

King Richard was originally not expected to become King of England. After a long internal struggle for power, Richard ascended to the throne in 1189 following the death of his father and his brother Henry. Richard had already pledged to go on Crusade back in 1187 following the news about Hattin, and had been making preparations since that time. In 1188, he imposed a "Saladin tax" on England that helped him to generate necessary revenue to fund his expedition. Once preparations were finalized, Richard and an army of soldiers from across the British Isles set out for the Holy Land in 1190.

After a brief layover in Sicily, he set sail for Acre but crashed at Cyprus on May 1st, 1191. Many Crusaders had already taken up residence on Cyprus. The island was a Byzantine territory ruled by the temperamental Despot Isaac Komnenos. Richard the Lionheart deposed Isaac and took the island for himself. He then sold it to the Knights Templar, who used it as a military base of operations for the rest of the

Crusades' duration. While he was on Cyprus he married Berengaria of Navarre, with whom he had no children.

On June 8th, 1191, Richard arrived at Acre, which had been taken by Saladin in January. Richard launched a fierce attack and retook the city after a brutal month-long battle. He demanded that Saladin pay ransom for his prisoners or they would be beheaded, as Saladin had done at Hattin. When Saladin refused to pay, Richard promptly answered Saladin by beheading the entire Muslim garrison at such a location that Saladin could watch it if he wanted to from a distance.

Richard then turned his attention to liberating the Crusader States' coastal cities from Saladin's rule. He began a march southward to Jaffa, in which Saladin attempted to draw Richard and his armies into a fight but failed to do so. Saladin formally ambushed Richard and engaged him in battle near the city of Arsuf in route to Jaffa in September 1191. It was a mistake that Saladin lived to regret, as Richard did not follow Saladin's provocations but held his ground and continued to march. Finally, the Grandmaster of the Knights Hospitaller, Garnier de Nablus, broke ranks and charged the Muslims against Richard's orders. Richard realized the charge could turn into a disaster, so he immediately responded by ordering the whole army to charge. This decision surprised Saladin, and his army was routed. Richard continued his march to Jaffa, which he swiftly conquered. He then went further south and took the city of Askalon.

By 1192, all the Holy Land's coastline was returned to Crusader control. However, King Richard wanted to return to England because his younger brother John was attempting to depose him.[47] Richard called a meeting with Saladin and the two formulated a three-year truce that allowed Jerusalem to remain in Muslim control but guaranteed safe passage for Catholic pilgrims. By October, Richard's work was done and he was on his way home. Saladin's health began to decline after the treaty, and he died in March 1193, unable to realize his dream of destroying the Crusaders.

Richard the Lionheart resumed his territorial wars in England against his brother John and other warring nobles. He contracted gangrene as the result of a wound inflicted from an arrow that was shot by a boy whose family was killed in Richard's wars. The sickness consumed Richard's body until he died in the arms of his mother on April 6th, 1199.

King Richard I of England, better known as Richard the Lionheart.[48]

Later Crusades

Six more crusades were launched. The worst of these was the Fourth Crusade in 1204, which was seized by opportunistic Venetian merchants who convinced and led the Crusader army to attack and pillage Constantinople. While the Church did not sanction the attack and soundly condemned what happened, serious damage was done to Catholic-Orthodox unity. This was doubly unfortunate, since many of the Popes had been working very hard on bringing about a reunification with the Orthodox during this time.

The Fifth Crusade was an abortive attempt between 1213 and 1221 to take over Egypt from Saladin's Ayyubid dynasty. However, the Crusade failed and many Crusaders as well as non-involved Muslims were killed in the fighting. The greatest benefit of this Crusade came from St. Francis of Assisi. The love and kindness he demonstrated to Kamal Ad-Din, Ayyubid Sultan of Egypt and nephew of Saladin, ultimately resulted in the Sultan's deathbed conversion to the Catholic Faith.

The Sixth Crusade in 1228 was the most successful in a temporal sense. The Holy Roman Empire under the leadership of King Frederick II with the help of the Teutonic Knights recaptured many Crusader territories on the Mediterranean coast. These included the cities of Bethlehem, Jaffa, Jerusalem, Nazareth, and Sidon.

The Seventh Crusade was another attempt at retaking Egypt in 1249, this time organized by King St. Louis IX of France. He was able to organize about 15,000 men to come on Crusade. Like the Fifth Crusade, it began by taking the Egyptian port city of Damietta, which they were able to successfully hold. Part of the army stayed at Damietta while St. Louis marched south with the rest of his army down the Nile to take Cairo. They were attacked by a combined army of Ayyubid and Mamluk[49] forces in route and were defeated near the city of Al-Mansourah in March 1250. Almost all the men were killed. St. Louis was taken prisoner but was later ransomed.

The Mamluks eventually annihilated Saladin's Ayyubid Dynasty in 1254 and established the Mamluk Dynasty. They were one of the most anti-Christian dynasties in Egypt's history. The Coptic Orthodox Church, which the majority of Egyptian Christians belong to, went into serious decline during this period. The Mamluks likewise waged a relentless jihad against the Crusader States.

The Eighth Crusade in 1270 was another abortive attempt organized by King St. Louis IX to take the city of Tunis from the Hafsid Dynasty. The siege initially worked well, but was forced to end early because of disease in the water supply that sickened many men and killed St. Louis. The benefit of the Crusade was that it opened trade between Tunis and Europe. Additionally, Catholic priests and missionaries were guaranteed safe residence and passage within Tunis.

The Ninth Crusade was organized in 1271 and ended in a 10-year armistice between the Crusaders and the Mamluks following the repulsion of the Mamluks at Acre. During the attack, the Mamluks attempted to conquer Cyprus, but were successfully repelled by the Crusaders. The Church attempted to ally themselves with the Mongols to fight the Mamluks as well as to Christianize the Mongols. This included sending missionaries and diplomats to China and Mongolia as well as inviting Mongol dignitaries to Europe, including their participation in the Council of Lyon in 1274. However, no alliance ever developed. The Crusader States were subject to ever more attacks from the Mamluks until the fall of Acre in 1291.

The Crusader States formally collapsed with the fall of Acre to the Mamluks in 1291. The last Crusader territory in the Holy Land to fall was Ru'ad Island off the Syrian coast in 1302. The Middle Eastern Christians, Catholic and Orthodox alike, suffered greatly with the loss of the Crusaders, as there was nobody left to protect them. Many converted to Islam, while others were forced to endure severe abuse.

While the 13th century ended with the destruction of the Crusader States, the Reconquista in the West was intensifying. This came particularly at the Battle of Las Navas de Tolosa in 1212, where the Spanish crushed the Almohads and permanently crippled Islamic Spain. The Almohads were eventually driven out of Spain and were replaced by the Marinid Dynasty from Morocco. But while in the past the subsequent Muslim newcomers were able to make significant military gains, the new Marinid invaders were unable to do so. Rather, they were contained in Spain's southernmost regions by the northern Spanish Catholic kingdoms.

There were also movements taking place in the Church. New religious orders emerged, including those that ransomed Catholics enslaved by Muslim pirates. There also was a new breed of Catholic explorers, scholars, and theologians that prepared the Church for her global mission that emerged in the coming centuries.

The Crusader ideal remained in Europe for several more centuries. It was vital in facing the Church's next great threat that emerged the same year that the last Crusader stronghold of Acre fell. This was the confederation of Turkish tribes led by a man named Osman in southwestern Anatolia. Osman had a dream that he would create a worldwide empire and become the next great protector and promulgator of Islam.[50] He was correct, for he became the founder of the Ottoman Empire that centuries later pushed Europe to the brink of extinction once again.

Our Lady of Mercy from the Church of St. Ferdinand in Cádiz, Spain. She appeared to St. Peter Nolasco, who founded the Mercedarian Order to combat the Muslim slave traders. Note that the heraldic symbol of the Kingdom of Aragón above her head is the Mercedarian emblem, and that the Cherubim on the bottom are carrying chains, as would be worn by captives.[51]

Martyrs

Bl. Albert Avogadro of Jerusalem
Feast Day: September 25th[52]

Bl. Albert Avogadro of Jerusalem was the Latin Patriarch Jerusalem from 1204 to 1215. He was born in 1149 and later became a canon lawyer. He was known for his mediation and diplomacy skills while serving as Bishop of Bobbio, Italy.

While serving as Patriarch, Bl. Albert's work reflected what he did in Europe. He was well-known for acting as a peacemaker between Catholics and Muslims, and he earned the respect of both groups. He also worked with St. Brocard to create the rule for the then recently-formed Carmelite Order. The rule came to be known as the Rule of Bl. Albert.

Bl. Albert died in 1215 after being stabbed to death by a mentally deranged man.

St. Berard of Carbio and Companions
(Accursius, Adjutus, Otho, Peter, and Votalis)
Feast Day: January 16th

St. Berard was born to a noble family and entered the Franciscan Order. Due to his knowledge of Arabic, he was commissioned to lead a group of priests to visit Morocco. Their mission was to preach to the Muslims and to invite Almohad Caliph Yusuf An-Nasir to embrace the Catholic Faith.

When they reached Morocco, their public preaching against Islam resulted in their imprisonment as well as an audience with Caliph Yusuf. The Caliph originally thought the men were mentally deranged, and he tried to negotiate with them to stop preaching and convert to Islam. However, they respectfully but adamantly refused. Out of anger, he had them beheaded in his court in 1220.

When their bodies were being shipped back to Europe through Portugal, a young priest named Fr. Fernando Martins de Bulhões saw them and was inspired to become a Franciscan. He later became known popularly as St. Anthony of Padua.

St. Daniel and Companions
(Agnellus, Donulus, Hugolinus, Nicholas, and Samuel)
Feast Day: October 10th

St. Daniel and his companions were Franciscan friars who sought to follow in the example of St. Berard and his companions. It is likely they were hoping for martyrdom, as they asked to preach in Almohad Spain and Morocco, which likely meant certain death.

After receiving permission, they traveled to Spain and arrived at the island of Ceuta. Here they preached publicly against Islam until they were arrested and brought before the local Sultan.[53] While in custody, they were asked to convert to Islam. When they refused, they were summarily beheaded in 1227.

Sts. John of Perugia and Peter of Sassoferrato
Feast Day: September 3rd

Sts. John of Perugia and Peter of Sassoferrato were Franciscans commissioned by St. Francis to preach to the Muslims in Spain. The men were seized by Muslims while in Valencia and were beheaded in 1231.

Bl. Raymond of Blanes
Feast Day: January 6th

Bl. Raymond of Blanes was a nobleman who joined the Mercedarians. While going to ransom enslaved Catholics in Granada, he was imprisoned and tortured to death. He died in 1235 on the feast of the Epiphany, and was the Mercedarian Order's first martyr.

St. Diego de Soto
Feast Day: January 15th

St. Diego de Soto was a Mercedarian from Toledo. He was tutored by St. Serapion prior to his martyrdom. Most of his work was done in southern Spain. He was arrested by the Muslims and imprisoned in 1237. When he refused to convert to Islam, he was starved to death in his prison cell. He is the Mercedarian Order's second martyr.

St. Serapion
Feast Day: November 14th

Born in London to a Scottish[54] family in 1179, St. Serapion served in the Third Crusade with King Richard the Lionheart's army. After returning to Europe, he served as a soldier in the Reconquista under King Alfonso VIII of Castile. It was during this time in Spain that he met St. Peter Nolasco, founder of the Mercedarian Order. In 1222, he joined the Mercedarians. He worked in southern Spain and North Africa until he was arrested in 1240 in Algeria.

According to tradition, St. Serapion told the Sultan two things after he was arrested and presented before him.[55] First, was that money was coming for his ransom from the

Mercedarian Order. Second, was that he would not convert to Islam, in spite of the Sultan's offers to him. When the money for his ransom did not arrive as quickly as the Sultan wished, he ordered St. Serapion crucified on an "X" shaped cross in the same manner as St. Andrew the Apostle perished. After his death, his remains were quartered.

St. Peter Rodriguez and Companions
Feast Day: June 11th

St. Peter Rodriguez was a Spaniard who was a member of the Order of St. James of the Sword. He was captured by Muslims along with seven companions. They were executed in 1242.

Sts. Raymond of St. Victor and William of St. Leonard
Feast Day: December 4th

Sts. Raymond of St. Victor and William of St. Leonard were French Mercedarians. On a mission to ransom enslaved Catholics in 1242, they were taken prisoner by Muslims in southern Spain. While in prison, they converted many Muslims to the Faith. When their captors asked them to convert to Islam and they refused, they were savagely beaten and decapitated.

St. Peter of St. Denis and Bl. Bernard of Prades
Feast Day: February 6th

St. Peter of St. Denis and Bl. Bernard of Prades were Mercedarians. They went to Tunis in order to ransom enslaved Catholics. In the process, the two were taken as hostage. Money was sent by the Order to redeem the two. Bl. Bernard was freed, but St. Peter was not. He stayed and continued preaching to the Muslims. His preaching enraged some of the Muslims, including the ruler of Tunis, Muhammad Alicur.[56] At his command, St. Peter of St. Denis was beaten with rods, paraded through Tunis while being mocked, and finally was beheaded, the corpse burned, and ashes discarded in 1247.

Sts. Ferdinand Perez and Louis Blanc
Feast Day: October 16th

Sts. Ferdinand Perez and Louis Blanc were Spanish Mercedarians from Castile and Aragón respectively. In 1250, they went to Tunis and were captured by Muslim pirates while in route.[57] When they refused to convert to Islam, they were beaten, tied with rocks, and drowned in the Mediterranean.

Bls. Raymond and William of Granada
Feast Day: October 21st

Bls. Raymond and William of Granada were Mercedarians. They were arrested after preaching among Muslims in public. When they refused to convert to Islam, they were executed around 1250.

Bl. Theobald of Narbonne
Feast Day: October 18th

Bl. Theobald was a Mercedarian from Narbonne. While on a mission in Tunis with St. Ferdinand of Portalegre[58] in 1253, he ransomed 129 Catholics enslaved by Muslims. He wanted to purchase more from two certain slave dealers, but instead found need of purchasing from other dealers because they had women and children. Enraged that Bl. Theobald did not buy more slaves from them, the two Muslims complained to the ruler of Tunis, who arrested Bl. Theobald.[59]

St. Ferdinand was allowed to go free with the 129 ransomed slaves, but Bl. Theobald was burned alive and finally stoned to death.[60]

Sts. Ferdinand of Portalegre and Eleutherius of Platea
Feast Day: April 12th

Sts. Ferdinand of Portalegre and Eleutherius of Platea were Mercedarian monks, the former of Portuguese birth in Portalegre, and the latter of French birth in Narbonne. The two were companions in their mission to ransom Catholics enslaved by Muslims. In 1257, they were captured by Muslim pirates while sailing to Algiers. The men were beaten, decapitated, and finally their bodies were thrown overboard into the Mediterranean.

Bl. Luis Gallo
Feast Day: December 3rd

Bl. Luis Gallo was a Mercedarian who ransomed Catholics enslaved by Muslims in Morocco as well as preached to and evangelized Muslims. In the year 1268, he was captured and imprisoned. When he would not convert to Islam, he was beaten and finally burned alive.

St. William the Wise
Feast Day: December 5th

St. William the Wise was a French nobleman of Italian descent who renounced his inheritance and became a

Mercedarian as a young man. On his first mission to Algiers in 1270, he was captured by Muslims. He was ordered stoned by Muslim children, and then his broken but still living body was burned alive.

Bl. Sancho of Aragón
Feast Day: October 21st

Bl. Sancho of Aragón was born in 1247 as the fourth son of King James I of Aragón. He became a Mercedarian while still a teenager, and by the age of 16 he was Archbishop of Toledo. He was killed at the Battle of Écija in 1275, which was a failed attempt to reconquer the city of Granada.

Bl. Peter of Cadireta
Feast Day: July 19th

Bl. Peter of Cadireta was born in Moya in northwestern Spain and became a Dominican. He was a close associate of the scholar and famed preacher St. Raymond of Peñafort. Most of his life was spent evangelizing the Albigensians in southern France, as well as preaching Crusades against them.[61] He was stoned to death by Albigensians in 1279 in the town of Seo de Urgell in northern Spain near the border of Andorra.

While he was not martyred at the hands of Muslims, Bl. Peter's missionary work involved a great deal of preaching to Spanish Muslims. He was one of a group of Dominicans who were sent to the *Studia Linguarum* founded by St. Raymond of Peñafort to study Arabic and Islam.

Bls. Monaldo of Ancona, Francis Petriolo, and Antonio Cantoni
Feast Day: March 15th

Bls. Monaldo of Ancona, Francis Petriolo, and Antonio Cantoni were Franciscan missionaries who were sent to what is now Erzincan, Turkey. Prior to the Armenian Genocide of 1917, Erzincan had a sizeable Christian population. The city was well-known to the Church, as William of Rubruck visited there during his travels to the Far East.

The missionaries reached Erzincan with the goals of bringing both the Armenians into full communion with the Catholic Church as well as converting the Muslims. They quickly won the admiration of the Armenians and continued to build constructive relations with them. However, the latter aim was more difficult. Nevertheless, the three men began preaching outside of a local mosque every Friday so that they would encounter the greatest number of Muslims to hear their message. Many Muslims were influenced by their preaching, and some did convert. However, a local Muslim judge took notice of them, and promised to publicly debate them the following week.

It was the week before Good Friday when the debate took place. To the surprise of the judge and his supporters, the missionaries crushed him in the debate. Out of anger, the judge and his supporters along with the Muslim leaders of Erzincan conspired to kill the missionaries.

The following week on Good Friday, the men were summarily arrested and summoned for a public trial. They were found guilty of blasphemy against Islam. The men refused to convert to Islam, and so received the death sentence. They were executed by being hacked to death with swords and their remains dumped for animals to feed upon. It is said there was a

Muslim man who tried for the sake of compassion to intervene and was also slain along with them. The year was 1286.[62]

While the majority of the Armenians were not Catholic, the Armenians immediately regarded Bls. Monaldo of Ancona, Francis Petriolo and Antonio Cantoni as saints and formally canonized them. They are venerated on March 15th in both the Catholic and the Armenian Apostolic Churches.

Sts. Mark Matthias and Anthony Valesio
Feast Day: April 10th

Sts. Mark Matthias and Anthony Valesio were Mercedarians sent to Tunis to preach to Muslims and ransom Catholics enslaved by Muslims. While in Tunis, they were arrested for evangelizing Muslims and brought before the Sultan, who told them to convert to Islam.[63] When they refused to convert, they were tortured and then executed. St. Mark Matthias was thrown from a castle's walls,[64] and St. Anthony Valesio was stoned to death. The year was 1293.

St. Peter Pascual
Feast day: December 6th

St. Peter Pascual was born in Valencia in 1227 and joined the Mercedarians while a priest. Prior to this he was tutor to Sancho, the son of King James I of Aragón. He preached across Spain and Italy, and ransomed many Catholics enslaved by Muslims. He also converted many Muslims. While serving as Bishop of Jaén, he was captured and beheaded at Granada in 1300 under Caliph Muhammad Al-Faqih.

Bls. James and Adolph
Feast Day: December 16th

Bls. James and Adolph were Mercedarians from Cataluña sent to Tunis to ransom enslaved Catholics. They ransomed many captives, but in 1314 they were captured by Muslims pirates and imprisoned. When they refused to convert to Islam, they were summarily executed.

A statue of Bl. Raymond Lull outside St. Michael's church in Palma, Majorca.[65]

Bl. Raymond Lull
"The Illuminated Doctor"
Feast Day: June 29th

Bl. Raymond Lull was a rich Spaniard from the island of Majorca. He was well-educated, married with two children, and was working as a tutor for King James II of Aragón's son when he had a vision of Jesus on the cross that prompted a religious conversion. He became a Third Order Franciscan and devoted his life to religious works in addition to his other studies. These included mathematics, computation, and alchemy.

Bl. Raymond Lull had a strong desire to convert Muslims and was an ardent supporter of the Crusades. He learned Arabic and studied the works of Averroes. Out of his search to find a systematic, logical response to Islam's claims he developed the beginnings of modern computation logic. This was expressed particularly in his seminal work, the <u>Ars Magna</u>. He was a great proponent of the union between faith and reason to develop a complete understanding about God.

He traveled three times to Tunis. The first time in 1285 he preached to Muslims publicly and barely escaped being lynched. The second time in 1304 he met with the Hafsid Caliph Muhammad I, and the two engaged in correspondence for some time. The third time in 1308 he traveled in secret as a spy gathering intelligence in preparation for a Crusader invasion that never happened. He went on a fourth and final visit in 1315, this time to Algeria, where he preached to angry Muslims and survived a public stoning. However, he never recovered from his injuries. He went home to Majorca, where he died at the age of 83.

St. Alexander of Sicily
Feast Day: April 1st

St. Alexander of Sicily was a Mercedarian from Palermo who was sent to redeem Catholics enslaved by Muslims in Tunis. In 1317, he was accused of insulting Islam. He was arrested and executed by being burned alive.[66]

Contenders

Bl. Arnaud Amalric
Feast Day: July 30th

Bl. Arnaud Amalric was a Cistercian monk and Papal Legate. He was born in the 12th century and eventually became Archbishop of Narbonne. He was known for his aggressive stances against heresy.[67] He took part in the great Catholic victory at the Battle of Las Navas de Tolosa in 1212, which routed the Almohads and put Islamic Spain into terminal decline. He died in 1225.

Bl. Berengar, the German of Bellpuig
Feast Day: October 20th

Bl. Berengar was a Spaniard with roots in Germany and the Catalan city of Bellpuig. He helped to fight and expel the Muslims from the island of Majorca under the leadership of King James I of Aragón in 1230. Later, he became a Mercedarian. While the exact date is unknown, he died in the late 13th century.

St. Ugo Canefri
Feast Day: October 8th

St. Ugo Canefri was born around 1148 to a noble Italian family near Piedmont, Italy. He joined the Knights Hospitaller and participated as a soldier in the Third Crusade. After returning home, he worked to care for the sick at a hospital in Genoa until his death in 1233.

St. Raymond Nonnatus
Feast Day: August 31st

St. Raymond Nonnatus was born in Spain in 1204. His name comes from the fact that his mother died while giving birth to him. In order to save his life, Raymond and was born by being cut out of his deceased mother's womb. He became a priest in 1222 and soon after joined the Mercedarians. He eventually became Master-General of the Order, and was a friend of St. Peter Nolasco.

During a mission to ransom enslaved Catholics in Algiers, St. Raymond sold himself into slavery so that another person might go free. While enslaved, he preached to and evangelized his captors and fellow slaves. When he would not stop preaching, the Muslims pierced his lips with a hot iron and placed a padlock through the hole in order to prevent him from speaking. He was also subject to frequent beatings during his eight months in captivity.

St. Raymond was eventually ransomed and was brought back to Spain. He died in 1240 while traveling to Rome to visit the Pope.

Bl. Tancred of Siena
Feast Day: September 9th

Bl. Tancred was born in 1185 in Siena. He became a Dominican following a vision of Our Lady standing beside St. Dominic during a homily at the Cathedral in Siena. He worked many miracles during his lifetime, including raising the dead. His work with Islam began in 1222 when he became head of the Dominicans in the Holy Land and the Crusader States. He made many converts from Islam to the Catholic Faith. He died in 1241.

St. Bernard Calbó
Feast Day: October 25th

St. Bernard Calbó was born in 1180 and became a jurist for the Archdiocese of Tarragona. In 1214 he became a Cistercian monk and was active in the Reconquista. He was a close associate of St. Raymond of Peñafort, and the two fought together at Valencia in 1238. After Valencia's fall, he helped to re-build the Church in the city by converting mosques into churches and evangelizing the locals. He died in 1243.

King St. Ferdinand III of Castile
Feast Day: May 30th

King St. Ferdinand III of Castile was born in 1198 in Salamanca, and was a great patron of the Catholic Faith. His contributions were numerous and vital in the Reconquista as well as to the Church within Spain and the restoration of Spanish culture.

St. Ferdinand ascended to the throne in 1217, taking the place of his father, King Alfonso IX, who was known as "The Slobberer." Five years earlier, Alfonso IX had inflicted the Almohads' greatest defeat at the pivotal Battle of Las Navas de Tolosa, which put Islamic Spain into terminal decline. After settling internal family disputes up to the time of his father's death in 1230, he intensified his support of the Reconquista. By 1248 he would conquer most of Spain, including Córdoba and Seville.

It is said that in addition to leading a life of prayer and fasting, he intensified practice of these disciplines before battle and personally saw to his men before leading them to war. The only Muslim controlled areas that remained by the end of his reign were the original Islamic strongholds, such as Granada, in the southernmost regions of Spain.

Whenever St. Ferdinand conquered an area, he sought to restore its previous Catholic roots as well as to sow new ones. As an example, he ordered translated and re-instituted the Liber Iudiciorum, or the Visigoth Code of law that governed Spain until the Islamic invasion of 711. He established the University of Salamanca, which was a project originally conceived by his father. He built many churches, including the Cathedral of Burgos, and restored former churches that were stolen by Muslims and turned into mosques. He strengthened all monastic orders within Spain, from the older ones such as the Benedictines and Cistercians to the newer ones such as the Dominicans, Franciscans and Mercedarians. He eventually became a Third Order Franciscan.

St. Ferdinand died in 1252 as the Almohad Empire was teetering on collapse.

King St. Ferdinand III of Castile[68]

Bl. Agnus of Zaragoza
Feast Day: March 14th

Bl. Agnus of Zaragoza was born in 1190 and became a Franciscan in 1220. He was an accomplished preacher, and because of this he was named a Titular Bishop of Morocco. As such, he was charged with both representing the Church in Morocco and evangelizing the Muslims. It is said that Bl. Agnus was highly respected by the Muslims.

As the Reconquista continued, Bl. Agnus was asked to help in re-establishing the Church's presence in areas of Spain that were liberated from Muslim control. He died in 1260.

King St. Louis IX of France
Feast Day: August 25th

King St. Louis IX of France was born in 1215. He became king at the age in 12 after his father died. He was raised for the most part by his mother, Blanche of Castile, in an environment of great piety and faith. He was known as both the "Most Christian King" and "King of the Franks," as he saw himself as restoring and preserving France's Catholic identity. He was known for using his personal fortunes to patronize art, culture, and architecture to build up the French nation and the Church. He is also known for having been a faithful husband to his wife, Margaret of Provence, through whom he had 11 children.

St. Louis decided to go on crusade in 1248 after hearing of the attacks on the Crusader States by the Mamluks and Ayyubids. While his heart was well-intended, St. Louis did not fully understand Islam or the realities of the Middle East. As a result, his attack on Egypt during the Seventh Crusade was a complete disaster and he was taken prisoner. After he was ransomed from captivity, he spent several years living in the

Crusader States and learning from the Catholic Military Orders. He also spent his own money to buy them weapons and fortify their garrisons.

Despite the massive setbacks, St. Louis' zeal for the Crusades never diminished. He opened contact with the Mongols and began the process of trying to organize an alliance between them and the Crusaders to combat the Mamluks. The negotiations surpassed his lifetime, and despite his efforts, no such alliance ever developed.

St. Louis organized the Eighth Crusade in 1270, during which he besieged the city of Tunis. However, he became sick with dysentery and died while on the Crusade.

St. Louis is the only canonized saint among the French kings. He was well-loved by the French people, and many of the geographic places named "St. Louis" are named after his memory.

St. Raymond of Peñafort
Feast Day: January 7th

St. Raymond of Peñafort was born in Cataluña in 1175 and became a Dominican monk in 1222. He is known for his aggressive efforts to evangelize both Spanish Muslims and Jews. In many respects, he followed in the path of Bl. Peter the Venerable by helping to develop the study of Islam as an academic discipline. One of his major accomplishments was the establishment of the *Studia Linguarum* in Tunis. This school taught Arabic and Hebrew to priests so they could study Islamic and Jewish texts as to facilitate missionary work. It was St. Raymond's work with Islam that inspired St. Thomas Aquinas to write the Summa Contra Gentiles.

St. Raymond also took part in the conquest of the city of Valencia from the Muslims with his associate, St. Bernard Calbó, in 1238. He died in 1275.

King St. Louis IX of France[69]

Pope Bl. Gregory X
Feast Day: February 16th

Pope Bl. Gregory X was born in 1210 and was elected Pope while participating in the Ninth Crusade. Although the Ninth Crusade failed to re-establish a strong Crusader presence in the Holy Land, Pope Bl. Gregory X nevertheless remained a strong supporter of the Crusades. His major project was to try to establish an alliance with the pagan Mongols, as they were sweeping across the Middle East during this time. He hoped that by working with the Mongols he would be able to stop the Muslim attacks against the Crusaders, as well as convert many Muslims and Mongolians to the Catholic Faith.

Pope Bl. Gregory X opened contact by sending a letter to the Mongolian Great Khan, Kublai, which was delivered by Marco Polo. It was helpful that many Mongols had good relations with and some were even members of the Assyrian Church of the East. The Mongolians began corresponding with Pope Bl. Gregory X, and more diplomatic missions were sent. One of the most famous ones was during the Second Council of Lyon in 1274. This was so because not only did the Pope invite members of the Orthodox Churches, but he also received a delegation of 13 men sent from the Mongolian Khanate to discuss a Catholic-Mongolian alliance.

Pope Bl. Gregory X died in 1276. His alliance with the Mongols never came to fruition, and the Crusader States formally disappeared fifteen years after his death.

Bl. Conrad of Ascoli
Feast Day: April 19th

Bl. Conrad of Ascoli was born to a noble Italian family in 1234 and joined the Franciscans. He was known as a teacher, preacher, and missionary. He petitioned to go to North Africa and preach to the Muslims, and his request was granted. Most of his time was spent in Libya, where he both made many converts and performed miracles. He died in 1289, and when his tomb was opened 82 years later in 1371, his body was found to be incorrupt.

St. Maria de Cervellón
Feast Day: September 19th

Known as "The Helper," St. Maria de Cervellón was a Spanish noblewoman and Third Order Mercedarian. She was known for praying for Catholics enslaved by Muslims, the Mercedarian brothers sent to the Muslim world to ransom them, and the Muslim slavers. In 1265 she took her vows and formed a community of sisters.

St. Maria de Cervellón died on September 19th, 1290. She is incorrupt, and her body can be found interred at the minor basilica of the Mercedarians in Barcelona.

St. Peter Armengol
Feast Day: April 27th

St. Peter Armengol was born in 1238 to a noble family. However, he soon began living a dissolute life as the leader of a gang of highway robbers that terrorized the Kingdom of Aragón. In 1258, he was captured by soldiers from King James I. Thanks to his father's intervention he was spared the death penalty. However, as a penance, he became a Mercedarian monk.

St. Peter made five trips to Spain and North Africa to ransom Catholics enslaved by Muslims. Between 1261 and 1266 he visited the cities of Algiers, Bejaa, Murcia, Oran, and Tangiers. It is known that between his efforts and those of the priests who accompanied him, a minimum of over 400 lives were saved. Additionally, St. Peter evangelized and converted many Muslims to the Catholic Faith.

In 1266 while in Bejaa, he was taken as ransom for a group of captives. Since the money needed to ransom him did not come in a timely manner, he was sentenced to death. The

Muslims hung him and they left his body for a day on the gallows. The money arrived the next day from a friar named William of Florence, who took St. Peter's body down only to find that he was still alive. St. Peter attributed his survival to the intercession of Our Lady and several angels that supported him. However, for the rest of his life he had a crooked neck.

Undaunted by this event, St. Peter continued to ransom captives but spent most of his next 40 years in contemplative life. He died in 1304.

Bl. Arnold of Queralt
Feast Day: October 26th

Bl. Arnold of Queralt was a Third Order Mercedarian and a knight. He was known for evangelizing Muslims, and was well-loved by fellow Catholics. He died around 1308.

Bl. Arnold of Rossinol
Feast Day: May 3rd

Bl. Arnold of Rossinol was a Spaniard of noble origins who became a Third Order Mercedarian. He ransomed many Catholics enslaved by Muslims, as well as repeatedly sold himself into slavery in Tunisia for this purpose. He died peacefully at the monastery of St. Mary in Valencia in 1317.

Inspirers

Sts. John de Matha and Felix of Valois
Founders of the Trinitarian Order
St. John de Matha Feast Day: February 8th
St. Felix of Valois Feast Day: November 4th

St. John de Matha was born to French nobility from Provence on June 24th, 1160. He was dedicated to God by his mother upon his birth, and grew up in a virtuous household. As a young man he went to Paris to study theology and was eventually ordained a priest. St. Felix of Valois was likewise born to French nobility from the house of Valois in 1127.

These two saints were brought together following a vision St. John had after saying said his first Mass. The vision was that he would establish a religious order dedicated to ransoming Catholics enslaved by Muslims. Moved by the Holy Spirit, he sought out St. Felix and asked to live in community with him in the woods. St. Felix accepted, and the two became companions. Eventually, St. John told St. Felix of his vision, and after praying and fasting together, they discerned his idea to be God's will. In 1197, the two men set out for Rome and presented their idea to Pope Innocent III, which he approved in 1198.

The Order was called the Order of the Holy Trinity for the Ransom of Captives, known as the Trinitarians. Its popularity spread rapidly across Europe. The Order's first voyage in 1201 ransomed 186 people. When St. John went by himself in 1202 to Tunis, he ransomed 110 people. The Order's actions enraged the Muslim slavers, since not only was he rescuing people, but he began successfully evangelizing both the captives and the Muslims. Not only did many captives return to the Faith, but some of the Muslim slavers converted as well.

When St. John returned for a second time in 1210, the Muslims sought to take revenge upon him. They severely damaged his ship while it was in harbor as to try to make his ship sink when sailing. However, not only did his ship arrive safely in Italy, but so did the 120 people he brought with him. St. Felix spent most of his time in Europe dealing with organizational matters.

St. John de Matha died on December 21st, 1213, and St. Felix of Valois died on November 4th, 1212. While most of the people who they rescued are not known, the work they did changed history. One person who is known is Miguel de Cervantes. While sailing home from the Battle of Lepanto, he was captured by Muslim pirates. Thanks to the Trinitarian Order, he was ransomed and returned to Spain, where he wrote his famous novel <u>Don Quixote</u>.

Both saints and their Order inspired the establishment of the Mercedarian Order.

St. Francis of Assisi
Feast Day: October 4th

St. Francis of Assisi, founder of the Franciscan Order, is one of the most beloved Catholic saints whose life and reputation is very well-known. In addition to the many great works he performed in Europe, he went to the Holy Land to meet with the Sultan of Egypt during the Fifth Crusade.

St. Francis arrived in Damietta, Egypt, in August 1219 with a group of Crusaders. The Crusaders had already been in a year-long siege against Damietta, and had even turned down offers from Egyptian Sultan Al-Kamil, a nephew of Saladin, to have Jerusalem in exchange. The Crusader reinforcements from

Europe launched a failed attack on the city, which to St. Francis' horror resulted in many innocent people being killed.

The Little Flowers of St. Francis, which was written by St. Bonaventure, says that following a temporary ceasefire, St. Francis marched into Egypt and began to preach on Cairo's streets. He was arrested and cast into prison, but he was soon released and received an audience with Sultan Al-Kamil.

St. Francis quickly befriended Al-Kamil, who was a learned man himself. After many discussions, Al-Kamil took an interest in the Faith. It is even said that St. Francis challenged the Sultan to a trial by fire to prove the truth of the Catholic Faith over Islam, and he walked across a bed of hot coals unharmed.

When he was leaving, St. Francis promised to send two friars to baptize Al-Kamil. He returned to Europe, and died several years later in 1226. Twelve years later, in 1238, Sultan Al-Kamil also found himself on his death bed, and as the Little Flowers says:

At the same time St. Francis appeared to two of his friars, and ordered them without delay to go to the Sultan and save his soul, according to the promise he had made him. The two set out, and having crossed the sea, were conducted to the Sultan by the guards he had sent out to meet them. The Sultan, when he saw them arrive, rejoiced greatly, and exclaimed: "Now I know of a truth that God has sent his servants to save my soul, according to the promise which St. Francis made me through divine revelation." Having received the faith of Christ and holy baptism from the said friars, he was regenerated in the Lord Jesus Christ; and having died of his disease, his soul was saved, through the merits and prayers of St Francis.[70]

St. Francis of Assisi walking safely over hot coals in the presence of Sultan Kamal Ad-Din, who converted to the Faith on his deathbed.[71]

St. Anthony of Padua
Feast Day: June 13th

St. Anthony of Padua was born Fernando Martins de Bulhões to Portuguese nobility in 1195 in Lisbon. During his life, he was a great teacher and miracle-worker. After his death, he was proclaimed a Doctor of the Church. However, what is seldom known is that it was his interactions with Islam that shaped his pastoral career.

While a new priest and Augustinian canon, St. Anthony saw the bodies of St. Berard of Carbio and his companions as they were brought back to Europe following their martyrdom. Upon seeing this, he became filled with evangelical zeal to suffer martyrdom by Muslims for the sake of Christ as they did. This desire was probably enhanced by his upbringing in Portugal, as well as the fact that he was a descendant of the First Crusade leader Godfrey of Bouillon.

St. Anthony left the Augustinian canons and became a Franciscan. Soon after he asked and was granted permission to go and preach in Morocco. However, he never arrived. The first time his travel was stopped by grave illness, and the second time his ship was blown off course and crashed in Sicily. He eventually made his way to Padua in northern Italy. It was in Padua that he spent the rest of his life as a priest, teacher, and miracle-worker. He died in 1231.

Our Lady of Puig
Feast Day: April 7th

In October 1238, King Alfonso I of Aragón set out to conquer the city of Valencia from the Muslims. The Catholics took an image of Our Lady into battle from the neighboring town of Puig. They prayed to her, asking for her intercession that they would be victorious. The Catholics won, and the Reconquista's strength continued to grow. Sts. Raymond of Peñafort and Bernard Calbó also took part in this battle.

St. Peter Nolasco
Founder of the Mercedarian Order
Feast Day: January 28th[72]

St. Peter Nolasco was a soldier who fought in the Reconquista for the Kingdom of Aragón. Following a vision of the Blessed Virgin holding a set of manacles, he founded the Royal, Celestial, and Military Order of Our Lady of Mercy and the Redemption of the Captives in 1218, known as the Mercedarians. His order was approved by Pope Gregory IX, and it was similar to the Trinitarian Order. However, the two major differences were that its membership was oriented towards the laity as opposed to priests, and that it also embraced aspects of the Catholic Military Orders. St. Peter and his brothers would travel across Europe preaching and raising money for the Order. The money was then given to Mercedarian brothers who traveled to Muslim Spain and North Africa where they bought he freedom of Catholics enslaved by Muslims. If they ran out of money, Mercedarians pledged to sell themselves into slavery to the Muslims so another man might go free.

The Mercedarians' repute grew quickly, and many people joined them. The order also produced many martyrs, as the members pledged to give their lives if necessary. While most of the people that the Order helped are unknown, the Mercedarians saved untold numbers of people from horrendous suffering. St. Peter Nolasco died on May 6th, 1245.

Our Lady of Ransom
or Our Lady of Mercy
Feast Day: September 24th

The feast day of Our Lady of Ransom[73] commemorates the vision of Our Lady to St. Peter Nolasco, founder of the Mercedarian Order, on August 1st, 1218. Over the next five years, the Mercedarians became renowned across Europe for ransoming Catholics enslaved by Muslim pirates.

Bl. William of Bas
Feast Day: December 3rd

Bl. William of Bas was General of the Mercedarian Order following St. Peter Nolasco's death. He greatly assisted in the redemption of captives as well as garnished support for the Order from powerful rulers and common persons alike. He died peacefully in 1260 in Barcelona.

St. Thomas Aquinas
Feast Day: March 7th

St. Thomas Aquinas is perhaps the most renowned theologian and philosopher in Catholic history. He is known as the "Angelic Doctor" and is famous for his monumental Summa Theologica, which provides a philosophical and rational approach to a broad range of questions about the Catholic Faith in a detailed manner. He is one of the most prolific writers the Church has ever had.

St. Thomas was born in 1225 to a noble Sicilian family that was related to the Hohenstaufen Dynasty of the Holy Roman Empire. In 1244, he entered the Dominican Order. The next year he was sent to the University of Paris where he met and began studying under Bl. Albertus Magnus, known also as Albert the Great. St. Thomas' philosophical training and love of God he had as a child blossomed while at university. He began writing around 1251 and wrote almost non-stop until his death in 1274.

Most of St. Thomas' writings were about the Catholic Faith. However, he was influenced by Islamic thinkers. This is shown particularly in the <u>Summa</u>, where he addressed various claims made by Avicenna,[74] Averroes,[75] and Alghazel[76] vis-à-vis the Catholic Faith in his questions and answers.

In addition, St. Thomas wrote explicitly about Islam on two occasions. The first was in the introduction to his book <u>Summa Contra Gentiles</u>, which he was inspired to write through the influence of the Dominican missionary to Spanish Muslims and friend St. Raymond of Peñafort. In his brief criticism, St. Thomas described Islam as a false religion because Muhammad performed no miracles and sought converts to Islam through force of arms or promises of carnal pleasure.[77] The second and more targeted work is his book <u>De Rationibus Fidei contra Saracenos, Graecos, et Armenos ad Cantorem Antiochenum</u>, which in ten chapters addresses disagreements between the Catholic Faith with Islam, the Greek Orthodox, and the Oriental Orthodox Armenians.[78] Eight of its chapters concern Islam.

Bl. Ambrose of Siena
Feast Day: March 20th

Bl. Ambrose of Siena was born in Siena in 1220 to a noble family. He became a Dominican monk at a young age and was known for being an excellent preacher. His preaching skills were so highly acclaimed that Pope Bl. Gregory X asked him to preach the Eighth Crusade. He died in Siena in 1286.

Our Lady of Loreto
Feast Day: December 10th

Many churches and pilgrimage sites were destroyed as the Muslim Mamluks from Egypt swept over the Holy Land following the end of the Crusader States in 1291. One of such places at great risk was the original house in which Our Lady had grown up in in Nazareth. It was a popular place of pilgrimage visited by many people in the Holy Land, including St. Francis of Assisi and King St. Louis IX of France.

As the Mamluks were rampaging across the Holy Land, what happened with the house is yet another testimony to the Assumption of Mary. As the Lord did not allow His mother's body to suffer corruption, neither did He allow her earthly home be destroyed. Miraculously, the house was picked out of the ground and carried to Tersatto, Croatia, where its landing was witnessed by several shepherds and location noted by the townspeople.[79] Those who visited the house experienced many miracles. Three years later, the house was again miraculously moved to just outside of Lecanati, Italy, where the same miracles continued.

Finally, the house was moved again, this time by human efforts, to Loreto, Italy, where it resides today and is known as the Sanctuary of the Holy House. It is a place of great pilgrimage, and countless miracles still continue to happen there.[80]

St. Peter of Amer
Feast Day: June 8th

St. Peter of Amer was a nobleman from Barcelona who entered the Mercedarian Order during St. Peter Nolasco's lifetime. While his birthdate is not known, he was born sometime between 1220 and 1240.

He freed many Catholics enslaved by Muslims by selling himself into slavery. Once money arrived for his ransom, he proceeded to buy more captives until he sold himself again. He was also known for his governance skills, and was eventually elected head of the Barcelona chapter of the Mercedarians. He died at the monastery of St. Mary of Puig in 1301.

The Shrine of the Holy House in Loreto[81]

Notable Mention

John of Plano Carpini, Benedict of Poland, and William of Rubruck.
John d. 1252
Benedict d. 1280
William d. 1293

John of Plano Carpini and Benedict of Poland were Franciscan friars commissioned by Pope Innocent IV to evangelize the Mongols. While their interactions with Islam were few, their travels to the Mongols and life among the Muslims were extensively documented. Like Marco Polo, their travels fueled the spirit of exploration which came over Europe in future centuries.

William of Rubruck was a Franciscan friar from Belgium who originally went with King St. Louis IX of France on the failed Seventh Crusade against Egypt in 1248. Following the Crusade and with King St. Louis' assistance, he was commissioned to travel to the Far East to convert the Mongols. His travels took him from Ukraine to Karakorum, the capitol of the Mongolian Empire.

As with previous missionaries, William made extensive documentations of Mongolian society, Muslims, and Islam. He made many converts, and was famous for winning a debate about the Catholic Faith versus Islam at the court of the Great Khan, Möngke.

Fr. Raymond Martí
d. 1284

Born in 1220, Fr. Raymond Martí was a Dominican theologian and student of Arabic and Hebrew. While most of his evangelization efforts were concentrated among Spanish Jews, he likewise spent a considerable time studying Islam and evangelizing Spanish Muslims. He was well-versed in Islamic theology, and trained many Dominicans for work among Muslims.

The Knights of Ru'ad Island

The Fall of Acre in 1291 officially marks the end of the Crusades for historians. However, the Knights Templar continued to fight for the Church for eleven more years across northern Israel, Lebanon, and Syria. After much effort, the Knights made their last stand at the Siege of Ru'ad Island on September 26th, 1302.

Only a very small number of soldiers took part, and the battle originally was not supposed to have taken place. This was because the Knights Templar had negotiated a surrender of the island with the Mamluks in exchange for their lives. However, the Mamluks reneged on their agreement, and a battle broke out which quickly overwhelmed the small force. The Templar Knights who were not killed were taken back to Egypt and imprisoned. None of them converted to Islam, and over the next five years until 1307 they slowly dwindled away in prison, dying from abuse and hunger.

Fr. Riccoldo di Monte da Croce
d. 1320

Fr. Riccoldo di Monte da Croce was born in 1243 to a noble Florentine family. He entered the Dominicans in 1267 and was one of the last Catholic figures of the Crusades as well as one who ushered in the new era of the Church's expansion to the Far East and beyond.

Fr. Croce's travels began in 1287 in the Holy Land. During his time, he witnessed the Fall of Acre to the Mamluks. After this, he traveled to Mosul and Baghdad, where he attempted to execute three goals at the request of the Pope. The first was to convert the Mongols to the Catholic Faith. The second was to establish an alliance against the Mamluks and with the Mongols, as previous popes and missionaries had attempted to do. The third was to bring the Assyrian Church of the East back into communion with the Church.

Unfortunately, Fr. Croce had few successes. The Mongols were uninterested in either conversion to the Catholic Faith or an alliance with the Church. Likewise, most of the Assyrians did not want to seek re-union with Rome. However, there was one Assyrian Patriarch named Mar Yaballaha who did. He was excommunicated by the Assyrian Church of the East, but was received into the Catholic Church.

Fr. Croce wrote detailed accounts about his encounters in the Middle East and with Islam in his travelogue, the Liber Peregrinacionis. He also wrote two more books specifically about Islam, entitled the Contra Legem Saracenorum (Against the Legends of the Saracens), and the Confutatio Alcorani (Confutation of the Quran). After returning to Europe in 1302, he continued his work with the Dominicans until he died in Florence in 1320.

Section III: The Expansion

The Expansion Begins

The struggle between the Catholic Faith and Islam did not end with the Crusades in 1291. Rather, the idea of a Crusade became the defense of Europe from Muslim invasion. This was vital given several major world-changing events in both the east and west.

In the east, this was in two parts. The first was that in spite of repeated efforts by the Church to evangelize the Mongolian conquerors, they showed little interest in the Catholic Faith. However, many of them were attracted to Islam, and eventually they mass converted to Islam. This brought pressure and persecution to the newly established Catholic missions in the Far East. The second and more dangerous threat was the geometric rise of the Ottoman Turks, whose empire was born the same year the Crusades formally ended. The Ottomans became the bane of the Europeans as they grew in power and turned into the Ottoman Empire.

However, the old idea of a crusade to spread the Faith outside of Europe never died either. This idea took particular hold as Spain and Portugal expelled Islamic rule through the successful completion of the Reconquista. Upon Islam's end in both nations, the Spanish and the Portuguese not only conquered the world militarily, but they brought the Catholic Faith with them. This time the Faith literally spread to all the ends of the Earth and went further than all of the Crusader period missionaries ever did.

The Catholic response to Islam both on Europe's borders and across the world was slowed by the rise of Protestantism during the 16th century. This was a period when the Papacy was thrust into the quarrelsome and power-hungry throes of Italian politics, which helped instigate the Protestant movement. Regardless of the real problems with corruption at the time, the long-term effect of the Protestant movement was that it sharply divided fellow Christians against each other and destroyed Christian unity. When the Ottoman Empire became aware of the Protestant movement, they directly funded it because they correctly saw it as a means to divide, conquer, and Islamize Europe.

Thankfully, Europe was still able to retain enough unity to respond to the Ottoman invasions. The Ottomans were not conclusively defeated until the Battle of Vienna on September 11th, 1683.[1] After this point, a power shift came into full motion towards Europe and away from the Ottomans. This happened at the same time Catholic and Protestant missionaries began exploring Muslim nations and cultures all over the world. These missionaries did tremendous work on culture, history, language, and religion. This helped to form many modern academic fields of study, which include anthropology, archaeology, historiography, and philology. At the time, this work was broadly classified as the "study of the East," or "Orientalism."

But however many advances were made, the social divisions that developed in Europe became much more serious. People gradually found themselves at animosity with each other over fundamental questions of faith, morals, and the ability to conclusively pronounce and define absolute truth. This initially manifested in the Church through the Protestant movement. People began to perceive both the Church and all Christianity as a confused system of beliefs with a morality subject to popular interpretation at a given place and time. The effects of these thoughts and ideas eventually came to fruition in the following centuries.

The Rise of the Ottomans

In the same year the Crusader States collapsed, a Turk named Osman united the Muslim tribes of southwestern Anatolia under his leadership. Osman had a dream one night that his small confederation would grow into the greatest Empire on Earth and become the guardian of Islam.[2] This was the beginning of the Ottoman Empire, which became the most feared, powerful, and dangerous Islamic power since the Umayyads of the 7th and 8th centuries. Under Osman's leadership, the Ottomans set out on a massive campaign to conquer the remnants of the Byzantine Empire and the world.

The Byzantine Empire was weak at this point and had great difficulty in managing its own affairs, let alone the Ottomans. In an attempt to improve relations with the Ottomans, Byzantine Emperor John VI Kantakouzenos married his daughter Theodora to Osman's son and successor to the Ottoman Sultanate, Orhan. However, the effect of this decision was to encourage the Ottomans to marry Christian women. As with the Islamic invasion of Spain in the 8th century, the Ottomans built themselves into the native Byzantine population. This ultimately facilitated the Byzantine Empire's demise and the Islamization of Anatolia.

As the Ottomans conquered the lands around the ever-shrinking Byzantine Empire, they encountered an interesting situation in the Balkan Peninsula. Many peoples were vying with each other for power. In addition to the Byzantines, the greatest competitors were the Bulgarians and the Serbians, who were both comparatively weaker than the Ottomans. There was also the influence of the Bosnians, Croats, Hungarians, Ukrainian Cossacks, and Moldavians. In the Black Sea region there were the Crimean Tartars, and controlling the Adriatic and Mediterranean Sea regions there were the Venetians. Finally, there were the Knights of Rhodes on the island of Cyprus.

With some exceptions to the Knights of Rhodes, all of these groups were fighting with each other for power. Given all this division, the Ottoman expansion into Europe was quite simple. It was only for the Ottomans to systematically play off these divisions until they absorbed each warring principality into their empire. The Byzantines were the easiest to manipulate, as they were the weakest and also the most desired by the Ottomans.[3] By 1338 all of northwestern Anatolia was under Ottoman control. By the time of the Battle of Adrianople in 1365, all that was left of the Byzantine Empire was Constantinople and the surrounding villages.

The role which treachery played in Islam's growth during this time cannot be understated. As during the Crusades, it was the self-interested power struggles between warring nobles that allowed for Islam to conquer Eastern Europe. Each power allied with and against each other and the Ottomans so long as it benefitted each one's immediate situation. The short term results were wins and losses with each other and against the Ottomans, and even significant personal gains. But it was a disastrous long-term strategy because eventually each power found itself either a vassal of or completely conquered by the Ottomans. Those who suffered the worst were the common people in the form of executions, enslavement, and a loss of rights.

Three subsequent crusades were launched at the behest of Popes Clement VI and Bl. Urban V against the Ottomans. The first was the siege and capture of Smyrna from the Ottomans. The second was a raid against the city of Alexandria, Egypt. The third was a mission to aid the Byzantine Empire in regaining territories lost to the Ottomans along the Black Sea coastline. All three attempts were successful in their missions, but none was able to establish a long-term presence.

The 14th century ended with a shadow of looming downfall but the hope of a new beginning. In the East, there was but a temporary reprieve before the Ottomans conquered the last vestiges of the Byzantine Empire. In the West, the spark of hope was growing for a new era of prosperity in Spain and Portugal as Islam was driven from the Iberian Peninsula.

A bust of Osman I
Under his command, the Ottoman Empire was born the same year the Crusades formally ended. [4]

Martyrs

Bl. William of Castellammare
Feast Day: August 8th

Bl. William of Castellammare was a Franciscan from Naples who went to the Holy Land in order to preach to and evangelize Muslims. In 1364 he began preaching in Gaza, which since the earliest days of Islam had been a hotbed of Muslim activity. Upon preaching he was arrested and told to convert to Islam or die. He refused and was tortured to death, after which his body was burned.

St. Nikola Tavelić and Companions
(Adeodat of Rodez, Peter of Narbonne and Stephen of Cuneo)
Franciscan Martyrs of Jerusalem
Feast Day: November 14th

Sts. Nikola Tavelić, Adeodat of Rodez, Peter of Narbonne and Stephen of Cuneo were Franciscans sent to evangelize Muslims in the Holy Land in 1383. They learned Arabic and prepared to preach on November 14th, 1391. Sources say that this was the festival of "Bairam," although the word "Bairam" is a general Turkish word meaning "festival." According to the dating on the Islamic calendar, this day corresponded with the Islamic holiday Eid Al-Adha.[5]

While St. Nikola and his companions were preaching, they were attacked by a Muslim mob, arrested, and placed before a judge, who immediately sentenced them to death. The next day the men were dragged out of their prison cell, lynched, and their remains burned by the Jaffa Gate in Jerusalem.

Bls. John of Cetina and Peter de Dueñas
Feast Day: May 22nd

Bls. John of Cetina and Peter de Dueñas were Franciscan missionaries sent to preach in Muslim Spain. Both were martyred in 1397 in Granada.

The Jaffa Gate of Jerusalem
It was near here that St. Nikola Tavelić
and his companions were martyred.[6]

Contenders

St. Venturino of Bergamo
Feast Day: March 28th

St. Venturino of Bergamo was born in Bergamo, Italy in 1304 and entered the Dominican Order in 1319. He was known for his preaching abilities and conversions he made within Europe. In 1344, he was commissioned by Pope Clement VI to preach a crusade against the Ottomans.

His preaching resulted in the Smyrniote Crusade. With the help of the Venetians and the Knights Hospitaller, the city of Smyrna, known now as Izmir, was re-captured in October 1344. It remained under constant Ottoman siege until 1351. St. Venturino accompanied the Crusaders to the city and fought alongside them.

Having fulfilled his mission, St. Venturino died in 1344 in Smyrna. The city remained under Christian control until 1402, when it was re-taken by the Ottomans.

A view of Smyrna and the mountains
Today it is the city of Izmir, Turkey.[7]

Inspirers

Bl. John of Montecorvino
Feast Day: November 29th

Bl. John of Montecorvino was born in 1246. He became a Franciscan and traveled to Central Asia and the Far East to spread the Catholic Faith. Most of his life was spent traveling, and he was one of the most accomplished missionaries of the late 13th and early 14th centuries.

In 1286, the Vatican made contact with Bar Sauma, who was a Uyghur diplomat for the Mongols and a monk of the Assyrian Church of the East. The Franciscan Order sent Bl. John as a missionary and diplomat to him. With Bar Sauma's help, Bl. John traveled to the Far East, eventually arriving in China after a long journey through Ethiopia, Persia, India, Bangladesh, and Central Asia. He opened many churches and established the first Catholic dioceses in the Far East. It is unknown how many converts he made to the Faith, both of Muslims or pagans, but it is likely to have been well over ten thousand.

Bl. John's work with the Muslims was primarily among the Uyghur people, who are descended from Turkic stock and are the majority ethnic group in western China. Bl. John was the first to translate the Bible into the Uyghur language as well as conduct Catholic missionary work among them. While the Mongolian Khan Timur[8] did not convert, he encouraged the spread of the Catholic Faith and became good friends with Bl. John.

Bl. John died in Beijing in 1328. Unfortunately, most of the Churches and missions he established were destroyed. Within China, this happened when the Ming Dynasty under Emperor Hongwu came to power and overthrew the Mongols.

Because the Ming associated Christianity with the Mongols, they expelled all missionaries and Christians from Ming-controlled territory. This decision may have been influenced by the Salur, a Turkic people living in China that recently converted to Islam and was favored by Emperor Hongwu. This was not the only time that the Chinese government allied with the Muslims against the Catholics, as it repeated during the Boxer Rebellion in 1900.

Outside of Ming territory, an Uzbek-born Chagatai Turk and convert to Islam named Tamerlane[9] began waging his own jihad across all of Central Asia. While Tamerlane was cruel to anybody who opposed him, including fellow Muslims, he had a particular disdain for Christianity. The end of Assyrian Christianity in Central Asia and western China as well as Bl. John's Catholic missions can be directly traced to Tamerlane's persecutions. Unfortunately, many Catholics were killed or converted to Islam.

Bl. Bartholomew of Bologna
d. 1333[10]

Bl. Bartholomew of Bologna was a Dominican monk who was sent as an ambassador and missionary to Armenia. He was a noted preacher who converted many Muslims and helped to form a closer union between the Catholic Church and the Armenian Church. He learned the Armenian language and made many translations, including works of St. Thomas Aquinas, into Armenian. He died in 1333.

Our Lady of Guadalupe, Extremadura
Feast Day: September 8th

Our Lady of Guadalupe is traditionally known by the famous apparition of the Blessed Virgin to the Aztec Indian St. Juan Diego in 1531. After several encounters she emblazoned an image of herself on his robe, which he brought to Juan de Zumarrága, the first bishop of Mexico. Upon seeing this, the bishop commissioned a church built to her honor in the place where she appeared. What is less known is that Our Lady of Guadalupe in Mexico has direct roots to another image by the same name found in Extremadura Province, Spain.

For most of the Reconquista, Catholics and Muslims fought intense battles over the arid, central province of Spain known as Extremadura. But prior to the Islamic invasions, there was a statue of St. Mary said to have been made by the Gospel writer St. Luke. It was brought to Spain by St. Leander of Seville in the 4th century, where it was venerated for centuries until the Islamic invasions in 711. The shrine where her statue resided was destroyed and the statue disappeared. Legend said that the Catholics buried the statue somewhere in Extremadura in order to keep it from being destroyed by the Muslims.

In the 14th century, Mary appeared to a shepherd named Gil Cordero from the town of Cáceres. She told him to have priests dig by the banks of a tributary of the Guadiana River that flows through Extremadura to the south. This tributary was known as the Wolf River, or "Guadalupe," from the Arabic "wadi," meaning "oasis," and Latin "lupus," meaning "wolf". Gil told this to his local priest, who dug where he told him and found the Statue.

A shrine and monastery was built to the Blessed Virgin in 1326, and its popularity grew rapidly. In 1340, King Alfonso XI of Castile allied with King Alfonso IV of Portugal and prayed to Our Lady of Guadalupe for victory over the Muslims, who were attempting yet another invasion from Morocco. The battle was on October 4th, and was known as the Battle of Río Salado. It was a decisive victory for the Catholics and a tremendous defeat for the Muslims.

Thanks to Our Lady of Guadalupe, Spain and Portugal were saved yet again from invasion. Many churches in Spain and across the Spanish world have been devoted to her.

Our Lady of Guadalupe, Extremadura[11]

Pope Bl. Urban V
Feast Day: December 19th

Pope Bl. Urban V was born in France in 1310 and became Pope in 1362. He was a great patron of education, culture, and art. During his papacy, he sought to rekindle the crusader zeal in order to oppose the invading Ottomans as they crashed over the Dardanelles and into the Balkans. This was during a time when Western Europe was occupied with the Hundred Years' War and was recovering from the Black Plague.

Pope Bl. Urban V's preaching was able to organize two successful crusades. The first crusade was to the city of Alexandria, Egypt, and is known as the Alexandrian Crusade. It did not result in the establishment of a permanent military outpost in Alexandria, nor was it intended to. Rather, it was successful in weakening the Mamluk Empire. King Peter I of Cyprus with the help of the Knights of Rhodes led the attack in 1365 and successfully looted the city. The result was a small conflict between Cyprus and the Mamluks over shipping routes, but it was quickly and peaceably resolved.

The second crusade was the Savoyard Crusade, led by Count Amadeus VI of Savoy between 1366 and 1367. It was a success in not only taking back territory from the Ottomans, but it helped to strengthen the Byzantine Empire. The Crusaders conquered a strip of land stretching from the Gallipoli Peninsula up to Kozyak, Bulgaria, but failed to capture Varna.

Count Amadeus attempted at the request of Pope Bl. Urban V to help bring about a reunion of the Catholic and Orthodox Churches. However, he was unable to do so. Count Amadeus was nevertheless hailed as a hero by both the Byzantines and the Pope alike, and he returned to France with his soldiers triumphant and well-received.

The gains made by the Savoyard Crusade were quickly lost. The first losses came on account of conflicts with Bulgaria. The second losses resulted from infighting between the Byzantine Empire's rulers as the Ottomans continued to flow into the Balkans. By 1377, the Ottoman Sultan Murad I had retaken most of Count Amadeus' hard-won gains. Pope Bl. Urban V died in 1370.

A statue of Count Amadeus VI killing an Ottoman soldier[12]

Notable Mention

Marco Polo
d. 1324

Born in 1254, Marco Polo is best remembered for his travels to China and the Far East over a seventeen-year period. He was also one of the first Catholic laypersons to make such a journey. He documented Muslim life and Islam, as well as his experiences with pagans and the Assyrian Church of the East in his <u>Travels</u>.[13]

Marco Polo inspired a sense of adventure and travel within the Church and across Europe. He was and continues to remain one of the most important Catholics who explored the Far East.

A bust of Marco Polo[14]

King Louis I of Hungary
d. 1382

King Louis I of Hungary was born in 1326 and became king in 1342. He was unique in that while he focused on the centralization of his power, he ruled with humility and integrity. Most of his life was spent in wars against the Ottomans. His actions set a precedent that was carried out by future Hungarian kings.

At the time, the Byzantine Empire was in serious decline as the Ottomans were absorbing all the territories surrounding Constantinople. The Wallachians,[15] Bulgarians, and Serbians were fighting viciously with each other in an attempt to expand into the power vacuums that opened. The Ottomans skillfully exploited the situation by supporting one group to facilitate a conquest only to conquer those who they helped give victory to. King Louis I was aware of this, and so he conquered parts of northern Serbia, Wallachia, and northern Bulgaria in an attempt to set up a buffer region between Hungary and the Ottomans. He attempted to establish a united front with other kingdoms in order to fight the Ottomans, but this was never realized. He also assisted Savoyard Crusade leader Count Amadeus in his battles against the Ottomans.

King Louis I had a strong devotion to King St. Ladislaus of Hungary,[16] after which Louis modeled his actions and rule. Upon his death in 1382, he was buried beside St. Ladislaus' tomb. He is one of the great Catholic and Hungarian kings who stood up to the Ottomans.

Generations of Fame and Infamy

The 15th century was an age of milestones. It positively marked the final destruction of Islamic Spain and Portugal as well as the beginning of the global spread of the Catholic Faith. It also marked the Byzantine Empire's fall to the Ottomans as they conquered Eastern Europe.

The Ottoman Empire would have overrun the Byzantine Empire much earlier were it not for the Central Asian Muslim conqueror Tamerlane's victory over the Ottomans in 1402 at the Battle of Ankara. It was only one of a few crushing defeats the Ottoman received until the late 17th century. During the Battle of Ankara, Sultan Bayezid was captured and died a year later. This threw the Ottoman Empire into a thirteen year state of anarchy. Eventually Bayezid's son Mehmet I took power, followed by his grandson Murad I, who re-organized the empire and in 1421 resumed war against the Byzantines.

While the Catholics and Orthodox in the Balkans had conflicted with each other, many of them recognized the need to unite or be destroyed by the Ottomans. Each area had its own resistance movement, but all worked together in varying capacities. George Kastrioti, known as Skanderbeg, led the resistance in Albania. Catholic warrior John Hunyadi maintained a strong border with the Ottomans in Hungary. Along the Black Sea coast, the Orthodox Saint-King Stephen of Moldavia formed another patch of resistance. Further south, the Wallachian Prince Vladimir III Țepeș, known better as "Dracula," waged a total material and psychological warfare against the Ottomans.[17]

The resistance had its successes and failures. The greatest victory was the Siege of Belgrade in 1456, when St. John Capistrano, a Franciscan monk, led a peasant army with John Hunyadi that routed the Ottoman army at the city of

Belgrade in Serbia. This was both a tremendous material and psychological loss for the Ottomans. Belgrade would eventually fall in 1521, but the successful resistance at the city kept the Ottomans contained in the Balkans long enough to prepare for further incursions.

The greatest loss was the fall of Constantinople in 1453, which was aided by treachery. Constantinople was besieged by the Ottomans, and the Byzantines received an offer from a Hungarian cannon-maker[18] to buy his cannons in order to attack the Ottomans. However, the Emperor did not have the money to afford them. As such, the businessman made the same offer to the Ottomans, which they accepted and used to blast through Constantinople's massive walls.

It is said that during the last Mass in the Hagia Sophia, the great church of eastern Christendom, a great light miraculously shone upon the church. The light then lifted up from the church and into Heaven, which some interpreted as the presence of the Holy Spirit leaving the building as the Ottomans encroached. The next morning, Constantinople was overrun by the Ottomans. The Hagia Sophia was desecrated into a mosque by order of Ottoman Sultan Mehmet II "The Conqueror."[19]

At the same time, the opposite course of events was happening in Spain and Portugal. By 1481, Islamic Spain was reduced to only a few strongholds along the southernmost Spanish coastline. King Ferdinand and Queen Isabella, whose marriage united Spain under one kingdom, spent the next decade systematically dismantling each remaining bastion of Islam until the fall of Granada in 1492. Spain and Portugal had done in the West what the Ottomans had done in the East with the Byzantine Empire. The two nations would independently take the struggle with Islam and the Church's mission to the ends of the Earth.

Martyrs

Sts. Peter Malasanc and John of Granada
Feast Day: May 25th

St. Peter Malasanc was born in Lleida, Spain in 1348 and entered the Mercedarian Order as a young man. St. John of Granada was also a Mercedarian, born of a father who converted from Islam to the Catholic Faith.

Sts. Peter Malasanc and John of Granada were sent to North Africa beginning in 1415 to ransom enslaved Catholics. In 1427 while in route to Oran, they were captured and sold into slavery. A year later while they were sailing with their Muslim captors, the ship was ambushed by Genoese merchants. During the ambush, the Muslims summarily hung the men and cast their bodies into the sea.

Bl. Ferdinand, the Holy Prince of Portugal
Feast Day: June 5th

Bl. Ferdinand was born in 1402 to King John I of Portugal and his English wife, Philippa of Lancaster. He was made prince of two districts in the Province of Leiria, Portugal. His brother was Henry the Navigator, who was one of the most famous cartographers of the 15th century and was actively engaged in the Portuguese Reconquista.

Based on his observations, Henry saw an opportunity to attack and seize Tangiers from the Marinids. Preparations began in 1432, and he eventually received the blessing of Pope Eugene IV for his expedition in 1437. However, the length of time it took him to plan the invasion proved to be a critical error. The

Marinids became aware of his plans some time ago, and were able to prepare for the Portuguese arrival.

The Portuguese Siege of Tangiers lasted for a month. Initially the Portuguese were successful, but the Moroccan army was simply too large and better armed. During the battle, Bl. Ferdinand and several of his associates were captured by the Muslims. Interestingly, the son of Abu Zakarya Al-Wattasi, the Governor of Tangiers, was likewise captured by the Portuguese. The battle ended in a truce by which the Portuguese promised the return of Al-Wattasi's son and to surrender the island of Ceuta in exchange for Bl. Ferdinand. However, the agreement was never realized.

As a result, Bl. Ferdinand spent six years in a Moroccan prison. The Muslims mistreated him in particular because of his relationship to Henry and the Portuguese nobility. He died in prison from the abuse in 1443.

Bl. Anthony Neyrot
Feast Day: May 10th

Bl. Anthony Neyrot was born in Rivoli, Italy in 1425. He entered the Dominican Order as a young man and was ordained a priest. However, he was unhappy and became restless, so he petitioned the Order to send him to Sicily. When this did not work out, he requested to go to Naples.

During the trip to Naples, Bl. Anthony was captured by a Tunisian slave raiding ship in 1458. The fate of the other passengers is not known, but it is said that Bl. Anthony was imprisoned and eventually presented to the Tunisian Caliph.[20]

Bl. Anthony was liked by the Caliph, but for unexplained reasons did something which angered him. It is said that Bl. Anthony was arrogant towards him, and the Caliph threw him into prison where he slowly starved on a meager diet of bread and water. To save his own life, Bl. Anthony apostatized from the Catholic Faith and converted to Islam. Following Bl. Anthony's conversion to Islam, he was immediately released, restored to good graces with the Caliph, married off to a Turkish noblewoman, and given a residence with a salary from the Caliph. Bl. Anthony even began to translate the Quran.

However, Bl. Anthony's spiritual restlessness that he experienced as a priest only intensified following his apostasy. One night in late 1459, he had a vision of his old teacher from Italy, St. Antoninus of Florence. He conversed with Bl. Anthony, and told him that unless he repented of his apostasy, Bl. Anthony's soul would be damned.

After the vision, Bl. Anthony resolved to follow his teacher's warning. He first secretly made contact with a Dominican priest, who heard his confession. After this, he sent his wife back to her family. On Holy Thursday, 1460, Bl. Anthony put on his old Dominican habit that he had since packed away and went before the Caliph. He renounced Islam, and proclaimed that he had returned to the Catholic Faith and his life as a Dominican.

The Caliph's superficial and conditional friendship with Bl. Anthony was immediately exposed. In a fit of rage, the Caliph ordered him to renounce the Catholic Faith. When Bl. Anthony refused, he had him summarily stoned to death. As Bl. Anthony was being stoned, he dropped to his knees and prayed that he would have the strength to remain faithful to his death.

Bl. Anthony's body was later purchased by Genoese merchants and brought back to Rivoli. Not only did he receive a dignified burial, but he became an honored man by his extended family and the town.

Bls. Antonio Primaldo, Bishop Stefano Argercolo de Pendinellis, and the 800 Martyrs of Otranto
Feast Day: August 14th

For a long time, the Ottomans attempted to establish a military base in Italy so as to facilitate an invasion of Rome. The Ottomans came close to realizing this goal when they invaded the port city of Otranto on Italy's Salento Peninsula on August 14th, 1480 under the command of Gedik Ahmet Pasha. The invasion was personally commissioned by the infamous Sultan Mehmet II "The Conqueror." This was the same Sultan who led the final battle that destroyed Constantinople and the Byzantine Empire in 1453.

Otranto initially attempted to resist the invasion, but the city could not stop the Ottomans. After the Ottomans took control, all of Otranto's men over the age of 15 were gathered, which numbered 800 in total. The Bishop, Bl. Stefano, approached the Ottomans and told them to repent of their sins and become Christians. After he finished speaking, the Ottomans summarily decapitated him and warned the 800 others to convert to Islam or suffer the same fate. They even brought an apostate Catholic priest named "Giovanni" from the neighboring Province of Calabria to testify in favor of Islam and against the Catholic Faith.

After listening to the Ottomans, an old man named Antonio Primaldo stood up before the villagers and exhorted them to stand strong in their Catholic Faith. He reminded them that it was better to be martyred for the sake of Christ than to lose their souls by renouncing the Faith. In his words, this was their final test and the time to choose eternal life or eternal damnation. The 800 men and the villagers stood with Antonio, which fueled the Ottomans' rage against them.

The next day the Ottomans brought the 800 men up to Minerva Hill outside the city to start the beheadings, and the first one was Antonio. According to the account, after Antonio was beheaded, his corpse miraculously stood back up and would not fall down until all 800 persons were beheaded. It is said that after seeing this miracle, only one of the Ottomans renounced Islam. It was a soldier named Berlabei,[21] who became Catholic on the spot and as a result was executed that same day by impalement.

The Ottoman possession of Otranto did not last. One year later, they were driven out by King Ferdinand I of Sicily, son of King Alfonso V of Aragón. But most importantly, all 800 men kept their Catholic Faith when pressured to convert to Islam, fulfilling Jesus words:

"Those who seek to save their lives will lose them, but those who lose their lives for my sake will find them."[22]

Bl. Arnold Serra and Companions
Feast Day: May 20th

Bl. Arnold Serra and his companions were Spanish Mercedarians sent to Tunisia to ransom captives and preach the Faith. Little is known about details, but they were arrested and imprisoned while preaching in Tunis in 1492. They were promised release if they renounced the Catholic Faith and converted to Islam, but they refused. As a result, they were starved to death in prison.

Contenders

John Hunyadi
Athleta Christi
d. August 11th, 1456

John Hunyadi was born in Hungary in 1407 as the illegitimate son of Holy Roman Emperor Sigismund and Hungarian noblewomen Erzebet Morzsinay. He was made Governor of the Kingdom of Hungary at a young age, and beginning in 1437 spent the rest of his life in wars against the Ottomans. He was known as the "White Knight," and remains one of the most energetic and passionate Catholic figures in the Church's struggle with Islam in Eastern Europe.

John lived during a difficult time. In order to fight the Ottomans, he also had to battle his way through the tangled, confused alliances of the perpetually quarreling Eastern European kingdoms. But in spite of this, he managed to secure many alliances as well as build up the Kingdom of Hungary. One of his closest friends was Skanderbeg, who professed the Catholic Faith with his men during the Battle of Niš in 1443 and directly aided John in his victory over the Ottomans.

John's greatest victory over the Ottomans came at the end of his life with the Siege of Belgrade in 1456. Together with St. John Capistrano, the two led a peasant army of 60,000 to victory over the Ottomans. While Belgrade eventually fell in 1521, his actions delayed further invasion of Eastern Europe until the Battle of Mohács in 1526.

John Hunyadi died several weeks after the Siege of Belgrade in 1456 due to a bout of plague. Before his death, Hunyadi implored his kinsmen:

Defend, my friends, Christendom and Hungary from all enemies… Do not quarrel among yourselves. If you should waste your energies in altercations, you will seal your own fate as well as dig the grave of our country.[23]

Pope Pius II bestowed the title of "Champion of Christ" upon John Hunyadi following his death.

John Hunyadi's statue in Budapest, Hungary
The bottom is a commemoration of the Siege of Belgrade.
St. John Capistrano can also be seen in the relief.[24]

St John Capistrano
Feast Day: March 28th[25]

The "Warrior Priest" was born in Italy in 1386. Initially, he was a secular man who worked for the government of Perugia. When a war broke out between Perugia and Rimini, St. John was sent to act as a peace mediator but was arrested and imprisoned. During his time in prison, he prayed about his life situation and had a vision of St. Francis that implored him to enter into religious life. He had been recently married, but since he had not yet consummated his marriage, he received a dispensation for an annulment. Following this, he immediately entered the Franciscan Order.

St. John Capistrano was known in his previous life for fighting corruption, and this translated into his priestly vocation. He earned a reputation for combating the various heresies plaguing the Church of the time. He was a vibrant and powerful preacher and writer who made many converts and was a champion of Catholic orthodoxy.

In 1453, the Ottoman invasion of Constantinople was both a military and psychological blow to the Church. Not only was Europe geographically open to a massive Ottoman invasion, but the holiest city of eastern Christendom after Jerusalem was now formally in Muslim possession. Empowered by their victories, the Ottomans began a massive push up the Danube River towards Belgrade in Serbia. If Belgrade fell, Eastern and Central Europe would be completely open to the Ottomans.

St. John Capistrano, scholar and preacher that he was, recognized the threat. In 1454, he picked up his pen for the last time and, having returned it to his desk, exchanged it for a sword. He spent the next two years of his life preaching a crusade against the Ottomans. He petitioned the Catholics to come to the aid of the Hungarians, who under John Hunyadi were holding back the Ottomans. Few noblemen responded, but he managed to gather an army of 60,000 peasants. With little to no military training and their Catholic Faith as a guide, they marched under St. John's leadership to Belgrade.

When they reached Belgrade, they were met by John Hunyadi with 4,000 of his own professional soldiers. However, they were ill-prepared to stand up to the over 100,000 battle-hardened Ottoman infantrymen and 5,000 Janissaries.[26] Like many of the crusades of the past, it looked more suicidal than hopeful.

When the battle started, known as the Siege of Belgrade, it did not go as expected. Initially, St. John's men held their positions and managed to repel the Ottomans. However, some of the soldiers broke orders by sneaking out of the citadel in order to harass the Ottoman camp. More men followed, and this quickly developed into a full-scale battle on the ground. Before St. John knew it, his men were pouring out of Belgrade and into the Ottoman camp. When he realized what was happening and that the peasant soldiers' harassment was working, he ordered a charge. It is said that as he led the charge, St. John shouted with his sword in hand "The Lord who made the beginning will finish the end!"

The Ottomans collapsed in sheer terror at the charge and retreated in panic. Not only did the Ottomans lose over 13,000 soldiers and about half of their ships, but their pride was checked by an old priest with a rag-tag army of farmers that, with God's help, crushed the greatest military power of the age.

St. John died several weeks after the battle from plague, as did John Hunyadi. But the deeds he did were never forgotten. Prior to the siege, Pope Callixtus III ordered all church bells across Europe rung at noon as a reminder to pray for St. John's army. Following the battle, he ordered that the ringing of the church bells at noon continue in thanks for the victory at Belgrade. This tradition has survived through today.

It is also interesting to note that St. John Capistrano's preaching against the Ottomans inspired a young Polish man named Szymon who came to hear him. Szymon became a priest and made pilgrimage to the Holy Land with the hope that he might suffer martyrdom by the Muslims. While he was never martyred, he returned to Poland and grew in popularity up to his death in 1482. He is now known as St. Szymon of Lipnica.

A statue of St. John Capistrano outside of St. Stephen's Church in Vienna, Austria with a dead Muslim beneath his feet. [27]

Skanderbeg
Athleta Christi
d. January 7th, 1468

Skanderbeg[28] was born George Kastrioti to a noble Albanian family of Italian descent in 1405. At the age of twenty-five, his father, Gjon Kastrioti, desired to preserve his political power in Albania as the Ottomans invaded. He and his entire family converted to Islam, despite being raised as Catholics. Gjon changed his name to Hamza, and George was given the name Iskander, which is the Turkish form of the name Alexander.

Under the devşirme[29] system, Skanderbeg was forced to serve in the Ottoman army beginning at age eighteen. He quickly distinguished himself as a great soldier and military leader. Because of this, he was referred to as Skanderbeg.[30] Nevertheless, his "conversion" to Islam was nominal and forced by his familial circumstances. Secretly, Skanderbeg was still Catholic and he sought a chance to defect from the Ottomans.

This opportunity came at the Catholic victory of Niš in 1443. During the battle, Skanderbeg defected with 300 men and assisted in leading John Hunyadi and the Hungarian army to victory. After the battle and in John's presence, Skanderbeg and his men publicly rejected Islam, re-affirmed the Catholic Faith, and vowed to fight with John for the liberation of Albania from Ottoman rule.

Skanderbeg executed possibly the greatest single-handed resistance to the Ottomans and one of the most skilled guerilla wars in world history. Using tactics similar to those the Muslims used during the Crusades, he continually crushed the Ottomans every time they attempted to stop him. Like John Hunyadi, he fought his way through the twisted alliances of

Balkan politics, never compromising his intentions. His resistance earned him an audience with Pope Callixtus III, and the two discussed plans for a crusade in 1457. However, nothing came of this. Skanderbeg also placed himself as a vassal to King Alfonso V of Aragón, who was able to help finance him for some time.

Skanderbeg never ceased his resistance, in spite of the setbacks he encountered. Eventually, the Spanish reduced their financial commitments to Skanderbeg because the resistance was becoming very expensive. Within his own family, many of Skanderbeg's relatives remained as Muslims and fought against him. Those who converted to the Catholic Faith and worked with him suffered much, including one case of a nephew that after being captured by the Ottomans was skinned alive, cut into small pieces, and thrown to dogs as food. Pope Pius II tried to re-organize a crusade to help Skanderbeg in 1464, but this attempt also never materialized.

Ottoman Sultan Mehmet II "The Conqueror" became so frustrated with Skanderbeg that he personally led an army against him in 1466. Three times the Ottomans attempted and failed to take Skanderbeg's fortress at Krujë. When they could not destroy Skanderbeg, the Ottomans began waging a total war against the Albanian people, whether or not they supported Skanderbeg, to try and force an end.

Skanderbeg died of malaria in 1468 while planning a new series of assaults against the Ottomans. His army was able to hold out against the Ottomans for ten more years. Because of the strong resistance, the Ottomans brutally mistreated the Albanian people when they took power. Many people were enslaved and abused up to the point of death. Likewise, many converted to Islam in order to save themselves.

The Albanians executed two rebellions, one in 1492 and one in 1501, which failed to dislodge the Ottomans. Albania remained under Muslim control until the Great Albanian Awakening in 1912, while the Ottoman Empire was in its death throes and Europe was on the eve of World War I. The memory of Skanderbeg's resistance was so strong that modern Albanians invoked his memory as they cast off four centuries of rule under the Ottomans. He remains the most widely acclaimed national hero of Albania.

Skanderbeg's statue in Tiranë, Albania's capitol. Albania's flag on the left is also Skanderbeg's heraldic crest. [31]

Bl. Catherine of Bosnia
Feast Day: October 23rd

Bl. Catherine of Bosnia was born in 1425 to a royal Serbian family. Her father was the Eastern Orthodox noble Stjepan Vukčić, and through her mother she was directly related to the Serbian Orthodox St. Prince Lazar of Serbia.

Bl. Catherine's life was filled with tension, as due to her familial relations she was at the center of the fighting between the Albanians, Bulgarians, Byzantines, Hungarians, and Serbs with each other and against the Ottomans. She was married to Stephen Thomas in 1446, who became King of Bosnia. Following a period of infighting over claims to the Bosnian throne due to the Ottoman advance, Bl. Catherine and her husband converted from Orthodoxy to the Catholic Faith. She became a great patron of the Catholic Church, and was a particular supporter of the Franciscan Order in Bosnia. Thanks to her assistance, the Ottomans came to respect the Franciscans, and they were allowed to remain in Bosnia to continue their mission even after the country was overtaken by the Ottomans.

At the time, the majority of Bosnia's population subscribed to a gnostic-type Christian heresy known as Bogomilism. The Bogomils were neither friendly to the Catholics nor the Orthodox, and the three groups continually fought with each other. When Islam arrived through the Ottomans, the Bogomils allied with the Ottomans to fight the Catholics and the Orthodox in 1463. After assisting the Ottomans, the Bogomils then mass converted to Islam. This crisis struck very close to Bl. Catherine's family.

Because of the self-interested alliances made between members of Catherine's family and the Ottomans for political power and gain, some of her family had already converted to Islam. This included her brother Stephen Hercegovic, who took the Turkish name Hersekzade Ahmed Pasha and married the daughter of Ottoman Caliph Bayezid II. While the sources are unclear, it appears that Bl. Catherine's apostate brother abducted Bl. Catherine's two young children, Sigismund and Catherine, and took them to Istanbul. Once there, the children were forcibly converted to Islam and integrated into the Ottoman Empire. Little Catherine died in Skopje, Macedonia, possibly from illness. Sigismund was given the name Ishak-Bey

Kraloğlu, and became a vizier to Sultan Mehmet II "The Conqueror."

Bl. Catherine left for Italy after Bosnia's fall, and stayed there until she died in 1478. She was buried in the Basilica of St. Mary of the Altar of Heaven in Rome. She left the throne to Sigismund, saying that if he returned to the Catholic Faith in which he was raised, he would be the rightful heir to it. However, he rejected his mother's offer and chose to remain as a Muslim.

Bl. Pacificus of Cerano
Feast Day: June 4th

Bl. Pacificus of Cerano was born in Cerano, Lombardy, Italy in 1420 and became a Franciscan friar in 1445. He was a brilliant preacher, and helped St. John Capistrano preach the crusade which became the Siege of Belgrade in 1456. He died in Sardinia in 1481.

Bl. Angelo Carletti di Chivasso
Feast Day: April 12th

Born in Piedmont, Italy in 1411, Bl. Angelo Carletti di Chivasso became a Franciscan Friar around 1441. He worked for most of his life as a writer, theologian, and later vicar-general within the order. After the Ottoman massacre of Catholics at the city of Otranto in 1480, he began preaching a crusade against the Ottomans in 1481 at the request of the Pope. King Ferdinand I of Naples, who was son of King Alfonso V of Aragón, was petitioned to drive out the Ottomans. A little more than a year after Otranto's anniversary, the Ottomans were expelled from Italy. Bl. Angelo died in 1495.

Inspirers

Bl. James of Tahust
Feast Day: August 28th

Bl. James of Tahust was a Mercedarian from Valencia. He served as Master General of the Order for four years. During this time, he traveled to the major North African slave ports and ransomed many Catholics enslaved by Muslims. His preaching also converted many Muslims to the Faith. One of those converts was made while he was on his deathbed in 1405. This man eventually became a Mercedarian, and he is now known as Bl. Muhammad Abdalla.[32]

Our Lady of Europe
Feast Day: May 5th

Our Lady of Europe is venerated at her shrine in Gibraltar. She is intimately connected to the Spanish Reconquista during the 14th and 15th centuries. The shrine stands at Europa Point, which is Gibraltar's southernmost end and is the last border between Spain and Morocco. It was originally a church, but depending on which group controlled the area, it alternated between a church and a mosque for many centuries until the Spanish conclusively seized it in 1468. Many miracles are attributed to her, particularly with soliciting help in rescuing Catholics from Muslim pirates.

In 1704, the church and the original statue of Our Lady was commandeered and destroyed by the British Empire, which used the church as an armory. The British finally returned the shrine to the Spanish in 1962. The church and statue were rebuilt, and it continues to serve as a place of pilgrimage.

Notable Mention

King Alfonso V of Aragón
d. 1458

King Alfonso V of Aragón was born in 1396 and became king in 1416. Like many European monarchs of his time, he was deeply involved in political infighting over succession and territorial expansion. But unlike many monarchs, he was also greatly concerned with defeating the Ottomans.

King Alfonso financially assisted the Catholic rebellions taking place in the Balkans, including Skanderbeg's resistance in Albania. His dedication to defending the Catholic Faith and Christianity as a whole against Islam reached all across the world. Eventually, he was even contacted by the Ethiopian Emperor Yeshaq I around 1450, who proposed an alliance against the Muslims.[33] According to the terms, Yeshaq's daughter would marry into King Alfonso's family in exchange for sending a group of craftsmen to assist in building up Ethiopia. King Alfonso agreed to the deal and sent a group, but they were killed in route. Since Ethiopia could not guarantee their safe passage, the agreement collapsed. Nevertheless, the contact between the Spanish and the Ethiopians later played an important role as Spain and Portugal expanded their empires worldwide.

Henry the Navigator
d. 1460

Henry the Navigator was born in 1394. He was the elder brother of Bl. Ferdinand, the Holy Prince of Portugal. Like his brother, Henry was a devout Catholic, patron of the Church, and a warrior for the Faith. His actions with Islam charted Portugal's imperial expansion and missionary efforts for the next several centuries.

Within Portugal, Henry was a fierce supporter of the Reconquista. He desired not just to liberate Portugal from Muslim rule, but also to take possession of Muslim territories in North Africa. Using his position as the leader of the Portuguese Order of Christ, he conducted many raids against the Moroccan coastline. His plan for a siege and invasion of Tangiers in 1437 however, failed miserably and resulted in the capture and death of his brother. [34]

Henry's title "The Navigator" comes from his work as a young man in stopping the slave trade in Catholic Europeans operated by Muslim pirates throughout North Africa. As he began to study the pirates' sea routes, he realized that the entire economic supply chain used by Muslims for centuries to import goods from the Far East could be interrupted. This was equally critical because European demand for eastern goods, particularly spices, enriched Muslim shippers and merchants while draining European treasuries. If a better way could be found to import goods from the East, then it would economically hinder the Muslims from carrying out their attacks against Europe.

By using information provided by Muslim pirates and merchants, sailors, and existing European knowledge, Henry created more detailed and accurate maps than had ever before existed. He explored the West African coastline and made the first maps of Serra Leone, Mauritania, and sub-Saharan Africa. He re-discovered the Madeira, Cape Verde, and Azores islands and had them colonized. Eventually, Henry concluded that an all-water route to India and the Far East by sailing around Africa was possible. He did not live to see this happen, but in 1498 the Portuguese explorer Vasco da Gama proved his theories correct.

Chivalric Orders of the Period

As during the Crusades, Chivalric Orders emerged to aid the Church's mission in the struggle with Islam. In the Balkan Peninsula, their purpose was to stop the continual Ottoman advance. In Spain and Portugal, the Orders established during the Crusades continued to serve their roles in aiding the Reconquista up to its successful completion in 1492.

The Order of St. George

The Order of St. George was founded in 1326 by Hungarian King Charles I. Its purpose was to repel the Ottomans during their continual attempts to invade Hungary. While the Byzantine Empire was weak during this period, it was still functional enough to repel many Ottoman attacks. The Order's role increased as the Ottomans pushed closer and more aggressively on Hungary's borders.

The Order of St. George was unique in that it was not specifically founded by the Church, but rather by the Hungarian monarchy. However, its goals were both political and religious, as it sought to defend both Hungary and the Church against the Ottomans. The Order's popularity spread throughout Europe, but it always retained a uniquely Hungarian character. The Order still exists today, albeit as a secular order of merit for the Hungarian nation.

Order of the Dragon

The Order of the Dragon was founded by Holy Roman Emperor Sigismund in 1408. It was modeled after the Crusader State Orders, only this time its focus was on repelling the

Ottomans. As its founding documents note, the Order's purpose was:

"...to crush the pernicious deeds of the same perfidious Enemy, and of the followers of the ancient Dragon, and (as one would expect) of the pagan knights, schismatics, and other nations of the Orthodox faith, and those envious of the Cross of Christ, and of our kingdoms, and of his holy and saving religion of faith, under the banner of the triumphant Cross of Christ..."[35]

The Order constituted many of Emperor Sigismund's allies in Eastern Europe. However noble its intentions were, it lasted only the duration of Emperor Sigismund's life, and was dissolved after his death in 1437.

Order of Sts. Lazarus and Maurice

The Order of Sts. Lazarus and Maurice has its origins in the Crusades to the Holy Land. The original Order of St. Lazarus was dissolved after the Crusades in 1291 on account of its lack of members and inability to support itself financially. Nevertheless, the few remaining members of the order settled in France and carried on the Order's memory in private. The Knights of St. Maurice were formed in 1434, but could not support themselves and were formally dissolved as quickly as they were formed. However, like the Order of St. Lazarus, the founding members carried on the Order's memory in private.

The two Orders eventually were re-established in 1572 by Pope St. Pius V, albeit this time as a unified Order of Sts. Lazarus and Maurice. The Order's mission was to protect the Pope from Muslim attacks. They earned a reputation as fierce warriors in battles with Muslim pirates off the Italian coastline. Additionally, the Order opened hospitals to care for the sick.

The Order was later secularized, and exists today as an Italian order of merit.

Order of Our Lady of Bethlehem

The Order of Our Lady of Bethlehem was founded in 1459. Its purpose was to protect the island of Lemnos in the Aegean Sea from Ottoman invasions. This was because Lemnos was both a major food-producing island and a transportation hub between Asia Minor and the Balkan Peninsula. At the time, the island was a hotly contested territory between the Venetians and the Ottomans.

The Order protected Lemnos for nearly three decades, and was critical in repelling a major Ottoman invasion in 1476. However, the attacks became more pronounced, and eventually the island fell to Ottoman control in 1479. The surviving members fled Lemnos, and the Order was disbanded.

Order of St. Stephen

The Order of St. Stephen was founded by the Tuscan Duke Cosimo di Medici in 1561. It was deeply involved in skirmishes with Ottoman naval vessels and combating Muslim slave ships. The Order directly participated in the Siege of Malta in 1565, the Battle of Lepanto in 1571, and many other assaults against North Africa and the Ottoman Empire.

The Order eventually focused its military activity on protecting the Italian coastline from Muslim raids. It was abolished in the late 18th century, but was later revived and now exists as a secular order of merit.

Endings and Beginnings

The late 15th and early 16th centuries were a turning point in the Church's struggle with Islam. The end of the Reconquista in 1492 was a great victory for the Spanish and Portuguese as well as the Church. However, three new issues immediately arose which threatened to undermine the Reconquista's gains and permit for Islam's resurgence in not just Spain and Portugal, but all across Europe.

The first problem was the Ottomans. The Catholic rebellions in Eastern Europe slowed but did not stop the Ottoman expansions. When the city of Belgrade fell in 1521, all of Eastern Europe was susceptible to attack. The Hungarians, who fought for centuries against the invasions, eventually were defeated at the Battle of Mohács in 1527 and were swallowed into the Ottoman Empire. Spanish King Charles I, also known as Holy Roman Emperor Charles V and heir to the Habsburg Empire, had to maintain his possessions in Spain as well as deal with the Ottoman threat. The Ottomans failed to take the Habsburg city of Vienna in 1529, but they remained a constant problem over the next 150 years.

The second problem was the issue of the Mudéjars and the Moriscos in Spain. The former were Muslims living in Spain after the Fall of Granada. The latter were Muslim converts to the Catholic Faith or the descendants of Muslim converts to the Faith. The former had isolated themselves into Muslim-only ghettos and were engaging in open rebellion against the Church and Spanish Kingdom. The latter group was more challenging because they constituted a mix of sincere converts to the Faith with superficial converts who supported the Mudéjar rebellions. The issue was both how to distinguish between the sincere versus rebellious Mudéjars and Moriscos, and if possible, how to genuinely bring them into the Church.

The third problem was the Protestant movement that began in 1517. While neither Luther nor Calvin[36] liked Islam, Protestants did ally with the Ottomans and other Muslim groups against the Catholics. This was such a problem that a popular phrase in Calvinist-influenced Holland about the conflict with the Ottomans and the Church was "Better a Turk than a Papist."[37] The Ottomans immediately detected these sympathies and established alliances with Protestant England and Holland, including direct correspondence with Queen Elizabeth I.[38] Perhaps the most insidious action was that the Ottoman Empire directly funded Calvinism and Calvinist revolutionaries in France, Hungary, Poland, Spain, and Wallachia. This was in addition to the fact that they were also supporting revolutionaries among the Spanish Moriscos. Catholic Counter-Reformation writers accurately called this phenomenon "Turco-Calvinism," in reference to the collusion between the two against the Church.[39]

The Church came into a position where it was literally under military siege from the Ottomans outside its borders and internally through their support of the Protestant movement. Due to the relationship with the Habsburgs, the Spanish were the only force powerful and unified enough to strategically resist the Ottomans. Fortunately, the Spanish experience of fighting Islam for eight centuries had given them considerable knowledge about Islam and how to combat its influence.

The first steps taken to deal with the Muslims in Spain began even before the Reconquista ended. Queen Isabella and King Ferdinand initially wanted to integrate the Mudéjars into Spanish society. The seldom-discussed Treaty of Granada in 1491 granted many religious liberties to Muslims. However, the treaty was revoked on account of the systemic, dangerous, and Ottoman-sponsored Mudéjar rebellions that broke out across Spain even as Granada was negotiating its surrender.

After nearly a decade, the Spanish concluded they could not successfully integrate the Mudéjars. At the suggestion of Cardinal Francisco Jiménez de Cisneros, the government ordered in 1500 that the Mudéjars had to either embrace the Catholic Faith and Spanish culture or leave Spain. Initially the decision was successful, but it created long-term problems that took nearly a century to remedy. While some persons left, many Mudéjars nominally converted to the Catholic Faith and transferred their rebellious activity to the Morisco population. This was confirmed in 1504 when the Grand Mufti of Oran, Abu Al-'Abbas Ahmad bin Boujam'ah drafted a fatwa to the Spanish Moriscos. The fatwa said that Moriscos could do everything Catholics did that violated Islamic teaching publicly as long as they secretly remained Muslims and continued their rebellions.[40] Because of the serious nature of the rebellions and their support by the Ottomans, the Spanish needed a method to distinguish between faithful versus rebellious Moriscos. This was both the reason for establishing and the original purpose of the Spanish Inquisition.

Within the Mediterranean Sea and beyond, the Spanish and Portuguese independently attacked Ottoman territories and Muslim pirates. However, because of the alliances the Ottomans established with the Protestant governments, they found themselves also fighting British and Dutch pirates under Ottoman contract. Many of these pirates converted to Islam and were just as traitorous in that they attacked and sold fellow Europeans into slavery in North Africa and Ottoman territories. These Muslim pirate converts became so ruthless that they even started to attack fellow British and Dutch citizens, and so forced their respective governments to drop their support of the Ottomans. Their infamy inspired literature and entertainment of the time, including the English play A Christian Turned Turk about the infamous English pirate Jack Ward, known by his Muslim name of Yusuf Reis.

In Eastern Europe, the Habsburgs continued to support resistance to the Ottomans while simultaneously dealing with Ottoman-funded Protestant movements in the same region. While there were many Europeans who genuinely believed in the Protestant cause, the Protestant movement survived in large part due to Ottoman support. From the Ottoman perspective, their support of the Protestant movement was merely an extension of their strategy to divide and conquer.

The religious wars in Western and Central Europe gravely damaged the Habsburgs as well as Christian unity. By the mid-17th century, the Habsburgs were barely able to maintain their own territories in Eastern Europe against the Ottomans, let alone combat them. Fortunately, the great Polish King John Sobieski III assumed many of the wars against the Ottomans that the Habsburgs had done in years past. Eventually, it was the Polish who came to the Habsburg Empire's rescue, and in doing so saved Europe from Ottoman invasion at the Battle of Vienna in 1683.

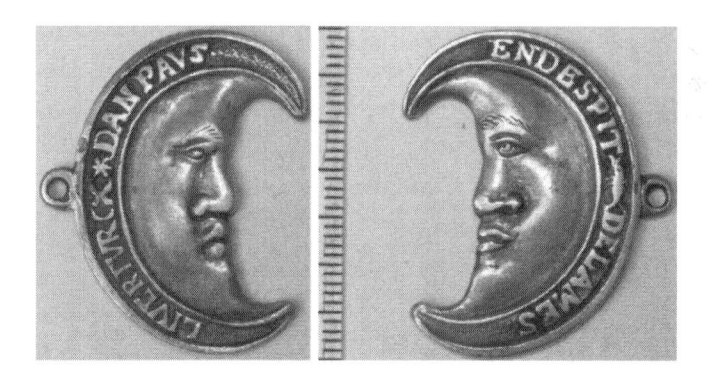

A medal worn by Dutch Protestant sailors around 1574. The side on the left reads "Better a Turk than a Papist" and the right reads "In spite of the Mass." The former phrase was conceived and often used by the Calvinist preacher Herman Moded[41] in his anti-Catholic sermons.[42] The metal is in the shape of the moon, which is a traditional symbol of Islam.

Martyrs

Bl. James of St. Peter
Feast Day: October 10th

Bl. James of St. Peter was a Dominican in Zaragoza. He was killed while saying Mass in 1516 by Muslim pirates who attacked his monastery.

Bl. Marc Criado
Feast Day: September 24th

Bl. Marc Criado was born in 1522 and was a missionary to the former Muslim strongholds in southern Spain. Many Muslims converted to the Catholic Faith on account of his preaching. His work was dangerous because the places he ministered to were often still major areas of Muslim rebel activity. One such area was Alpujarras, where Moriscos launched a massive rebellion that lasted from 1568 to 1571 and nearly overthrew the Spanish government. While he was preaching in Alpujarras in 1569 during the rebellion, he was kidnapped by a group of Moriscos. They tied him to a tree and slowly tortured him to death over the course of several days.

St. Jerome of Werden
Feast Day: July 9th

St. Jerome of Werden was born in 1522 in Werden, Holland. He entered the Franciscan Order as a young man and soon traveled to the Holy Land. At this time, the Holy Land was under the control of the Ottoman Empire, but the Franciscans were allowed to continue both their public ministry as well as evangelization. He earned a reputation as a great preacher and converted many Muslims to the Catholic Faith.

Upon returning home to Holland in 1572, St. Jerome was captured by Calvinist revolutionaries in the city of Gorkum along with nine other Catholic priests. At the order of Calvinist rebel William de La Marck, the men were summarily executed. He was one of the martyrs of Gorkum.

Servant of God Bishop John Andrew Carga
Feast Day: October 17th

Martin Carga was born in 1560 and entered the Dominicans at 18 with the name John Andrew. He was sent to Constantinople as an emissary and soon was appointed Bishop of Syros and Milos on the island of Cyprus in 1607. While Cyprus was under Ottoman control at the time, it had a large Catholic population. During a conflict with the Ottomans in 1617, Bishop Carga refused to divulge the location of certain Catholics to the Ottomans. It is possible they were Muslims who converted to the Catholic Faith. He was arrested and imprisoned. The Ottomans promised to release him if he converted to Islam. However, he refused to convert, and was executed by hanging.

St. Ketevan of Mukhrani, Queen of Georgia
Feast Day: September 26th (Georgian Orthodox)

St. Ketevan of Mukhrani, Queen of Georgia is an interesting case of Catholic-Orthodox unity. While she was not Catholic and her canonization is recognized by the Georgian Orthodox Church, her sanctity was recognized by Augustinian monks from Portugal's colony in Goa who witnessed her martyrdom and cared for her relics after her death.

St. Ketevan served as queen during a difficult time in Georgian history. Georgia was caught between the Shiite Safavid Persian Empire in the east,[43] the Ottomans in the west, and Russia in the north. Safavid Shah 'Abbas sought the support of the Christian Georgians in his wars against the Ottomans. This was complicated by the fact that Shah 'Abbas had kidnapped St. Ketevan's daughter Helen, forcibly converted her to Islam, and married himself to her. Additionally, there was a power struggle between St. Ketevan's two sons. Her first son Temuraz remained a Christian and was fighting to keep Georgia free from Muslim rule. His brother Constantine, however, converted to Islam and allied with Shah 'Abbas against Temuraz.

St. Ketevan attempted to keep peace in the situation while making no commitments to the Safavids, Ottomans, or Russians. However, she did not know that Temuraz had made contact with the Russians to seek an alliance against the Safavids in 1614. This information reached Shah 'Abbas quickly, and out of anger he sought to take revenge on St. Ketevan, her family, and the Georgian people.

Shah 'Abbas deposed St. Ketevan's family as rulers and replaced them with Georgian converts to Islam. He ordered a mass murder of the Georgian people, and over 60,000 Georgian Orthodox were executed and 100,000 were enslaved and deported to Persia. Temuraz escaped and continued to fight the Persians for the next half-century, but his sons Alexander and Leon were captured. At Shah 'Abbas' order they were abducted and castrated, but died of the wounds incurred in the process.

St. Ketevan suffered the worst of the punishment. She was deported with the other Georgians to what is today Shiraz, Iran, and was ordered to convert to Islam. However, she refused. For her execution, Shah 'Abbas ordered her publicly tortured to death by a serious of heinous punishments. He had her fingernails and toenails ripped off, her breasts cut off with scissors, eyes blinded, and finally scalded her naked body with a hot iron before impaling her with the same instrument.

There were several Augustinian friars visiting Shah 'Abbas on a diplomatic mission from Portugal's colony in Goa, India. One of them was a Fr. Antonio de Gouvea. He and his representatives witnessed the whole event and were convinced of her sanctity. After St. Ketevan was dead, he secretly exhumed her body and transported her badly mutilated relics to the Church of St. Augustine in Goa, India for veneration.

St. Ketevan's story and the honor given to her by Fr. Antonio emphasize the common unity shared by Catholics and Orthodox alike. While there are differences, her story shows that Catholics and Orthodox share a common faith in and love of Christ. It is this same love that likewise drives Islam's zeal to oppress and destroy Christianity wherever it spreads.

Bl. Giovanni da Prado
Feast Day: May 24th

Bl. Giovanni da Prado was a Franciscan and the first Apostolic Prefect of Morocco. He was killed by Muslims at Marrakesh in 1631.

Bls. Denis of the Nativity and Redemptus
Feast Day: November 29th

Pierre Berthelot was born in 1600 in France. He became a sailor in 1619 and traveled with the French to Portuguese-controlled Malacca, in what is today Malaysia.

During his travel to Malacca, Pierre had a religious conversion. After reaching his destination, he temporarily worked as a naval commander and cartographer for the Portuguese. However, he later abandoned this and joined the Discalced Carmelites in Goa in 1638 with the name Brother Denis of the Nativity. There he met Thomas Rodrigues da Cunha, known as brother Redemptus.

That same year, the two traveled together to evangelize the Muslims of Aceh Province on the Indonesian island of Sumatra. At the time, the island was ruled by the devout Muslim Sultan Iskandar Thani. During their missionary work the brothers were captured, imprisoned, and told to convert to Islam or die. When they refused, the Muslims slit Bl. Redemptus' throat and then beheaded Bl. Denis.

King St. Stephen III of Moldavia
His coat of arms, which can be seen in the center of the monument, is emblazoned on Moldavia's national flag today.[44]

Contenders

King St. Stephen III of Moldavia
Athleta Christi
Feast Day: July 2nd (Eastern Orthodox)

Born in 1433 to Moldavian royalty, King St. Stephen III of Moldavia is known for leading a heroic resistance of Catholic and Eastern Orthodox Christians against the Ottomans.

St. Stephen became King of Moldavia in 1457. Because Moldavia is a small nation, it found itself constantly besieged by its neighbors. In spite of these problems, he correctly perceived the Ottomans to be the greatest long-term threat not just to his temporal domain, but to the whole of Europe.

After much work, St. Stephen sought to pacify his neighbors by building alliances with them against the Muslims. Two of his greatest supporters were Hungarian King Matthias Corvinius and Prince Vladimir III Țepeș of Romania, better known as "Dracula." He provided military and financial aid to both countries, and encouraged Catholic and Orthodox Christians to unite with each other to combat the Ottomans.

In late 1474, the Ottomans attempted a full invasion of Moldavia by attacking its coastal border along the Black Sea. Ottoman Sultan Mehmet II "The Conqueror" fully expected to overtake St. Stephen's small force made up of Moldavians, Poles, and Hungarians. St. Stephen petitioned Pope Sixtus IV for help, but as with Skanderbeg's rebellion a decade earlier, the Pope was unable to assist him.

Nevertheless, St. Stephen's little army stood up courageously to the Ottomans. During the day of invasion on January 10th, 1475, known as the Battle of Vaslui, St. Stephen gave the Ottomans an even greater defeat than the one St. John Capistrano and John Hunyadi inflicted at Belgrade in 1456. At least half of the 80,000 Ottoman soldiers died in the failed invasion, not to mention those captured and supplies lost. It was said that Sultan Mehmet was so distraught after hearing of this loss that he isolated himself and spent every day after planning his next attack against Moldavia. St. Stephen refused to celebrate his victory, but chose to pray and fast and so that the victory would always be remembered as coming from God.

One year later, the Ottomans launched a massive attack against Moldavia at Valea Alba. The Ottomans were victorious, but they could not crush the Moldavian resistance. Eventually, the Ottomans slowly took over all of Moldavia and forced it to become a vassal state in 1498. However, this happened because St. Stephen was forced to fight against foreign attacks from Poland at the same time he was combating the Ottomans.

St. Stephen died in 1504. He was canonized by the Romanian Orthodox Church in 1992. Because of his work with Catholics and Orthodox in striving for Christian unity against the Ottomans, Pope Sixtus IV gave him the title of *Athleta Christi*.

St. Francis Xavier
Feast Day: December 3rd

St. Francis Xavier was one of the original members of the Jesuits. He was born in Spain in 1506, and he evangelized thousands of Muslims and non-Muslims throughout the Far East.

St. Francis Xavier arrived at Goa in May 1542, where he set up the Jesuits' first mission in the Far East. His work was spent mostly among the native Hindu and Muslim populations. St. Francis Xavier executed his duties with astonishing success, as he tailored his missionary efforts to meet the social and cultural differences of the Indian people while maintaining Catholic orthodoxy.

St. Francis often faced resistance from the Hindus and Muslims, and they attempted to assassinate him multiple times. He also had to struggle with the issue of false converts, since many Muslims superficially converted to the Catholic Faith in order to get food assistance from the mission while simultaneously opposing the Church they claimed to belong to. For this reason, St. Francis Xavier supported and requested for the Inquisition to come to India in order to help him distinguish between the true versus false converts. Unfortunately, it did not come during his lifetime, and when it did, the Portuguese so poorly executed it that many innocent people were unjustly hurt. However, this does not speak to St. Francis Xavier's character, as his life and actions testify to his unique care for the salvation and material welfare of his fellow man.

St. Francis Xavier died in 1552 following a bout of fever in China. By this time, he had traveled all throughout the Far East. He pioneered missionary work in Asia among Muslims and non-Muslims alike, and his work still blossoms today.

St. Joseph of Leonessa
Feast Day: February 4th

St. Joseph of Leonessa was born in 1556 in Leonessa, Italy. In 1573 he became a Capuchin monk and in 1580 he was ordained a priest.

St. Joseph always desired to go to the Ottoman Empire and preach to the Ottomans. For many years, this was only a dream. However, in 1587 he was commissioned to minister to the tiny Catholic population within Istanbul. Due to the

Ottoman depopulation of Constantinople during its fall in 1453, the Catholic community was limited to Venetian merchants on business and a few Eastern Catholic Greeks and Armenians. He accepted the assignment, but in addition to his duties to the Catholic community, he earnestly desired to present the Catholic Faith to Ottoman Sultan Murad III.

Unfortunately, St. Joseph did not seem to understand the kind of man Sultan Murad III was. Murad was an intelligent and pious Muslim man who was born to an apostate Italian Catholic mother.[45] He likewise was married to another Italian Catholic apostate. His zeal for Islam equaled his hatred of Christianity and obsession with destroying the Church. It was he who took the initiative in establishing a Protestant-Muslim alliance with Queen Elizabeth I of England and Calvinist Holland to try to divide and conquer Europe. Additionally, he openly supplied money and weapons to Calvinist revolutionaries across Europe.[46]

St. Joseph attempted to break into Murad's palace but was captured by the guards. He met with Sultan Murad, who accused him of being a spy and ordered him to be suspended head-first over a fire and roasted alive. However, when the Ottomans attempted to roast him, he was not burned by the flames. They kept the fire burning for three days, and although St. Joseph hung by his feet the entire time, no harm came to him. The Ottomans were in complete shock, and so afterwards they expelled him from Istanbul and gave him no further trouble.

After returning to Europe, St. Joseph lived out the rest of his life in penance and sacrifice. Many miracles were attributed to his prayers. He died peacefully in 1612.

Bl. Mark of Aviano
Feast Day: August 13th

Born Charles Dominic Cristofori in Aviano, Italy in 1631 to noble parents, he assisted Polish King John Sobieski III's victory over the Ottomans in 1683.

Bl. Mark became a Capuchin monk at 17. Most of his initial years were spent in Italy, where he developed a reputation as a preacher and scholar. He became very popular following the healing of a crippled nun by his prayers in 1676. He traveled across Italy praying for people and working miracles. However, his heart always desired to evangelize the Ottomans.

One day, Habsburg Emperor Leopold I requested Bl. Mark to visit and pray with him, as he and his wife were unable to conceive. Bl. Mark befriended the Emperor and soon became his close advisor in not just their personal business, but with all affairs in governing the Habsburg Empire. He exercised his responsibilities with great care, and he earned the Emperor's deepest trust.

When Pope Bl. Innocent XI called for a Holy League and specifically upon Polish King John Sobieski III to defend Vienna against the Ottomans, Bl. Mark directly organized and represented the Habsburg Empire's participation. It was by his leadership that the necessary defenses and preparations were made so that Vienna could stand up to the Ottoman siege before the Poles arrived.

When the Ottomans did attack, he fought alongside the Viennese and led the city's heroic defense. After the Ottomans were defeated, he personally oversaw the humane treatment of Ottoman war prisoners and more than once intervened to stop them from being abused. He also served as mediator between the Habsburgs and the Ottomans to discuss the situation of these same war prisoners.

Bl. Mark died in 1699. He represents well the dichotomy of the Catholic Faith, as he fought Islam with military force yet sought to ensure and defend the humanity and lives of the Muslim people.

Our Lady of Guadalupe
Note that she is standing on the crescent moon, which is a traditional symbol of Islam. The same posture can be seen with Our Lady of Almudeña, Patroness of Madrid, Spain.[47]

Inspirers

Our Lady of Guadalupe
Patroness of the Americas
Feast Day: December 12th

Our Lady of Guadalupe is well-known to many people in the Americas and across the Spanish world. She is the Patroness of the Americas, of the unborn, of the Mexican people, and is one of the most important Marian apparitions in Catholic history. However, what is less known is her connection to Islam and the conversion of the Muslims.

The title Our Lady of Guadalupe originally comes from a statue of Mary believed to have been carved by St. Luke and that was hidden following the Islamic invasion of Spain in 711. It was rediscovered by a shepherd, Gil Cordero, following an apparition of Our Lady to him. The original Our Lady of Guadalupe in Spain was a place of great pilgrimage, and King Alfonso XI of Castile attributed his victory over the Muslims at the Battle of Río Salado in 1340 to her intercession.

It has been often noted that Our Lady of Guadalupe who appeared in 1531 on St. Juan Diego's tilma was standing on a crescent moon. Many people have said this was interpreted by the Aztec Indians as crushing the serpent god which they worshipped. However, the name "Guadalupe" was given to her by Bishop Juan de Zumarrága, to whom St. Juan Diego presented his tilma and who commissioned the construction of the Church dedicated to her as she requested. Some say he called her "Our Lady of Guadalupe" because in the Nahuatl language the phrase "the one who crushes the serpent," "Te Coatlaxopeuh," sounded like "Guadalupe" to him.

While Bishop Zumarrága's thoughts on this matter are lost to history, it seems more likely that he called this apparition of Our Lady by the title of "Guadalupe" because of the crescent moon she is standing on in the image, in reference to Our Lady of Guadalupe, Extremadura. The crescent moon was one of the earliest and most often used signs by Muslims to represent Islam, and it has been carried on the flags of many Muslim invaders. On St. John Capistrano's crest, there is a picture of a sword piercing an inverted crescent moon. During the Battle of Lepanto against the Ottomans in 1571, the Italian naval commander Gianandrea Doria carried an icon of this same Mexican Our Lady of Guadalupe into battle with him.

As the Catholic Faith teaches, Our Lady has been the greatest intercessor for the Church in the struggle with Islam. Surely Bishop Zumarrága understood this well, especially when he saw Our Lady standing on the crescent moon. The Americas and Europe would be wise to seek her prayerful intercession as Islam rises again. For as Our Lady of Guadalupe makes clear, she will be the victorious leader for the Catholic Faith over Islam.

Our Lady of Victory
Our Lady of the Rosary
Feast Day: October 7th

Our Lady of Victory is a title given to the Blessed Virgin stemming from her prayerful intercession in winning the 1571 Battle of Lepanto against the Ottoman navy.

Lepanto happened as the result of an Ottoman attack on a Venetian fortress in Famagusta, Cyprus. Prior to this, the Ottomans and the Venetians had been engaging in skirmishes for quite some time. On October 1st, 1571 the Ottomans agreed to let a Venetian brigade go free from the fortress following terms of surrender. However, Ottoman Commander Lala

Karamustafa changed his mind at the last minute. Instead, he had the Venetian Commander Marco Bragadin flayed alive and his internal organs cut up and distributed as a prize to his soldiers before ordering his skin stuffed with straw and paraded through the streets of Famagusta on an ox.[48]

Outrage over the incident pulsated across Italy, and Pope St. Pius V called for the Holy League to sail to Cyprus and confront the Ottomans. Catholics from across Italy, Spain, France, Austria, and the Knights of Malta heeded the Pope's call. Prior to the battle, St. Pius V asked Europe to pray the Rosary and seek the intercession of Our Lady for victory. This prayer was critical, since the Ottomans had the world's largest and most powerful navy yet in history.

The Battle of Lepanto as it happened was an accident. This was because while the Holy League was sailing to Cyprus by way of the Ionian Sea, so also was the Ottoman naval fleet sailing towards Italy. The two fleets met on October 7th in the Gulf of Corinth, also known as the Gulf of Lepanto. A vicious naval battle ensued, and by the end of the day the Catholics defeated the Ottomans so badly that the Ottomans were left to throwing fruits as weapons. While the Holy League lost approximately seventeen ships and eight thousand men, they killed or captured half of the Ottoman navy, destroyed or captured seventy-five percent of their ships, and freed over ten thousand Christian slaves. The Ottomans still launched naval assaults against Europe, but the monopolistic control they possessed over the Mediterranean was now over.

It is said that on the day of the battle, St. Pius V stood up and, looking to Heaven, praised God because news of the victory was revealed to him before the Holy League returned. He instituted the feast of Our Lady of Victory, also known as Our Lady of the Rosary, in commemoration of the victory which she brought the Holy League at Lepanto.

Mary, Help of Christians
Feast Day: May 24th

The feast of Mary, Help of Christians can be traced back to the 4th century. However as a modern devotion, it dates to the battle of Lepanto in 1571, since Catholics sought Mary's help in defeating the Ottomans.

Pope St. Pius V
Feast Day: April 30th

Pope St. Pius V was born in 1504. He is remembered in helping to establish the Holy League to confront the Ottomans and in petitioning Europe to seek Our Lady's intercession for victory.

St. Pius formed the Holy League in early 1571, as he saw the Ottoman navy's rising power as a grave threat. He consistently worked to form the Order in both its spiritual and military character. Prior to the Battle of Lepanto, he ordered that the League's soldiers sent to confront the Ottomans were only men of high moral integrity. He also petitioned all of Europe to pray the Rosary for the soldiers before they went to battle. When Lepanto was won, knowledge of the victory was revealed to him before the news made it back to Europe, at which he jumped up and praised God.

In thanks for the victory at Lepanto, St. Pius instituted the feast of Our Lady of Victory, also known as Our Lady of the Rosary. Because of the assistance Our Lady gave the Holy League, St. Pius associated the feast of Our Lady, Help of Christians with Lepanto. Additionally, St. Pius asked the Lord to increase his personal sufferings so that more victories might be won over the Ottomans. He died in 1572.

St. John of Ribera
Feast Day: January 6th

St. John of Ribera was born in Seville in 1532. In 1568 he became Archbishop of Valencia. He held this position for the rest of his life. It was here that he directed the final end of Islam in Spain through the expulsion of the Moriscos in 1609.

The problems with Spain's Morisco population dated back to end of the Reconquista in 1492. Muslim rebellions were common throughout inner-city Morisco ghettos and across the southern Spanish countryside. Many of these rebellions were funded by either the Ottomans or the Moroccans, and on more than one occasion they nearly overturned the Spanish government. This was worsened by the fact that rebellious Moriscos conducted themselves as Catholics in public but practiced Islam and fomented their insurrections in secret.[49]

For over a century, the Church and Spanish government tried to integrate the Moriscos into society. Most of this work was either done by Church missionaries sent to Muslim areas or by the Spanish government through the Inquisition. While both efforts were helpful, the rebellions only intensified and became harder to control. Something had to be done to conclusively fix this problem.

St. John of Ribera knew the situation well. He was from southern Spain, and both growing up in that region and serving in the Church he witnessed repeated Morisco rebellions. St. John was also a great proponent of evangelizing the Moriscos, and he worked as a tireless advocate for them. Nevertheless, he also knew as Archbishop that the rebellions were ripping Spanish society apart, including his own city of Valencia. He could not continue to support the current approach, but neither would he support violence against the Moriscos.

Ultimately, St. John believed that it was best for Spain as well as the Moriscos that they be expelled to the Muslim world. He presented the idea of expulsion to King Philip III of Spain, who agreed with the suggestion. In 1609, over 200,000 Moriscos were deported to North Africa. Following this action, the Morisco revolts conclusively ceased as the last vestiges of Islam in Spain were vanquished.

Three points must be emphasized from St. John of Ribera's actions. First is that the expulsions happened due to Islam's inability to coexist long-term in Spanish society, as it sought to re-establish the Andalusian Caliphate through each subsequent rebellion in spite of a century of attempts to integrate them. Second is that the decision to expel the Moriscos was carefully thought out and was a last-resort decision that was unique to the Spanish situation. Third, St. John must be credited with saving many lives, as he stood against King Philip's advisors who encouraged massacring the Moriscos. He died in 1611.

Ven. Carlo Carafa
d. September 18th

Ven. Carlo Carafa was born in Marietta, Italy to noble parents in 1561. He entered into military service and distinguished himself in battle against the Ottomans, but he did not care much about religion. In 1600 he renounced his military life, became a priest, and devoted himself to working with the poor and sick. During this time he founded the Congregation of Pious Rural Workers to minister to Catholics living in rural areas.

In 1621, two major events happened in Ven. Carlo's life. First, his congregation was officially recognized by the Church. Second, he was transferred to teach at the diocesan seminary in Naples. Additionally, he began ministering to imprisoned

Ottoman soldiers and slaves captured in battles with Naples. He became a close friend and advocate for them, and many converted to the Catholic Faith on account of his influence. Ven. Carlo died peacefully in 1633.

Pope Bl. Innocent XI
Feast Day: August 12th

Pope Bl. Innocent XI was born in 1611 to a noble Milanese family and became Pope in 1676 as the struggle between the Poles and the Ottomans was raging. Through his prayers and support he united and provided military assistance to the Poles and the Habsburgs, allowing them to defeat the Ottoman Siege of Vienna in September 1683.

When Polish King John Sobieski went out to meet the Ottomans on September 9th, 1683, Pope Bl. Innocent entrusted the battle to Our Lady. He also asked for the Church to pray for the Polish army. After a fierce fight, the Catholics routed the Ottomans on September 11th and began the process of driving them out of Eastern Europe. He instituted the feast of the Holy Name of Mary in commemoration of the victory.

He died in 1689, as the Poles and Habsburgs pressed the Ottomans back into the Balkans. He is also the first pope whose body was incorrupt.

Holy Name of Mary
Feast Day: September 12th

The feast of the Holy Name of Mary has roots dating back to early 16th century Spain. However, it gained prominence following the Catholic victory over the Ottomans at the Battle of Vienna on September 11th, 1683. This was because Pope Bl. Innocent XI asked Polish King John Sobieski and the whole Church to entrust the battle to Our Lady's prayers. A year later, he instituted the feast in thanks for the victory she won at Vienna.

As such, the feast is commemorated annually on September 12th, one day after the Catholic victory.

King Ferdinand of Aragón and Queen Isabella of Castile. Through their marriage, they united Spain and began the final stages of the Reconquista which ended 781 years of Islamic rule.[50]

Notable Mention

Queen Isabella and King Ferdinand
"Los Reyes Católicos"
Isabella d. 1503
Ferdinand d. 1516

Queen Isabella and King Ferdinand were one of the most powerful Spanish royal couples, and their influence has long outlived them. They were the "last crusaders" in the West, as it was by their actions that Muslim Spain was vanquished and the Reconquista made victorious after eight centuries of warfare. By uniting Spain under one kingdom, they went on to establish a global empire that forever defined the character of the Western Hemisphere and the Americas.

Isabella and Ferdinand respectively came from the Kingdoms of Castile and Aragón, located in the central-north and northeastern divisions of Spain. Prior to their marriage Aragón was in healthy shape, but Castile was not. Isabella's half-brother, King Henry IV, was a spendthrift consumed with waging war against Portugal and soliciting the services of prostitutes. Henry's erratic and profligate behavior resulted in widespread lawlessness across Castile.

The future Queen Isabella sought to depose Henry and restore Castile to law and order. She secretly met with King John II of Aragón through the help of her friend Cardinal Rodrigo Borgia, who later became Pope Alexander VI. They arranged for a strategic marriage to John's son and Isabella's second cousin, Ferdinand. While such a marriage was forbidden by the Church because of close blood relations, Cardinal Borgia gave them a dispensation. The two were secretly married on October 19th, 1469, and began their fight for a unified Spanish throne.

For the next ten years, Isabella and Ferdinand fought King Henry, his daughter Joan, and the Kingdom of Portugal to establish their dominion. Finally in 1479 with Henry and Joan long deposed, they signed the Treaty of Alcáçovas with Portugal to end the territorial disputes developed between Castile and Portugal during Henry's reign. The royal couple then spent the next two years restoring law and order to Castile. By 1481, Castile was restored to order along with her treasury.

With Aragón and Castile united as one kingdom, Ferdinand and Isabella prepared for their final war against the remaining Muslim strongholds in southern Spain. An opportunity came in late 1481 when the Muslim Emirate of Granada attacked the Spanish city of Zahara de la Sierra and killed or enslaved the entire population. Because the monarchs had a peace treaty with Granada, this grave violation proved to be an ideal justification for Isabella and Ferdinand to commence their war.

Over the next ten years, Isabella and Ferdinand slowly conquered the costal ports surrounding Granada. This time, however, Morocco was unable to help because they were too busy fighting off Portuguese invasions. The Mamluks in Egypt likewise could not help because they were fighting both the Ottomans and the Portuguese at the same time. The Ottomans also were unable to help because in addition to the Mamluks, they were engaged in wars against the Persians in the east and the Hungarians in Europe.

Once the coastline was controlled, Isabella and Ferdinand moved inland and conquered the remaining cities one by one. After nine years, Granada was absolutely cut off from any outside support. However, Granada had very strong walls and was so surrounded by natural barriers that traditional siege methods would have been very difficult. Following the example of the Ottoman conquest of Constantinople in 1453,

Isabella and Ferdinand used black powder cannons and mines to take down the city's walls beginning in 1491. Nasrid Emir of Granada Abu 'Abdullah Muhammad XII, known as Boabdil, announced his surrender in late 1491. In January 1492, he formally placed the keys of Granada into the hand of Queen Isabella before departing for Morocco. It is said that as he rode away, he looked back upon Granada with great sadness and sighed before he finally left.[51]

With Andalusia reconquered, Ferdinand and Isabella then faced the tasks of how to manage rebuilding Spanish society and dealing with the situations posed by Islam. Many Muslims had left Spain for North Africa by this point, but many also stayed. The latter, known as Mudéjars, launched massive uprisings across Spain almost immediately after the Reconquista ended. What made these rebellions worse was that while the Moroccans and Ottomans could not send armed forces to assist them, through their network of spies and Muslim pirates they shipped money and weapons in order to aid the rebellions.

The other issue was the Moriscos, or Muslim converts to the Catholic Faith. Catholic missionaries had great successes in bringing Muslims to the Faith, and there were many sincere converts. However, many Muslims also converted superficially to the Faith in order to gain social acceptance while they secretly remained Muslims and supported the rebellions. This problem had persisted for years, and was the driving reason for the Spanish Inquisition's creation in 1478.[52]

These dynamics continually forced Isabella and Ferdinand to revise their approach to the Spanish Muslims. To their credit, they originally intended and tried to guarantee religious freedom for Muslims. This is illustrated by the Treaty of Granada in November 1491, which guaranteed full religious rights for Muslims. However, by March 1492 they rescinded the Treaty and replaced it with the Alhambra Declaration, which was the beginning of Queen Isabella and King Ferdinand's policy that Mudéjars had to embrace the Catholic Faith and Spanish culture or leave Spain.[53] By 1500, the Mudéjars were expelled from Spain, and only Moriscos were allowed to stay. Islam persisted in Spain until 1609 when the Moriscos were expelled following a century of revolts.

Queen Isabella died in 1503, and King Ferdinand in 1516. Their victory in finishing the Reconquista forever transformed the world, and history cannot be written without acknowledging their influence. Their memory continues among the Spanish people who celebrate the Reconquista on the feast day of St. George, the great soldier-saint of the Catholic Faith, every year on April 23rd.

Don Alfonso De Albuquerque
d. 1515

Don Alfonso de Albuquerque was a Portuguese sailor and nobleman born in 1453. He was called the "Lion of the Seas," and throughout his career in the Portuguese navy he directed the Portuguese Empire's formation in the Far East.

After Ottoman soldiers massacred the Italian city of Otranto in 1480, Don Alfonso assisted King Ferdinand of Aragón in driving the Ottomans out of Italy. For the next twenty years, he spent much time in battle against the Ottomans and Muslim pirates throughout the Mediterranean.

In 1503, Don Alfonso was sent to open relations with Kerala, India, on the Malabar Coast. The area's existence was well-known since the 13th century, as it has been visited by Bl. John of Montecorvino. At the time Islam had a strong presence in the area through the local Muslim rulers, who were also allies of the Ottoman Empire. The Muslims were aware that the

Portuguese were coming to build their own water-based trade routes around the land-based Ottoman ones, as Henry the Navigator proposed doing a century earlier.

Don Alfonso earned the title "Lion of the Seas" during his voyage to India and subsequent wars with the Muslims. In route, he conquered the island of Socotra between the horn of Africa and Yemen. Following this, he sent one of his soldiers, Tristão da Cunha, to fight the Muslims on Indian soil and was victorious at the Siege of Cannanore in 1507. Two years later at Diu Island in the Indian Ocean, he fought and crushed a united Muslim naval force sent by the Ottoman Empire, Mamluk Empire, the Muslim rulers in India, and even the Venetians who were supporting the Ottomans for trade reasons.[54]

Upon arriving in Portuguese India, Don Alfonso fulfilled his order from the King of Portugal and deposed the previous governor. He continued his wars further east, taking Malacca in what constitutes modern Malaysia. He made expeditions to Thailand and the island of Sumatra, and he pioneered what would become the Portuguese colony of Macau in China. Thanks to his work, the Church and Franciscan Order were able to establish a firm presence in Kerala, which led to the expansion of missionary efforts across India.

Don Alfonso also pushed into East Africa and up the Red Sea along the Arabian Peninsula's coast. He hoped to capture the city of Mecca and seize the Black Rock inside the Ka'ba as hostage until terms could be set for negotiating the return of the Holy Land to the Christians. However, the Mamluk Empire took immediate notice of his movements and repelled him at the port city of Jidda.

Don Alfonso continued to serve as governor of Portuguese India, but remained in conflict with his men and other members of the Portuguese nobility. When word reached him that he was to be replaced as governor, he died of grief on December 16th, 1515 and was buried in Lisbon, Portugal at the Church of Our Lady of Grace.[55] His memory lives on as a great Catholic explorer, conqueror, and contender for the Faith.

Francisco Cardinal Jiménez de Cisneros
d. 1517

Cardinal Cisneros was born in 1436 and entered the priesthood at a young age. In 1459 he was sent to Rome and worked there for many years, where he attracted the attention of Pope Pius II and Sixtus IV. He was so well-liked that Pope Sixtus IV gave him a special dispensation to be archbishop of any diocese he desired in Spain. With the Pope's letter in hand, he returned to Spain in 1474 and chose Toledo, as it was his home. Despite the Pope's letter, the Archbishop of Toledo did not approve of Cardinal Cisneros' choice. He jailed him for six years, but eventually released him because the Cardinal would not relinquish his claims.

Cardinal Cisneros' time in prison greatly deepened his Catholic Faith. In 1484 he became a Franciscan friar and took the name Francisco. He lived a life of intense asceticism and penance for souls as an anchorite. His repute soon brought him from the wilderness to the courts of Queen Isabella at her request in 1492. In 1495 he was made Cardinal and the Franciscan Provincial for all Spain. It was here in the courts of Queen Isabella and King Ferdinand that Cardinal Cisneros orchestrated the rebuilding of Spanish Catholicism and the formal uprooting of Islam from Spain.

The largest problem which Cardinal Cisneros faced was the issue of the Mudéjars and the Moriscos. Many of the Mudéjars were actively engaged in open rebellion, and many of the Moriscos secretly supported them. The rebellions, which began immediately after the Reconquista's end, were becoming more serious. Something had to be done to stop them.

Cardinal Cisneros responded by trying to remove any vestiges of Islam from Spain. This involved three parts. First was the expulsion of the Mudéjars from Spain. Second was the conversion of any Mudéjars who wanted to remain in Spain to the Catholic Faith, thus bringing them into the Morisco population. Third was the banning of Arabic from popular use and the suppression and destruction of popular, non-academic Islamic writings. By 1500, all of these actions had taken place.

Cardinal Cisneros' approach worked in part, but it also created a new problem. While some Mudéjars left Spain and some genuinely converted, many nominally converted but continued to secretly practice as Muslims. Thus the Mudéjars were gone, but the rebellious element among the Moriscos increased. This was worsened by the fact that in 1504, the Grand Mufti of Oran drafted a fatwa that permitted Moriscos to publicly convert to the Catholic Faith and live as Catholics so long as they secretly practiced Islam and continued to rebel.[56] Cardinal Cisneros spent the rest of his life working to root out the rebels among the Moriscos. He later regretted his earlier decision because it was both ineffective and violated Catholic teaching on freedom of conscience.

The other problem Cardinal Cisneros faced was that Islam's influence posed a threat to the Church's integrity. In one example, there were many Franciscans who were living with women in violation of their professed vows. Cardinal Cisneros ordered that in fealty to their vows, they disavow the women, do penance, and return to full communion with the Church. However, the monks aggressively opposed this, and at least a thousand Franciscans converted to Islam and left Spain for Morocco with their women. In response to this and the many other issues he faced, Cardinal Cisneros aggressively worked to reestablish the Church's presence in southern Spain.

Cardinal Cisneros, as his life attests, sought to preserve, protect, and expand the Catholic Faith in the midst of what was a tremendously difficult situation. While his actions were not always correct, he sought repentance for his errors and fearlessly guided the Spanish government, people, and the Church in rebuilding their nation after eight centuries of warfare. He died in 1517 while traveling to meet Holy Roman Emperor Charles V.

Pál Tomori
d. 1526

Pál Tomori was born in 1475 and was Archbishop of what is today Kalocsa, Hungary. He fought against the Ottomans during the Hungarian-Ottoman wars of the late 15th and early 16th centuries. He was killed in fighting at the disastrous Battle of Mohács in 1526.

Monument in Hungary to the Battle of Mohács[57]

The Habsburg Family and the Habsburg-Ottoman wars
1526 – 1918

The story of Islam and the Church in Eastern Europe could not be told without the Habsburg family, who ruled Austria for nine centuries until World War I. This dynasty of Catholic monarchs and their empire checked the Ottomans' dominance and eventually expelled them from the Balkan Peninsula.

The Habsburg family's story dates to the Swabian Count Radbot in 1020. He build a castle that he named Habsburg on the Aar River in what is today Switzerland near the German border. Through a series of strategic marriages, land purchases, and battles, the Habsburgs gradually acquired a massive empire across Central and Eastern Europe and became the Continent's most powerful family. Unfortunately, their territorial acquisitions by marriage meant repeatedly crossing bloodlines, and so they were also Europe's most inbred royal family.

The Habsburg family's military conflicts with the Ottomans began in 1526 following the Hungarian Empire's disastrous loss at Mohács. The Hungarian loss allowed the Ottomans to move into Habsburg territories around Hungary. Three years later, the Ottomans besieged the Habsburg capitol at Vienna. An Ottoman victory meant opening up Western Europe's gates to a massive invasion. While they were outnumbered almost four-to-one, the Habsburgs valiantly defended Vienna and won by nothing short of a miracle.

Following the Habsburg victory at Vienna, the nation of Hungary was split into two parts. The north and west went to the Habsburgs, and the south and east to the Ottomans. War continued between the Ottomans and Habsburgs until the fall of a Habsburg fortress at Szigetvár, Hungary on September 8th, 1556. Although the entire Hungarian garrison of 3000 men was wiped out, it was a pyrrhic victory for the Ottomans. Over 25,000 Ottomans were killed as well as Sultan Sulayman "The Magnificent," who led the original attack against Vienna in 1529. Habsburg Emperor Maximilian II and Sulayman's successor, Selim II, signed a temporary ceasefire with the Treaty of Adrianople.

The Habsburg wars with the Ottomans also continued in the Mediterranean. They funded the Knights of Malta and later, the Holy Leagues established by various Popes to combat the Ottomans at different times. Their funding and military support was instrumental in winning the Battle of Lepanto in 1571. The Habsburgs also mimicked the Ottoman strategy of supporting Calvinist revolutionaries in Habsburg territories by funding proxy wars through Catholic rebels against Ottoman-occupied Hungary, Moldavia, and Romania.

The Habsburgs and Ottomans engaged in skirmishes with each other for nearly a century until the Ottomans tried to attack Vienna in 1664 at the Battle of St. Gotthard. The Ottomans lost terribly and proposed a 20-year ceasefire, but this was simply to allow them to prepare for another assault on Vienna. In the meantime, the Ottomans turned their attention to conquering neighboring Poland, which was suffering from political infighting. Within less than two decades, the Ottomans established the Empire's furthest borders yet along the Carpathian Mountains in Poland's southern regions.

During this entire time, the Ottomans had also been preparing for yet another massive attack on Vienna. After completing preparations, the Ottomans besieged Vienna beginning on July 14th, 1683. The Habsburg Empire, which was suffering from conflicts due to the wars of religion in Western Europe, was weak and had great difficulty defending itself. Fortunately, with help from Pope Bl. Innocent XI and the Polish

King John Sobieski III, the Ottomans were defeated at the Battle of Vienna on September 11th, 1683.

The Habsburg reprieve at Vienna allowed them to replenish themselves in order to continue their war against the Ottomans. Working with the Polish Kingdom and other Christians in the Balkans, the Habsburgs successively crushed the Ottomans with each passing battle. When the Ottomans were forced to sign the Treaty of Karlowitz in 1699, the Habsburgs had taken Hungary, Romania, and parts of Bosnia, Croatia, and Moldavia from the Ottomans, with other parts going to the Poles or Venetians. The Habsburgs continued their wars against the Ottomans, winning yet more battles as the 18th century progressed. One of the most notable was the Battle of Petrovaradin, which liberated northern Serbia and after which the feast of Our Lady of Tekije was instituted.

Unfortunately, the Habsburg's defense of the Church and Europe facilitated their empire's collapse. The British, French, Germans, and Russians had been aggressively building their own empires worldwide. However, the Habsburg family's empire and the Ottoman Empire remained locked against each other as the surrounding territories were consumed by their neighbors. The constant pressure they were under forced them to enter into a web of alliances between the European powers. By the beginning of the 20th century the Habsburg family's empire, then known as the Austro-Hungarian Empire, was on the edge of collapse.

World War I ended the Habsburg family's empire as well as the Ottoman Empire. Nevertheless, the history of the Church and Islam could not be written without the Habsburgs, as it was by their efforts that the Ottomans were prevented from conquering Europe.

Christovão da Gama
d. 1542

Christovão da Gama was born in 1516 and was the son of the Portuguese explorer Vasco da Gama, who was the first European to completely sail around Africa to India. Christovão was a man of great faith, fearless determination, an explorer of East Africa, and martyr.

At the age of 16, Christovão sailed with his brother Estevão to India. Estevão, who was then the Portuguese Viceroy of India, had many years of experience in battle against the Mamluks and the Ottomans. Since he was impressed with Christovão's competence, Estevão gave Christovão a fleet and charged him with leading the Portuguese incursion into East Africa.

At the time, Ethiopian Emperor Gelawdewos was fighting Somali Ahmad ibn Ibrahim Al-Ghazi, leader of the Muslim Adal Empire which sought to conquer and Islamize Ethiopia. Many Ethiopians were Christians, having been converted by Coptic Orthodox missionaries over the centuries. Christovão's arrival in late 1541 could not have come at a better time. He routed Ahmad's forces at the Battle of Bacente in February 1542, which he attributed to the assistance of Our Lady.

Ahmad realized the Portuguese were a force to be contended with and sought help from the Ottoman Empire. He and Christovão continued to skirmish until August 1542, when Christovão was ambushed at the Battle of Wofla and was captured after suffering a broken arm. Ahmad proceeded to torture Christovão for several hours, first by plucking his beard out hair-by-hair, and then crushing his head with a large rock. He promised to relieve him of the torture if he converted to

Islam. Christovão said no and told him that Muhammad was a false prophet, after which Ahmad decapitated him.

Christovão's body was recovered by his soldiers, who regrouped with Emperor Gelawdewos. In February 1543, a united force of Portuguese and Ethiopians attacked Ahmad and his Ottoman mercenaries at the Battle of Wayna Daga. Ahmad was killed in battle, the Muslims were conclusively defeated, and Ethiopia was saved from Islamization.

Holy League[58]
1st League: 1538
2nd League: 1571 – 1573
3rd League: 1683 – 1699
4th League: 1717

The Holy League was a confederation of Catholic military officers and forces from across Europe who allied to combat the Ottoman Empire during the 16th through the 18th centuries. The Leagues lasted only the duration they were needed and were disbanded afterwards. The Popes directly assembled the Holy Leagues, often with great effort and expense. Were it not for the Holy Leagues, it is likely that Europe would have been overrun by the Ottomans.

The First Holy league was assembled in 1538 to combat the Ottoman Navy. Pope Paul III formed an alliance of Venetian and Spanish forces to confront Ottoman Naval Commander Khair Ad-Din Pasha[59] outside of the city of Preveza in western Greece bordering the Ionian Sea. Because of a lack of coordination, the battle was a disaster for the Catholics and victory went conclusively to the Ottomans. This allowed the Ottomans to move up the Ionian Sea and towards the Italian coastline.

The Second Holy League was assembled in 1571 by Pope St. Pius V and included a collection of Italian republics, the Habsburg Empire, and the Knights of Malta. It became famous for responding to the Ottoman massacre of a Venetian fortress at Famagusta, Cyprus. While sailing to Cyprus to confront the Ottomans, the two navies met in combat at the Gulf of Lepanto[60] in the Ionian Sea on October 7th, 1571. Prior to going to war, Pope St. Pius V offered the battle to Our Lady and asked the Church to pray the rosary for victory. The Battle of Lepanto was a crushing defeat for the Ottoman navy from which it never recovered. St. Pius instituted the feast of Our Lady of Victory, known also as the feast of Our Lady of the Rosary, on account of the victory at Lepanto.

The Third Holy League was assembled by Pope Bl. Innocent XI in response to the Ottoman Empire's aggression in Eastern and Central Europe. At the Pope's insistence, an agreement was instituted between the Polish Empire and the Habsburg Empire that the two come to each other's aid should the Ottomans attack. This could not have been better timed, as it was agreed upon in September 1682, exactly one year before the Ottomans marched to and besieged Vienna.

The Holy League responded immediately to the distressed Habsburg Empire. Polish King John Sobieski III led the battle, and was aided by German Catholics from Bavaria and Swabia and Italians from Tuscany. Pope Bl. Innocent XI offered the Battle to Our Lady. After a vicious fight ending on September 11th, 1683, the Holy League routed the Ottomans. But the war did not end there, as the Holy League pursued the Ottomans deep into the Balkans for the next 16 years, where they consistently crushed them. Eventually, the Ottomans were compelled to sign the Treaty of Karlowitz in 1699, which redefined territorial boundaries as well as guaranteed the Catholic Church's rights in Ottoman border territories.

The Fourth Holy League was in 1717, and fought in the Battle of Matapan by Cape Matapan in Greece. An allied force of Italian states, Portugal, and the Knights of Malta gave the Ottomans another severe blow to their already atrophied navy. This was the last of the Holy Leagues, as the Ottoman Empire then entered into terminal decline until its dissolution after World War I.

Sultan Yahya
d. 1648

Yahya was born in 1584 and was the eldest living son of Ottoman Sultan Mehmet III.[61] His mother, Elena, was a member of Sultan Mehmet's harem. She was descended from the Komnenos family, which ruled the Byzantine Empire during the Crusades and later the Empire of Trebizond along the southern Black Sea coastline until they were conquered in 1461 by the Ottomans. They were related to the Palaiologos family, who were not only the last rulers of the Byzantine Empire during the Fall of Constantinople, but were converts to the Catholic Faith who unsuccessfully tried to bring about a re-union of the Orthodox with the Catholic Church.[62]

Due to the Ottoman persecutions, many Catholics outwardly converted to and practiced Islam but secretly lived and practiced as Catholics. This was similar to what the Moriscos did in Spain after the Reconquista. Elena was one of these "crypto-Catholics," and while her son, Yahya, was regarded as a Muslim, she secretly cared for him as a Catholic.

When Sultan Mehmet III came to power in 1595 after Murad III's death, he ordered all 19 of his brothers and half-brothers brought to him, one by one, where he watched as his servants strangled each one to death. When word got out as to what Mehmet was doing, people in the Ottoman palace fled for fear they might suffer the same fate. Elena used this opportunity to escape the harem with Yahya to a monastery in Macedonia, where they lived in secret. Since they were finally out of the Sultan's palace, Yahya was baptized with the name of John and raised in the Catholic Faith.[63]

Mehmet died in 1603, and John went to Istanbul as a legitimate heir and faithful Catholic claimant to the Ottoman Sultanate.[64] However, since it was believed that he was dead for many years, the Sultanate was given to the next child, who became Sultan Ahmet I. Due to his late arrival and conversion to the Catholic Faith, John was unable to claim his throne, and was forced to flee Istanbul.

Following this incident, Sultan John spent the rest of his life preaching crusades against the Ottomans, raising funds, and working out anti-Ottoman alliances with European nobles and empires. He visited Florence, Kiev, Madrid, Paris, Prague, Rome, Venice, Vienna, and many more places to promote his cause and raise money. In 1622, disguised as a whirling dervish, he secretly visited Mecca and Medina to spy on the Ottomans.[65] He later did the same to sneak into Ottoman-controlled Saloniki and Istanbul. John also met with Popes Paul V, Gregory XV, Urban VIII, and Innocent X to discuss his plans. Throughout this time, he promised that if he became Sultan, he would Christianize the Ottoman Empire.

While Sultan John never realized his dreams, he did manage to lead a strong military resistance to the Ottomans in the Balkans. As early as 1615 he was leading unified regiments of Croatian and Albanian Catholics alongside Serbian Orthodox Christians against the Ottomans throughout Albania, Bosnia, Croatia, and Montenegro. He did this for the rest of his life.

Sultan John died in 1648, possibly of illness.[66] His resistance helped to slow the Ottoman advance in the Balkans and into Eastern Europe.

King John Sobieski III
"The Lion of Lechistan"
d. 1696

King John Sobieski III was born in 1629 and became King of Poland, which was known then as the Polish-Lithuanian Commonwealth. The Ottomans called King Sobieski "The Lion of Lechistan," and he was the Church's "Last Crusader" in that his victory over the Ottomans at the Battle of Vienna marked the beginning of the Ottoman Empire's decline.

King John's career began in 1648 after returning home from Poland's prestigious Jagellonian University. He joined the Polish military and distinguished himself as an expert cavalryman. Poland was in a unique and difficult place in its history. It was a large, heavily populated nation, yet suffered from the same problems that plagued the Habsburg Empire. Externally, she was attempting to defend herself against the German Prussians, the Swedes, the Russians, the Ukrainian Cossacks, the Crimean Tartars, and the Ottomans. Internally, Poland was fighting off Calvinist revolutionaries who were sponsored by both the Prussians and the Ottoman Empire. By the time King Sobieski inherited the Polish throne from his father in 1676, Poland had lost a third of its people to war and the country was laid waste from the destruction.

King John's first years on the throne were tumultuous. The Ottomans made considerable advances, thanks to their alliances with traitorous leaders among the Ukrainian Cossacks. By 1676, the Ottomans forced Poland to sign the Treaty of Żurawno, which gave preferential treatment to the Ottomans and Islam. Additionally, the Polish Parliament worsened matters because they were too consumed with internal political fighting.

King Sobieski set to work to save Poland and confront the Ottomans. He knew that any peace with the Ottoman Empire would be short lived, and so time was working against him. He rebuilt Poland's army, fortified defenses, and responded to Pope Bl. Innocent XI's request to work with the Habsburgs and defend each other when the Ottomans returned.

Beginning in 1682, a Hungarian Calvinist revolutionary funded by the Ottomans named Imre Thököly was fighting against the Habsburgs. Since Imre had pledged himself as a vassal to the Ottomans, the Ottomans used the Habsburg's resistance against Imre as justification to go to war. Fortunately, King Sobieski knew the Ottoman Empire's desire for Vienna, and so he was able to tailor his army's preparations in order to confront the coming Ottoman siege.

The Ottomans formally besieged Vienna beginning on July 14th, 1683. It was a terrible ordeal that lasted for months. Vienna was well-defended, but the city eventually ran out of food. The Ottomans had cut off any escape or shipment routes, so Vienna was isolated. Ottoman sappers continually attempted to blow up the city's walls using makeshift black powder mines, and there was little hope of communicating with the outside. To worsen matters, the treacherous Imre Thököly was helping the Ottomans to raid the Viennese countryside.

After a brief communication with Pope Bl. Innocent XI, King Sobieski prepared his army to leave for Vienna. Pope Bl. Innocent XI offered the battle to Our Lady and asked for Europe to pray for the Polish army, and King Sobieski made pilgrimage to the Shrine of Our Lady of Czestochowa. As King Sobieski and his army arrived at Vienna, they were met by several regiments of German and Italian Catholics who pledged to fight with him. He arrived at Vienna by night, and on the morning of September 11th, 1683, he opened war against the Ottomans.

The Ottoman sappers worked faster, but they could not repel the Polish army as King Sobieski slashed away at the Ottoman's flanks. For thirteen hours, King Sobieski continually pushed the Ottomans into a position of weakness and defense. Finally, at five o'clock PM, King Sobieski gathered 3,000 heavily armed horsemen and commenced the largest cavalry charge in military history. The panicked and stressed Ottoman soldiers fled in vain as they were trampled under hoof.

The Ottomans were forced to withdraw from Vienna. Sultan Mehmet IV ordered Karamustafa Pasha, the Ottoman military commander who led the battle strangled to death, decapitated, and the head delivered to him in a velvet bag. Together, the Poles and Habsburgs waged what became known as the Great Turkish War that pulverized the Ottomans in the Balkans and ended with the Treaty of Karlowitz in 1699.

King Sobieski died in 1696. Pope Bl. Innocent XI called him "The Savior of Vienna and Western European Civilization." But as King Sobieski said after his victory at the Battle of Vienna:

Vini, vidi, Deus vincit
I came, I saw, God conquered.

Section IV: Modern Times

A Church Between Worlds

Polish King John Sobieski III's victory over the Ottomans at the Battle of Vienna on September 11th, 1683 marked the beginning of the Ottoman Empire's end as well as the transition into modern times. In terms of Islam, this period is characterized by the Church's worldwide growth, particularly in Muslim areas, and the later destabilization of Europe's empires leading up to the First and Second World Wars.

Catholic missionaries traveled all across the world, but as far as Islam is concerned, the Church had the greatest successes in sub-Saharan Africa. Most of this missionary work was done by Irish, French, or Portuguese Catholic missionaries. Although it was difficult, the French in particular established some of the first permanent, successful missions. The long-term results were phenomenal, as the mass conversions from Islam to the Faith taking place throughout Africa today have their direct roots in these missions. These missions have long outlived the European colonial presence.

The same can be said about East Africa. Catholic missionaries converted many Muslims and became the most powerful advocate of the black Africans in the south. These people were often harassed and enslaved by the Muslims in North Africa. Under the Church's leadership, bishops and priests freed slaves, vocally protested, and militarily contested alongside the Africans for their rights and freedom. As with the French, the Church's presence long outlasted the European colonial presence, and its fruits continue to blossom today.

The area in which the Church faced great suffering was the Ottoman Empire's territories. The Ottomans always did persecute the Catholic and Orthodox Christians who lived within their borders, but this became more aggressive as the Empire fell into sharper decline. The suffering was greatest in eastern

Anatolia, which now encompasses the region of eastern Turkey, Armenia, and Georgia. The Christians who lived there since the time of St. Paul were significantly reduced through emigration and systematic persecution. This culminated in the mass murder of the Christians by the Ottomans beginning in 1915 during the Armenian Genocide.

The Church's foreign missions had great successes, but the Church in Europe struggled due to the rise of destructive philosophies such as atheism and socialism. Many people saw the Church as an antiquated relic hindering European "progress." These persecutions took many forms, but they spread across Europe as the centuries progressed, beginning with the French Revolution. With Islam no longer an active threat, Europe forgot the danger it posed and began to romanticize about the Muslim world and Islam while forgetting history.

While the Battle of Vienna in 1683 saved Europe, it can also be said to mark a decline in European culture and the Church. By the Second World War's end in 1945, the Church survived but no longer held the moral or social influence it once had on the Continent. Many Western Europeans turned away from God and religion altogether, let alone Christianity. In combination with other social and cultural factors, this allowed for Islam to re-emerge within two decades after the Second World War as a threat to Europe once again.

Martyrs

Bl. Gomidas Keumurgian
Feast Day: November 5th

Bl. Gomidas Keumurgian was born in 1656 to an Armenian Apostolic family. In 1696 he entered into the Catholic Church under the Armenian Rite and became a priest. His conversion angered the Armenian Patriarch, who brought the matter to the Ottoman authorities. Under Ottoman law, the Catholic and Orthodox faiths were permitted to exist but nobody could convert to any religion except Islam. Conversion to any other religion was punishable by death. When brought before the Ottoman authorities, Bl. Gomidas was told if he converted to Islam then all charges of apostasy would be dropped. He refused, and he was beheaded in 1707.

Bl. Gomidas was loved by both Catholic and Orthodox Armenians alike. After his death, it was Armenian Orthodox priests who received and buried him. Bl. Gomidas' death strengthened the Catholic Faith so much that many Armenians were brought into full communion with the Church.

Bls. Franciscan Martyrs of Damascus
(Nicholas Alberga, Engelbert Kolland, Ascanio Nicanore, Emmanuel Ruiz, Peter Soler, and Carmelo Volta, (Postulants) John Fernandez and Francis Pinazo, (Lay Franciscans) 'Abd Al-Mu'ti Massabki, Francis Massabki, and Raphael Massabki)
Feast Day: July 10th

Lebanon has always held a unique place in the Middle East because it is the only nation which never lost its Catholic identity in spite of being surrounded by a sea of Islam. It is a place where comparatively speaking to many other nations, Catholics and Muslims lived in relative peace with each other.

One of the largest and most powerful Muslim groups in Lebanon was the Druze, which is a heretical sect of Shiite Islam that emerged in the 11th century.

The Ottoman Empire governed Lebanon during the 19th century through the Druze. However, the Ottomans were losing control over Lebanon to the British and French empires. The Ottomans especially disliked the French since they supported the majority Catholic and Orthodox Maronite people of Lebanon. Through the Druze administrators, the Ottomans imposed onerous taxes and regulations on the Catholics to assert their dominance. This action angered the Catholics. By the mid-1850's, relations between the Catholics and the Druze devolved into open hostility.

In May 1860, a dispute between two children, one Catholic and one Druze, exploded into an anti-Catholic pogrom. Ottoman imperial soldiers assisted Druze militias in the mass murder and destruction of Catholic persons, homes, and institutions across Lebanon and Syria. By August 1860, over 30,000 people were killed, 100,000 people were refugees, and countless homes, churches, and buildings were destroyed. The only reason the massacre ended was that the French forced the Ottoman Empire to permit their intervention.

The Martyrs of Damascus were six Franciscan friars, two postulants, and three lay brothers who were killed during the height of the pogroms on July 10th, 1860. While saying their evening prayers together at the Franciscan monastery in Damascus, Syria, marauding Druze broke into the convent, tortured, and executed the men.

Bl. Salvatore Lilli and Companions
(Ieremias Boghos, David David, Toros David, Khodianin Kadir, Baldji Ohannes, Kouradji Tzeroum, and Dimbalac Wartavar)
Feast Day: November 19th

Bl. Salvatore Lilli was born in 1853 and became a Franciscan at the age of 17. Initially, he was sent to the Franciscan mission in the Holy Land. However, he only stayed a short time before returning to Italy. Afterwards, he was sent to the city of Maras[1] in the Ottoman Empire. At the time, the city had a large Armenian Catholic population with a mix of Orthodox Christians and Muslims. He earned everyone's respect, and was even allowed to build a church in the city.

Since the late 1870's, Armenian Christians had been rising up against the Ottomans. The Ottomans responded by sponsoring mass executions of any and all Christians in an area deemed to have rebel activity. These pogroms were administered by Ottoman provincial governors and equally targeted Catholics, Orthodox, and Assyrians alike. The worst persecution prior to the Armenian Genocide was the Hamidian massacres between 1894 and 1896.

Bl. Salvatore Lilli was living in Maras when the Hamidian massacres started. He helped many Catholics and Orthodox escape from the Muslim death squads. However, on November 22nd, 1895 he and a group of fellow Armenian Catholics were arrested by a Muslim death squad and told to convert to Islam or die. The men refused to convert, and they were stabbed to death with bayonets and their remains burned.

Bl. Archbishop Ignatius Maloyan and 447 Companions
Feast Day: June 11th

Bl. Archbishop Ignatius Maloyan was born in Mardin, Turkey to an Armenian Catholic family in 1869. He became a priest in 1904 and was made a bishop in 1911. At the time, the Ottoman Empire was on the eve of the Armenian Genocide that murdered over a million people and exterminated Christianity from Anatolia.

When the Genocide began on April 24th, 1915, Mardin was one of the first towns attacked because of its large Christian population. Dr. Mehmet Reshid, the Ottoman governor of Diyarbakir Province in which Mardin was located, oversaw the Genocide's first stages. When he was asked in an interview why he persecuted Christians, he said that Christians were "microbes" and that as a doctor, it was his job "to kill microbes."[2]

Dr. Reshid charged Mamduh Beğ, Chief of Police for Mardin, with executing his orders in the city. On June 9th, 1915, he rounded up 447 Armenian Catholics and told them to convert to Islam or die.[3] Bl. Bishop Maloyan urged them to stand strong in their Faith, and he told Mamduh that he and his fellow Catholics were prepared to suffer for Christ.

Mamduh forced Bl. Bishop Maloyan and his followers to march to their death. Despite being tired, Bl. Bishop Maloyan managed to say Mass and even distribute communion. Following the Mass, Mamduh forced them to walk for several more hours to their grave. He gave them one last chance to convert to Islam or die. Fortunately, not a single person converted.

Mamduh was particularly angry at Bl. Bishop Maloyan, so he forced him to watch the execution of all 447 before his death. Bl. Bishop Maloyan was then subjected to a series of slow and heinous tortures. When he was near death, Mamduh gave him one last chance to convert to Islam. Bl. Bishop Maloyan replied "Into Your hands, Lord, I commend my spirit." In a fit of rage, Mamduh summarily shot him.

Bl. Bishop Maloyan is the first beatified Catholic who was murdered in the Armenian Genocide.

Servant of God Bishop Flavianus Michael Malke
d. August 28th, 1915

Servant of God Bishop Flavianus Michael Malke, also known as Ya'qub, was born to an Assyrian Orthodox family in 1856 in Qal'at Mara, now in Turkey. He became a deacon in 1878 and began to work as a teacher at the Saffron Monastery, which was home to the Syriac Orthodox Church. Eventually, he entered into the Catholic Church under the Chaldean Rite and became a Chaldean Catholic priest in 1883.

This was a tumultuous time for Christians living in the Ottoman Empire, as the Ottomans viciously persecuted Christians of all denominations as their empire fell into greater decline. Bishop Malke witnessed the Ottoman violence and experienced it himself, as his mother was murdered during the Hamidian massacres in 1895. Nevertheless, he persevered in his vocation and was eventually made Bishop of Mardin.

When the Armenian genocide began, many local Muslim leaders encouraged Bishop Malke to flee, as they knew the massacres the Ottoman government was planning to execute. However, he refused, saying:

*"Never would I leave my flock and save my soul,
for this is contrary to my faith and my work"*

Eventually, the Ottomans arrived and rounded up Bishop Malke along with the Christians of Mardin. They were marched to the outskirts of the city of Cizre, where they were told to convert to Islam or die. Bishop Malke refused, and so he was first beaten and then beheaded. The rest of Mardin's Christians were shot to death with machine guns. Among those executed was Bishop Philippe-Jacques Abraham.

Bl. Archbishop Ignatius Maloyan
Martyred in the Armenian Genocide[4]

Contenders

Bl. Mariam Baouardy
Feast Day: August 25th

Bl. Mariam Baouardy was born in I'bilin, Israel to devout Melkite Catholic parents. Her parents both died when she was two, and she was left to the care of her extended family, as was her only surviving brother, Boulos.

When Bl. Mariam was 13, she was living with her uncle in Alexandria, Egypt. He wanted to marry her off without her consent, but she refused. He became very angry with her and, after berating and beating her, forced her to be his servant girl. Her brother Boulos was living with other family, and she wrote a letter asking him to visit. She gave the letter to one of her uncle's Muslim servants to deliver, who secretly read it and deceitfully asked Bl. Mariam to tell her about her problem, as he was romantically interested in her. After listening to her story, he suggested that she convert to Islam in order to escape. She realized his intentions, and responded to him by saying:

"Muslim? No, never! I am a daughter of the Catholic Apostolic Church, and I hope by the grace of God to persevere until death in my religion, which is the only true one."

At this, the Muslim servant violently attacked Bl. Mariam, drew his sword, and slit her throat. The wound was so deep that she was nearly decapitated. He then dumped her dead body in an alley. The day was September 8th, 1858, the Birthday of the Virgin Mary.

However, while Bl. Mariam was dead, she saw herself being picked up by the Blessed Mother in the presence of a host of angels and Jesus. Her throat was miraculously stitched back together, and Our Lady brought her to the Franciscan church of St. Catherine before she disappeared.

Bl. Mariam consecrated her life to the Blessed Virgin on that day, and began to seek a vocation as a religious sister. She eventually entered the Carmelite Order with the name Sister Mary of Jesus Crucified. She endured many sufferings, and finally died on August 27, 1878 at 33 years old uttering "My Jesus, my Mercy" as she died.

St. Daniel Comboni
Feast Day: October 10th

St. Daniel Comboni was born in Limone Sul Garda,[5] Brescia, Italy, in 1831. He was the only surviving of eight children. He became a priest in 1854 and in 1857, he was sent to Sudan.

St. Daniel Comboni spent the rest of his life in the Sudan, working among what at the time was a majority Muslim and pagan population. He firmly established the Church in Sudan, particularly in the south, and was a tireless champion of the Sudanese people. He played a key role in working to stop the infamous trade in black Africans by Muslim slavers.

St. Daniel Comboni died of illness in 1881. His work long outlived his life, as today the Church has grown strong in southern Sudan and throughout Africa. Among the additional fruits were the Comboni Missionaries, who have continued St. Daniel Comboni's work after his death.

Inspirers

Our Lady of Tekije
Feast Day: August 5th

Our Lady of Tekije's feast comes from a church in Petrovaradin, Novi Sad Province, Serbia. It was originally a mosque, but was captured and converted to a church dedicated to Our Lady in 1701. In 1716, a combined force of Austrian, Croatian, and Hungarian Catholics led by the Habsburg Prince Eugene of Savoy united with a force of Serbian Orthodox Christians and gave the Ottomans a great defeat at the Battle of Petrovaradin.[6] The feast was instituted in commemoration of the victory.

Our Lady of Tekije church, also known as Our Lady of the Snows, is unique because it was a unifying point for both Catholics and Orthodox in the struggle with Islam. As such, the church is both a Catholic and Orthodox church, and both Catholic and Orthodox Masses are celebrated within it. The church is a living testament that through Our Lady, not only can the two Churches be formally reunited, but that Islam can be stopped with her prayerful intercession.

St. Charbel Makhlouf
Feast Day: July 17th

St. Charbel Makhlouf is one of the greatest Lebanese Catholic saints. Born in 1828 to a poor family with the name Joseph, he became a monk in 1851 and was ordained a priest in 1859.

St. Charbel lived in Lebanon during the horrendous wars between the French-supported Maronite Catholics and the

Ottoman-supported Druze. Upon seeing the destruction, St. Charbel prayed for the salvation of both the Catholics' and the Muslims' souls alike. In addition to this, he imposed strict fasting and penances upon himself until his death in 1898.

St. Charbel's holiness has been recognized by both Catholics and Muslims. His body remains incorrupt, and persons of both religions still venerate his tomb today.

Marian Shrine of Mariamabad
Feast Day: September 8th

The Marian Shrine in Mariamabad, Pakistan was founded in 1892 by Capuchin monks from Belgium. It has become nationally recognized and is visited by both Catholics and Muslims alike. Both groups have reported many miracles stemming from pilgrimages made to the Shrine. While there have been attacks by Muslim mobs and even Pakistani police against pilgrims visiting the Shrine, experiences have been usually peaceful. Through the intercession of Our Lady, many Muslims have come to friendship with Christians and even entered into the Catholic Faith.

St. Josephine Bakhita
Patroness of Sudan
Feast Day: February 8th

St. Josephine Bakhita was born around 1869 in Darfur, Sudan to pagan nobility of the Daju tribe. She was captured by Muslim slavers around 1878 and was forced to convert to Islam. By 1883, she had been sold at least five times, and not a day passed that she was not beaten or abused by her different masters. She was so horribly abused that she even forgot her own name. She was eventually renamed *Bakhita* by one of her masters, which means "lucky" in Arabic.

St. Bakhita's last Muslim master was an Ottoman military officer who needed to sell his slaves before returning to Turkey. He put her for sale on the market in Khartoum. Fortunately for her, she was bought by Callisto Legnani, the Vice-Consul of the Italian Embassy to work as a servant. Callisto showed her great love, and St. Bakhita admired him.

When Castillo was summoned to return to Italy in 1885 he desired to free St. Bakhita, but she persistently asked to follow him to Italy. Upon arrival in Italy, he gave her to a friend named Augusto Michieli, and she served as a nanny for his children. This continued until 1888, when the Michieli family moved to Sudan and St. Bakhita was entrusted to the care of the Canossian Sisters. During this time she was baptized, confirmed, and wanted to join the Canossian Sisters. However, when the Michielis returned, they said she was still their slave. The Canossian Order with the Bishop of Venice brought a legal dispute over St. Bakhita's status, and the Italian courts ruled that St. Bakhita was never a slave because Italy did not recognize slavery and that despite her being born in Sudan, she was born after slavery had been legally outlawed in Italy.

St. Bakhita entered the Canossian Sisters three years later in 1893. She was consecrated as Sister Giuseppina Margherita Fortunata, with Fortunata meaning "Bakhita" in Italian. She lived out the rest of her life in peace until her death in 1947. Throughout her life she was known for her humility, generosity, and love. When asked about her captors, she said that she would thank them because through her capture that she eventually became a Catholic. She was canonized by Pope Bl. John Paul II in 2000. Pope Benedict XVI's encyclical <u>Spe Salvi</u> opens with St. Bakhita's story as a model for Christian hope.

Notable Mention

The Shihab Family
Circa 1799

The Shihab family was and remains one of Lebanon's most powerful and influential Muslim royal families. Among their reputes is that many Shihab family members converted to the Catholic Faith from Islam.

The Shihabs are the direct descendants of Abu Bakr, the second Caliph of Islam and close friend of Muhammad, the founder of Islam. In the 12th century, the family converted from Sunni Islam to the Druze religion, which is a sect of Shiite Islam. By the 16th century, the Shihab's became the most powerful Muslim family in Lebanon.

When the French began to colonize Lebanon and Syria in the 18th century, the Shihab family embraced Francophone culture and education. While the Shihabs were Muslims, they befriended the French Catholic missionaries and permitted them to operate in their territories. It was through this friendship that the Shihabs began to learn about the Catholic Faith. Finally in 1799, Shihab family patriarch Prince Bashir bin Qasim Shihab II converted with a large portion of his family to the Faith and entered the Maronite Rite of the Catholic Church.

While not all of the Shihabs became Catholic, the Shihab family's conversion greatly influenced Catholic-Muslim relations in Lebanon. Today, the Shihab family still remains one of Lebanon's most powerful families with both Catholic and Muslim persons in it. They are a living testimony to the hope for the conversion of the Muslims through friendship and love with Catholics.

Joanna Nobilis Reinhardt

a.k.a. Begum Sumru and Farzana Khan
d. January 27th, 1838

Born Farzana Khan in 1753 in Kotana, Kashmir Province, India, she was the Muslim daughter of an Arab named Latif Ali Khan. Her father died when she was six, and she moved to Dehli with her mother. In Dehli, she became a nautch girl where she worked as a dancer for religious and social events by day and a child prostitute by night. One of her clients was a French-employed mercenary from Luxembourg named Walter Reinhardt. He fell in love with Farzana and married her. He was 45, and she was 14.

Walter was referred to by the Indians as "Sumru." This is a corruption of the French "Le Somre," in reference to his swarthy complexion. Although Walter was nominally Catholic, many of his actions in India completely opposed the Faith he professed. The first and obvious problem was that he was patronizing child prostitutes, as seen by his relationship with Farzana. The second problem was that he was a bigamist, since when he married Farzana, he was simultaneously married to another Indian Muslim woman who he already had a son with and chose to ignore. The third problem was that as a mercenary, he was ruthless in exploiting the conflict between the declining Mogul Empire and the governing British Empire for personal gain. He is particularly hated by the British, because while working for Mir Qasim, the British vassal ruler of Bengal, he participated in the massacre of a large group of British soldiers taken as prisoners following a skirmish in 1763 in Cheria in the Bihar Province.[7]

In spite of Walter's significant personal problems, he loved Farzana dearly and was as much a teacher and friend to her as he was her husband. Walter's brutality subsided as the years passed, and he acquired a large amount of land in Sardhana, Uttar Pradesh Province in northern India. At the same time, Walter slowly returned to the Catholic Faith and eventually used his money to patronize Catholic missionary efforts in northern India. All of these actions influenced Farzana. When Walter died in 1778, she was selected to control Walter's territories by the European powers who had divided up India at this point.

Farzana was soon referred to by the Indians as Begum Sumru, coming from the title given to her deceased husband.[8] She was still a Muslim, but she continued her husband's patronage of Catholic missions and the Church in northern India. She began to study the Catholic Faith and in 1781 was received into the Church. When she was baptized, she took the name Joanna Nobilis, named after St. Joan of Arc. She also reconnected with Walter's son from his first wife, whose name was Zafar Khan. Due to her influence, Zafar not only forgave his father, but he converted to the Catholic Faith and adopted his father's full name, Walter Reinhardt, as his own.

Begum Sumru became known as a warrior-princess, administrator, and diplomat who ruled her kingdom with great care while leading fierce battles against British, Muslim, and Sikh armies. She was the only female ruler in India during her time, and she was admired by both European and Indian alike. In addition to being a great ruler, her Catholic Faith was an important part of her rule. While she was a fierce warrior, she also respected the human dignity of her enemies and even cared for them after she would defeat them in battle. Her patronage of the Catholic Church was so great that she is regarded as the founder of the Church in northern India. Many of the religious orders, churches, and missionaries who worked in northern India were directly supported by her assistance. One of her greatest projects was building the Basilica of Our Lady of Graces in Sardhana, Uttar Pradesh Province, India.

She died on January 27th, 1838. She is remembered as one of the greatest female and Catholic rulers of the Far East.

Fr. François Bourgade
d. 1866

Fr. François Bourgade was born in 1806 in France. He was one of the first French missionaries to North Africa. In addition to his missionary work in Tunis which began in 1838, he was also an archaeologist and historian. He was a pioneer in uncovering the forgotten pre-Islamic history of ancient Carthage, and he wrote prolifically about his discoveries. He died in 1866.

Fr. Carlos Cuarterón
d. 1880

Fr. Carlos Cuarterón was born in Cádiz, Spain in 1816 to a family of sailors. At the age of 25, he sailed across the world to the Spanish colonies in the Philippines. While working in the Far East, he ransomed many persons enslaved by Muslims. This practice motivated him to become a priest. In 1855 he was ordained, and the following year he sailed to the island of Borneo to establish a mission within the tiny Sultanate of Brunei. While the mission did not have the impact he desired, he continued his efforts until he fell ill with pneumonia in 1879. He then returned to Spain and died three months later in 1880.

Br. Marie-Clement Rodier
d. 1904

Br. Marie-Clement Rodier was born in 1839 and was a French missionary from the Congregation of the Holy Spirit. He worked as a missionary to Algerian Muslims as well as ran an orphanage. He was also known for his horticultural skills. Through a series of experiments with various fruit trees that grew on the orphanage's property, he created a new variety of mandarin orange. The fruit was named after him and is one of the most popular citrus fruits sold today, known as the clementine. He died in 1904.

Bishop Philippe-Jacques Abraham
d. August 28th, 1915

Bishop Philippe-Jacques Abraham was born on January 3rd, 1848 to an Assyrian Catholic family. He was consecrated a priest in the Syro-Malabar Rite in 1875 and became Bishop of Gazireh near Mardin in 1882.

When the Ottomans commenced the Armenian Genocide, Bishop Abraham tried to save the Christians with help from local Muslims but could not. Eventually, he was rounded up and taken to the Ottoman city of Cizre along with Servant of God Bishop Flavianus Michael Malke. When he refused to convert to Islam, Bishop Abraham was shot and his corpse was dragged through Cizre's streets.

Bishop Addai Scher
d. 1915

Bishop Addai Scher was born in Shalaqwa, Irbil Province, Iraq in 1867 to an Assyrian Catholic family. He became a Dominican in 1880 and went to study in Mosul, Iraq. He returned in 1889 and was ordained a priest, and in 1902 became the Chaldean Catholic Archbishop of Siirt in the Ottoman Empire. He traveled for several years across Europe and Istanbul, and during this time he wrote about religion.

When the Armenian Genocide began in 1915, Bishop Scher bribed various Ottoman officials to help the Catholics and fellow Christians escape. He was helped by a Muslim named Osman Ağha. Bishop Scher was hated by the Ottomans for his actions, and they set out to find and arrest him.

One day, Ottoman soldiers received a tip that Bishop Scher was hiding in Ağha's home. After raiding the house and discovering him, he was arrested and tortured by the Ottomans. Finally, they cut off his head and brought it to the local governor as a prize before massacring Siirt's Christian community. Ağha was later beaten to death by the same soldiers.

Bishop Mar Toma Audo
d. 1918

Bishop Mar Toma Audo was born in Alqosh, Iraq in 1855 to an Assyrian Catholic family. He was ordained in 1880, and became Archbishop of Urmia in what is today Iran. He wrote extensively about the Assyrian people, including a dictionary of Assyrian, and translated Catholic theological works into Assyrian. He was murdered on July 27th, 1918 in the Armenian Genocide.

Filippo Dormeyer
d. March 11th, 1920

Filippo Dormeyer was born in 1845 and became a Cistercian monk. He was living in Syria when one day, a band of Muslims came to the monastery where he lived and asked him if he was a Christian. When he said "Yes," they responded "Then we will do to you what has been done to him." They crucified him to the monastery's door lintels, where he hung for two days until he died.

Fr. Franciscus Georgius Josephus van Lith
d. 1926

Fr. Franciscus Georgius Josephus van Lith was a Jesuit missionary born in 1863 in Oirschot, Holland. He pioneered missionary work with the Javanese people of Indonesia.

Fr. van Lith's work began in 1896 on the island of Java. He synchronized the cultural and social customs of the Javanese to the Catholic Faith. He baptized and catechized hundreds of Javanese Muslims into the Faith, built Catholic schools, and created friendly relations with the Muslims. He also advocated for the rights of both Catholic and Muslim Javanese in Indonesian society.

Fr. Van Lith died in 1926. He is remembered for having successfully established the Church's presence in the world's most populous Muslim nation.

Nothing has changed

The only thing we learn from history
is that we learn nothing from history.
– Georg Hegel

After World War II, European nations invited large numbers of Muslims from North Africa and South Asia to help rebuild the Continent. As the mid-20th century progressed and Europe drew itself further away from its roots, even more Muslim immigration happened in the name of tolerance and diversity. However, this did not change the historical threat which Islam still posed.

The social and political preferences that have been given to Islam have placed Europe at a historical "crossroads." There are now large Muslim communities in all Western European nations. Mosque construction is outpacing church construction, and some bishops have sold churches to Muslims to become mosques. Most births in Europe today are among Muslims, while many non-Muslims are having few to no children. The European disdain of the Catholic Church has increased at the same time the practice of Islam has risen.

If the current trends continue, Western Europe will become Muslim-majority in several generations. This has not yet become a serious problem in Eastern Europe, but it has the potential to spread there. The same situation is true for the United States and Canada, where criticism of Islam has been progressively silenced.

The Church has engaged and continues to engage in extensive missionary work among Muslims. While evangelization has been a slow process, many Muslims have converted to the Catholic Faith. Interestingly, the Faith has grown strongest in many former Muslim strongholds in sub-Saharan Africa, India, and other parts of Asia while it has been progressively rejected by the European people. These trends have been noticed by both Muslim missionaries and the Church.

Nothing has fundamentally changed in the relationship between the Church and Islam. All that is different is the attitude of the people and their willingness to address the situation with Islam at this particular time in history. The future of the Church and Islam in Europe and the world is unknown except for one variable from St. Matthew's Gospel:

Thou art Peter, and upon this rock I shall build my Church, and the gates of Hell will not prevail over it.[9]

Photos from protests in London over Pope Benedict XVI's Regensburg lecture on September 12th, 2006. The disdain Islam has for the Catholic Faith and all Christianity is no different than it was during Muhammad's life. Islam must be addressed lest this picture become the future of Europe and the Americas as it did to the Middle East during the 7th and 8th centuries.[10]

The Faithful

Fr. Paul Mulla
d. February 24th, 1959

Fr. Paul Mulla was born Mehmet Ali Mullazade on Crete to a noble family of mixed Turkish, Albanian, and Greek roots in 1882. He was raised as a Muslim and was trained in Islamic philosophy and theology as well as the western scholarly tradition. At the age of 17, he met the French intellectual Maurice Blondel, and the two became lifelong friends.

Fr. Paul already had an interest in the Catholic Faith from his academic studies, which intensified through the influence of Maurice. To his surprise and pleasure, the rich intellectual, philosophical, and spiritual tradition of the Catholic Faith was persistently more fulfilling than anything that Islam could offer. Eventually Mehmet realized that:

The egalitarian conception, in the Quran, of a revelation of the divine unity, repeated in a discontinuous series of messages to the people and generations of men...results in what is in effect practically a historical unreality.[11]

Fr. Paul converted to the Catholic Faith in 1905. Eight years later he was ordained a priest. He taught Islamic Studies at the Pontifical Institute for Oriental Studies in Rome, and was a great proponent of Catholic-Muslim dialogue until his death.

Fr. Nelson Javellana
d. November 3rd, 1971

Fr. Nelson Javellana was a Filipino priest and Oblate of Mary Immaculate. He was murdered in Cotabato Province, Philippines by Muslim terrorists in 1971 seeking to establish a separate Islamic republic on the island of Mindanao.

Br. Sean Devereux
d. 1993

Br. Sean Devereux was born in 1964 in England. He was a schoolteacher who became a Salesian missionary in Africa. He spent the rest of his life there as an advocate for children and war refugees.

During the Somali Civil War in 1993, Br. Devereux was working with UNICEF through the Salesians in the city of Kismayo, which was a stronghold of Muslim rebel activity. His efforts were focused on helping to get food to the city's people, who were starving as a result of the Muslim rebels having cut off supplies and seized any remaining food supplies for themselves.

On January 2nd, Br. Devereux was shot in the back of the head outside where he was staying with UNICEF.

Br. Henry Vergès and Sr. Paul-Hélène Saint-Raymond
d. May 8th, 1994

Br. Henry Vergès was a Marist monk born in 1930 who worked since 1969 as the director for St. Bonaventure School in Algiers. Sr. Paul-Hélène Saint-Raymond was born in Paris in 1927. She joined the Little Sisters of the Assumption in 1952 and since 1963 she lived throughout Algiers, Tunis, and Casablanca as a nurse to children and premature babies. The two were murdered by Islamic Salvation Front (ISF) terrorists on May 8th, 1994.

Srs. Caridad Álvarez-Mártin and Esther Paniagua-Alonso
d. October 23rd, 1994

Sr. Caridad Álvarez-Mártin was born in 1933 and entered the Augustinian Missionary Sisters in 1955. She spent most of her life in Algeria working among the poor and elderly. Sr. Esther Paniagua-Alonso, a fellow Augustinian Missionary Sister, was born in Spain in 1949 and entered the Augustinian Missionary Sisters in 1970. She spent most of her time working in Algeria as a nurse for handicapped children. Both sisters were going to Mass on October 23rd, 1994 when they were murdered by ISF terrorists.

Martyrs of the Missionaries of Africa
(White Fathers Brs. Christian Chessel, Jean Chevillard, Alain Dieulangard, and Charles Deckers)
d. December 27th, 1994

Brs. Jean Chevillard, Alain Dieulangard, Charles Deckers, and Christian Chessel were missionaries with the White Fathers in Tizi Ozou, Kabylia, Algeria. All of them worked extensively with the Kabylia Berbers, both in education as well as building interfaith outreach. They were all loved and respected by the Muslim people.

On December 27th 1994, ISF terrorists broke into the White Father's missionary house and found the four brothers in the courtyard. They were shot to death with submachine guns.

Srs. Angele-Marie and Bibiane
d. September 3rd, 1995

Sr. Angele-Marie was born Jeanne Littlejohn in 1933 and took the name Angele-Marie upon entering the Sisters of Our Lady of the Apostles in 1957. She was sent to Algeria in 1959 where the taught embroidery at an orphanage and school operated by the Order. Sr. Bibiane was born Denise Leclercq in 1930 and took the name Bibiane upon entering the Sisters of Our Lady of the Apostles in 1959. She went to Algeria in 1961 and also taught sewing and embroidery, as well as worked with Algerian mothers and newborn babies. Both sisters were murdered by ISF terrorists on September 3rd, 1995 as they were leaving Mass.

Sr. Odette Prevost
d. November 10th, 1995

Sr. Odette Prevost was born in 1932 and entered the Little Sisters of the Sacred Heart in 1953. Since 1958, she worked in interfaith outreach between the Moroccans and Algerians. As Sr. Prevost was going to Mass on November 10th, 1995, she was shot to death by ISF terrorists.

Martyrs of Our Lady of the Atlas
(Brs. Christian de Chergé, Luc Dochier, Michel Fleury, Christophe Lebreton, Bruno Lemarchand, Paul Favre-Miville, Célestin Ringeard)
d. May 21st, 1996

The Martyrs of Our Lady of the Atlas, also known as the Martyrs of Tibhirine, were seven French monks belonging to the Order of the Cistercians of the Strict Observance in Tibhirine, Algeria. They were kidnapped and murdered by ISF terrorists.

The monastic community was already very small. All of the monks knew for a long time that they might suffer martyrdom because of their lived witness as Catholics in a Muslim nation. Each of the brothers had been in Algeria since at least the 1980s, and all were harassed or captured by Muslim terrorists at least once during their time. However, they were all committed to building peaceful interfaith relations with the Muslims as well as working with the poor, the outcast, and those suffering from serious illnesses.

On March 27th, 1996, ISF terrorists broke into the monastery and kidnapped the seven monks. For nearly two months, the monks were held as hostages. On May 21st, 1996, after a failed attempt to rescue them, the monks' throats were slit in revenge. The Islamic Salvation Front's leader Jamal Zaytuni, known as Abu 'Abd Ar-Rahman Al-Amin and was the one who ordered the executions, said that the monks could be legitimately killed because they were infidels attempting to Christianize the Muslims by their mere presence.

Following the event, the monastery was closed and the community relocated to Midelt, Morocco. The 2010 film <u>Of Gods and Men</u> was based on the Martyrs' story.

Bishop Pierre Claverie
d. August 1st, 1996

Bishop Pierre Claverie was born in 1938 in Oran. He became a Dominican in 1959 and was ordained in 1965. Since he was born in Algeria, he felt a personal connection to the country. He pledged to live in Algeria as a witness to Christ and to minister to the small and dwindling Catholic community.

Three months after the Cistercian monks of Our Lady of the Atlas were martyred by ISF terrorists, Bishop Claverie was also murdered. As he was returning home, the ISF detonated a remote-controlled bomb which killed him and his driver on August 1st, 1996.

Bishop Benjamin de Jesus
d. February 4th, 1997

Bishop Benjamin de Jesus was Bishop of Sulu, Jolo Island, Philippines. He was shot to death by Muslim Abu Sayyaf terrorists outside of the Cathedral of Our Lady of Mount Carmel on February 4th, 1997.

Servant of God Fr. Rhoel Gallardo and the Claret School Martyrs
d. May 3rd, 2000

Servant of God Fr. Rhoel Gallardo was a Claretian missionary priest working in the heavily Muslim area of Basilan, Mindanao Province, Philippines. In early 2000, he and 52 persons from the school operated by the Claretians, staff and students alike, were taken as prisoners by Muslim terrorists. All but Fr. Gallardo and three teachers were released. The remaining four were shot to death.

A Final Thought

As the Church enters into the third millennium, many challenges lay ahead. But nothing has happened with Islam that has not happened in the past. The reality which the 7th century Church faced is the same in the 21st century. The only notable difference between those of the past and today is the desire and response of the Church to Islam. This is wholly a matter of human decision. God presents man with circumstances, and empowers man through his free will to select his fate.

It is for the sake of mercy that Catholics must engage with Muslims, as they are made in God's image and likeness. But there is no such place of honor for Islam, as it denies and curses the divinity of Christ. In the words of the Córdoban martyrs Aurelius, Felix, George, Liliosa, and Natalia:

"Any cult which denies the divinity of Christ, does not profess the existence of the Holy Trinity, refutes baptism, defames Christians and derogates the priesthood, we consider to be damned."

It is enough that each man must render unto God an account of his life during the Final Judgment. Every man is ultimately saved by God's grace, and the Final Judgment is reserved for God alone. Yet it was Christ who said He will deny before His Father those who deny Him in this life.[12]

Catholics are mandated to represent Christ to people of all religions in the context of each man's particular vocation and life situation. Islam is no exception. The men and women of Lions of the Faith are a sampling of those who have witnessed for Christ's love to Muslims throughout history. Their lives exemplify models to guide the Church's relationship with Islam as much today as in the past. It is left for the Church to seek their prayerful intercession and guidance in her dealings with Islam and Muslims, as the salvation of many depends on this.

Works Cited

Research for <u>Lions of the Faith</u> was a challenging task because of the volume of texts, diversity of textual differences, linguistic issues, and access to resources. Fortunately, many of these saints listed were already written about in some capacity. It was for <u>Lions of the Faith</u> to compile, expand upon, and present in a succinct fashion this information in cooperation with the available biographical and historical resources.

As far as sources are concerned, most of the research was derived from the following texts:

<u>Acta Sanctorum</u> (A.S.)

Compiled by the Bollandists, this is one of the largest texts on saints and their life stories, having been written over the course of 297 years. It contains many documents directly copied from the original manuscripts, and is a wealth of primary source information.

<u>Acta Sanctorum</u>. Published by the Bollandists, Society of Jesus. Antwerp and Brussels. Vols. 1-68. 1643-1940. Available through Proquest Online via Chadwyck-Healy Databases, UK.

<u>Bibliotheca Sanctorum</u> (B.S.)

This was published between 1961 and 1969 as per request of the Second Vatican Council. It is a very complete compilation of saints throughout Church history, made up of primary source documents and research from the Bollandists.

Bibliotheca Sanctorum. Istituto Giovanni XXIII. Pontificia Universita Lateranense. Rome. 12 Vols. 1961-1969.

Martyrologium Romanum (M.R.)

The Martyrologium Romanum was first published by Pope Gregory XIII in 1583, and was the replacement to the 6th century Martyrologium Hieronymianum written by St. Jerome. It was updated several times until 1748 under Pope Benedict XIV, and has since remained the standard martyrology of the Catholic Church. During the Second Vatican Council, the Council voted to update the martyrology. For this book, the original 1748 martyrology was used.

Pope Gregory XIII. Martyrologium Romanum. 1583. Republished by Pope Benedict XIV in 1784. Venice.

Memoriale Sanctorum (M.S.)

Written by St. Eulogius, the Memoriale Sanctorum is the most comprehensive source of information about the Martyrs of Córdoba.

St. Eulogius of Córdoba. Memoriale Sanctorum. Republished in Corpus Scriptorum Muzarabicorum by Juan Gil. Instituto Antonio de Nebrija. Madrid. 1973. Pages 395-415.

Mercedarian Historical Survey (M.H.S.)

This book is a detailed history of the Mercedarian Order. It is an excellent source of information about saints from Order, especially those who are not as well-known by the public.

Order of the Blessed Virgin Mary of Mercy (1218 – 1992): A Historical Synthesis. Historical Institute of the Mercedarian Order. Mercedarian Press. Leroy, NY. 1998.

Catholic Encyclopedia (C.E.)

This early 20th century work sources many original texts and provides a keen insight into the lives of the saints. The Catholic Encyclopedia was updated and is now sold under the title of the New Catholic Encyclopedia (N.C.E.). Both texts were used in writing Lions of the Faith.

Catholic Encyclopedia. Robert Appleton Co. New York. 1907-1912.

New Catholic Encyclopedia. The Catholic University of America. Published by Thomson/Gale. Detroit. 2nd edition. 2003.

Two other sources served as important references to inspire research about potential saints for Lions of the Faith. The first was the famous Anglo-Catholic hagiography Butler's Lives of the Saints, written by Fr. Alban Butler in the 18th century and reprinted many times since. The second was the Our Sunday Visitor's Encyclopedia of Saints, which likewise provided an easy-to-read but excellent starting point for research.

Butler, Fr. Alban. Butler's Lives of the Saints. Republished and updated by Paul Burns for Liturgical Press. Collegeville, MN. 2003.

Bunson, Matthew et al. Our Sunday Visitor's Encyclopedia of Saints. Our Sunday Visitor Publishing. Huntington, IN. 2003.

Potentially useful information about each saint was included as it was deemed necessary. The above abbreviations were used to help reduce unnecessary referencing and to facilitate research if somebody wanted to read more about a particular person. All of the saints and persons here are organized in the order they appear in the book.

In addition to the above-listed sources, some research for Lions of the Faith came from sources that were old, obscure, or difficult to access. Since information of this nature can unintentionally possess inaccuracies, persistent efforts were made to verify facts and claims. This work was very successful and rewarding. If there are any factual errors in the text, please notify the publisher so that corrections may be made for future editions.

Various photos and drawings were used in different sections. All works are attributed to their respective authors or sources and are used in context of the specific permissions granted them, which is noted in the endnotes. Please inform the publisher immediately if there are any errors concerning said information.

Section I: The Rise of Islam

Sts. Florian, Calcanicus, and the 56 Martyrs of Eleutheropolis
B.S. LX Difensori di Gaza
M.R. December 17th

St. Torcatus
    da Costa, Antonio Carvalho O.P. Corografia Portugueza e Descripcam Topografia. Vol I. 2nd edition. Domingos Goncalves Gouvea. Braga, Portugal. 1868. Page 19.
    da Cunha, Rodrigo. Cataloga e Historia dos Bispos do Porto. Episcopal Office. Porto, Portugal. 1742. Pages 191-199.
    Silva, Augusto Santo. A Paixao Segundo São Torcato. Sociologia- Problemas e Practicas. Number 13. 1993. Pages 9-17.

Another text which was unavailable for use was the Vida Preciosa e Glorioso do Martiro São Torcato, written in 1835. It can be found in the Portuguese National Library.

The story of Our Lady of Covadonga, Pelagius of Asturias, and Oppas the Bishop of Seville
    Aradi, Zsolt. Shrines of Our Lady Around the World. Farrar, Straus, and Young. 1954. Pages 43-45.
    C.E. Diocese of Oviedo Vol. XI. Pages 363-364.
    Gibbon, Edward. The History of the Decline and Fall of the Roman Empire. Vol VI. Philadelphia. 1805. Pages 381-408.
    Trongoso, Don Juan. Glorias y Triunfos de España. Vol. III. Madrid, Spain. 1849. Pages 67-86.
    Wolf, Kenneth B. Conquerors and Chroniclers of Early Medieval Spain. Liverpool University Press. Liverpool. Second Edition. 1999. Pages 163-170.

St. Sophronius
    A.S. March 11th
    B.S. Sofronio, Patriarca di Gerusalemme
    M.R. March 11th
    N.C.E. St. Sophronius

St. James the Greater
    A.S. July 25th
    B.S. Giacomo il Maggiore
    C.E. St. James the Greater
    M.R. July 25th
    Trongoso, Don Juan. Glorias y Triunfos de España. Vol. III. Madrid. 1849. Pages 87-106

St. Emilian of Cogolla
    Baring-Gould, Sabine. The Lives of the Saints. Vol. 13: November. John Hodges. 1877. Page 292.
    B.S. Emiliano della Cogolla
    de Sandoval, Prudencio. Fundaciones de los Monasterios del Glorioso Padre San Benito. Madrid. 1601.

Sts. 'Abd Al-Masih and Barbar
    Sahas, Dr. Daniel J. Hagiological Texts as Historical Sources for Arab History and Byzantine-Muslim relations. The Case of a Barbarian Saint. Byzantine Studies. 1996-1997. Pages 50-59.

Jabalah ibn Al-Aiham
    Al-Baladhuri, Ahmad ibn Jabir. Futuh Al-Buldan. See also P.K. Hitti's translation, The Origins of the Islamic State. Columbia University Press. New York. 1916. Vol I. Pages 208-210.

Asakir, Ibn. Tarikh Dimashq. Dar Al-Fikr. Damascus. Reprinted 1998. Vol. 57. Page 368.

St. Eurosia
    A.S. June 25th
    B.S. Eurosia di Jaca

St. Fructus
    A.S. October 24th
    B.S. Frutto
    Trongoso, Don Juan. Glorias y Triunfos de España. Vol. III. Madrid. 1849. Pages 46-66.

St. Eusebia
    A.S. October 4th
    B.S. Eusebia
    N.C.E. St. Eusebia of Saint-Cyr

St. Porcarius and Companions
    A.S. August 12th
    B.S. Porcario
    M.R. August 12th

St. Theofrid of Orange
    A.S. Listed under October 19th
    B.S. Teofrido
    de Blemur, Jacqueline Bouëtte. L'Annee Benedictine ou le View des Saints de l'Ordre de Saint Benoist. Vol VI. November. Paris. 1673. Pages 393-395.
    M.R. November 18th

St. Ebbo
    A.S. August 27th
    B.S. Ebbone

St. Urbicius.
    B.S. Urbicio
    Faci, Roque. Aragón Reyno de Christo y Dote de Maria Santissima. Vol II. Zaragoza. 1750. Pages 266-271.

St. William of Gellone
    A.S. May 28th
    B.S. Guglielmo, Monaco a Gellone
    C.E. St. William of Gellone

St. Beatus of Liébana
    A.S. February 19th
    B.S. Beato di Liebana
    Emerson, Richard, and McGinn, Bernard. The Apocalypse in the Middle Ages. Cornell University Press. Ithaca. 1992. Pages 217-233.

Charles Martel
    C.E. Charles Martel
    Gibbon, Edward. The History of the Decline and Fall of the Roman Empire. Vol VI. Philadelphia. 1805. Pages 408-430.
    Strauss, Gustave L. Charles. Muslim and Frank, or, Charles Martel and the Rescue of Europe. London. 1854.
    Wolf, Kenneth B. Conquerors and Chroniclers of Early Medieval Spain. Liverpool University Press. Liverpool. Second Edition. 1999. Pages 141-149.

Odo the Great
  Blake, Jean-François. Eudes, Duc d'Aquitaine. Paris. 1892.
  de Vic, Claude et al. Histoire Generale de Languedoc. Vol II. Toulouse. 1840.
  Panckouke, C.L.F. Victoires, Conquetes, Revers et Guerres Civiles des Français depuis les Gaulois Jusqu'en 1792. Vol XII. Paris. 1821. Pages 254-277.

St. Peter of Damascus
  B.S. under Pietro, Prete di Capitolas
  Kennedy, Hugh. The Byzantine and Early Islamic Near East. Ashgate Publishing. Hampshire. 2006. Page 71.
  M.R. October 4th

St. Peter Mavimenus
  A.S. February 21st
  B.S. under Pietro, Prete di Capitolas
  M.R. February 21st

Sts. Constantine and David, Princes of Georgia
  B.S. Santi Martiri David e Constantino in Georgia
  Dowling, Theodore. Sketches of Georgian Church History. Society for Promoting Christian Knowledge. 1912. Reprinted 2005 by Adamant Media Corporation. Pages 121-122.

St. Abu of Tbilisi
  Rayfield, Donald. The Literature of Georgia- A History. Clarendon Press. Oxford. 1994. Pages 35-37.
  Vasiliev, Alexander. The Goths in the Crimea. Mediaeval Academy of America. Cambridge, MA. 1936. Pages 96-99.

St. Ashot of Iberia

    Rapp, Stephen. Studies in Medieval Georgian Historiography: Early Texts And Eurasian Contexts. Peeters Publishers. Leuven. 2003.

    Toumanoff, Cyril. Date of the Death of the Curopalates Ashot. Le Museon. Peeters Publishers. Leuven. 1956. Vol. LXIX, 10-2. Pages 83-85.

Al-Mu'eiyyad and St. Theodore of Edessa

    Abel, Armand. La Portée Apologétique de la 'Vie' de St. Théodore d'Edesse. Byzantinoslavia Journal. Vol. 10. 1949. Pages 229-240.

    At-Tabari, Muhammad ibn Jarir. The History of Al-Tabari: Incipient Decline. Vol. XXXIV. Trans. Joel L. Kraemer. SUNY Press. Albany. 1989. Pages 210-224.

    Patrich, Joseph. The Sabaite Heritage in the Orthodox Church from the Fifth Century to the Present. Peeters Press. Louvain. 2001. Pages 147-169.

    Vasiliev, A.A. The Life of St. Theodore of Edessa. Byzantion Journal. Vol. 16. 1942-43. Pages 165-225.

St. Anthony Ruwah

    B.S. Antonio Rawah

    La Passion Arabe de S. Antoine Ruwah. Le Museon. Peeters Publishers. Leuven. 1961. Vol. LXXIV. Pages 108-133.

St. Elias of Heliopolis

    B.S. Elia il Giovane, Martire a Damasco

    Byzantine Authors: Literary Activities and Preoccupations. Ed. John Nesbitt. Brill. Leiden. 2003. Pages 83-107.

St. Bacchus Dahhat
    B.S. Bacco Dahhat
    Kofsky, Arieh and Stroumsa, Guy. Sharing the Sacred: Religious Contacts and Conflicts in the Holy Land. Yad Izhak Ben Zvi. 1998. Pages 150, 198.
    Patrich, Joseph. The Sabaite Heritage in the Orthodox Church from the Fifth Century to the Present. Peeters Press. Leuven. 2001. Page 70.

Forty-two Martyrs of Amorion
    At-Tabari, Muhammad Ibn Jarir. History of Al-Tabari: Storm and Stress along the Northern Frontiers of the 'Abbasid Caliphate. Vol XXX. Trans. Clifford Bosworth. SUNY Press. Albany. 1991. Pages 118-119.
    B.S. Martiri di Amorio
    M.R. March 6th
    Skylitzes, John. A Synopsis of Byzantine History. Trans. John Wortley. Cambridge University Press. 2010. Pages 78-81.

St. Archil of Kakheti
    B.S. Arcil di Georgia
    Rayfield, Donald. The Literature of Georgia- A History. Clarendon Press. Oxford. 1994. Pages 112-114.
    Toumanoff, Cyril. Studies in Christian Caucasian History. Georgetown University Press. 1963. Pages 394-395.

St. John Damascene
    A.S. May 6th
    B.S. Giovanni Damasceno
    C.E. St. John Damascene
    M.R. December 4th

St. Peter of Mount Athos
    A.S. June 12th
    B.S. Pietro Eremita sul Monte Athos
    de Mendieta, Emmanuel Amand. Mount Athos: The Garden of the Panaghia. Akademie-Verlag. Amsterdam. 1972. Pages 56-57.

Conversion of the Banu Habib
    de Souza, Philip and France, John. War and Peace in Ancient and Medieval History. Cambridge University Press. Cambridge. 2008. Page 149.
    Hamdanids. Encyclopedia of Islam. Version II. 2000. Brill. Leiden. Volume III. Page 126.
    Sahas, Dr. Daniel J. Hagiological Texts as Historical Sources for Arab History and Byzantine-Muslim Relations. The Case of a Barbarian Saint. Byzantine Studies. 1996-1997. Pages 50-59.
    Treadgold, Warren. Byzantium and its Army: 284-1081. Sanford University Press. Sanford. 1995. Page 34.

Sts. Adulphus and John
    A.S. September 27th
    B.S. Adolfo e Giovanni
    M.R. September 27th
    M.S. Book III, Chapter XVII.

St. Perfectus
    A.S. April 18th
    B.S. Perfetto
    M.R. April 18th
    M.S. Book II, Chapter I.

St. Isaac of Córdoba
    A.S. <u>June 3rd</u>
    B.S. <u>Isacco, Monaco a Cordova</u>
    M.R. <u>June 3rd</u>
    M.S. Book II, Chapter II.

St. Sancho the Soldier
    A.S. <u>June 5th</u>
    B.S. <u>Sancio</u>
    M.R. <u>June 5th</u>
    M.S. Book II, Chapter III.

Sts. Habenitus, Jeremiah, Peter, Sabinian, and Wistremundus
    A.S. <u>June 7th</u>
    B.S. <u>Pietro, Walabonso, Sabiniano, Wistremondo, Abenzio e Geremia</u>
    M.R. <u>June 7th</u>
    M.S. Book II, Chapter IV.

St. Sisenandus
    A.S. <u>July 16th</u>
    B.S. <u>Sisenando</u>
    M.R. <u>July 16th</u>
    M.S. Book II, Chapter V.

St. Paul of St. Zolius
    A.S. <u>July 20th</u>
    M.R. <u>July 20th</u>
    M.S. Book II, Chapter VI.

St. Theodemir
- A.S. July 25th
- B.S. Teodemiro
- M.R. July 25th
- M.S. Book II, Chapter VI.

Sts. Alodia and Nunilo
- A.S. October 22nd
- B.S. Nunilone e Alodia
- M.R. October 22nd
- M.S. Book II, Chapter VII.

Sts. Flora and Maria
- B.S. Flora e Maria
- M.R. November 24th
- M.S. Book II, Chapter VIII.

Sts. Gumesindus and Servus-Dei
- A.S. January 13th
- B.S. Gumesnido e Servidio
- M.R. January 13th
- M.S. Book II, Chapter IX.

Sts. Aurelius, Felix, George, Liliosa, and Natalia
- A.S. July 27th
- B.S. Giorgio, Aurelio, Felice, Natalia e Liliosa
- M.R. July 27th
- M.S. Book II, Chapter X.

Sts. Christopher and Leoviglid
    A.S. August 20th
    B.S. Cristoforo e Leovigildo
    M.R. August 20th
    M.S. Book II, Chapter XI.

Sts. Emilias and Jeremiah
    A.S. September 15th
    B.S. Emilia e Geremia
    M.R. July 15th
    M.S. Book II, Chapter XII.

Sts. Rogelius and Servus-Dei
    A.S. September 16th
    B.S. Rogelio e Serviodeo
    M.R. September 16th
    M.S. Book II, Chapter XIII.

St. Fandilas
    A.S. June 13th
    B.S. Fandila
    M.R. June 13th
    M.S. Book III, Chapter VII.

Sts. Anastasius, Digna, and Felix
    A.S. June 14th
    B.S. Anastasio, Felice, e Digna
    M.R. June 14th
    M.S. Book III, Chapter VIII.

St. Benildus
    A.S. June 15th
    B.S. Benilde
    M.R. June 15th
    M.S. Book III, Chapter IX.

St. Columba
    A.S. September 17th
    B.S. Colomba di Cordova
    M.R. September 17th
    M.S. Book III Chapter X.

St. Pomposa
    A.S. September 19th
    B.S. Pomposa di Cordova
    M.R. September 19th
    M.S. Book III, Chapter XI.

St. Abundius
    A.S. July 11th
    B.S. Abbondio di Cordova
    M.R. July 11th
    M.S. Book III, Chapter XII.

Sts. Amator, Louis, and Peter
    A.S. April 30th
    B.S. Amatore, Pietro, e Ludovico
    M.R. April 30th
    M.S. Book III, Chapter XIII.

St. Sandilia
    A.S. September 3rd
    B.S. Sandulfo
    M.R. September 3rd

St. Witesindus
    A.S. May 15th
    B.S. Witesindo
    M.S. Book III, Chapter XIV.

Sts. Elias, Isidore, and Paul
    A.S. April 17th
    B.S. Elia, Paolo, e Isidoro
    M.R. April 17th
    M.S. Book III, Chapter XV.

St. Argymirus
    A.S. June 28th
    B.S. Argimiro
    M.R. June 28th
    M.S. Book III, Chapter XVI.

St. Aurea
    A.S. July 19th
    B.S. Aurea di Cordova
    M.R. July 19th
    M.S. Book III, Chapter XVII.

Sts. Roderick and Salomon
    A.S. March 13th
    B.S. Rodrigo e Salomone

M.R. March 13th

St. Eulogius of Córdoba
    A.S. March 11th
    B.S. Eulogio di Cordova
    M.R. March 11th
    Paulus, Alvarus. Vita Eulogii. Republished in Corpus Scriptorum Muzarabicorum by Juan Gil. Instituto Antonio de Nebrija. Madrid. 1973. Pages 330-344.

St. Leocritia
    A.S. March 15th
    B.S. Leocrizia
    Dunbar, Agnes Baillie Cunninghame. A Dictionary of Saintly Women. Volume I. London. 1904. Page 468.
    M.R. March 15th

St. Laura
    A.S. October 19th
    B.S. Laura
    Dunbar, Agnes Baillie Cunninghame. A Dictionary of Saintly Women. Volume I. London. 1904. Page 457.

St. Victor of Cerezo
    A.S. August 26th
    B.S. Vittore di Cerezo
    Florez, Enrique. España Sagrada: Contiene las Iglesias Colegiales, Monasterios, y Santos de la Diocese de Burgos. Vol XXVII. Madrid. 1772. Pages 734-754.
    M.R. August 26th

St. Daniel of Arles
>Florez, Enrique. España Sagrada. Vol. XLV. 1832. Pages 185-189.
>Roig i Jalpí, Joan Gaspar. Resumen Historial de las Grandezas y Antiguedades de la Ciudad de Gerona. Barcelona. 1675. Pages 385-392.

Sts. Andrew, Anthony, John, and Peter
>A.S. September 23rd
>B.S. Andrea, Giovanni, Pietro, e Antonio
>M.R. September 23rd

Sts. Pelagius the Boy Martyr and Hermogius
>A.S. June 26th
>B.S. Pelagio di Cordova
>de Mariana, Jean. Histoire Generale d'Espagne. Vol II. Book VII. 1725. Page 122.
>Ebert, Adolf. Histoire Général de la Literature du Moyen Age en Occident. Paris. 1884. Pages 316-319.
>Hrotsvitha. The non-Dramatic Works of Hrotsvitha. Trans. Sr. Gonsalva Wiegand. University of Illinois Urbana-Champaign. Doctoral Thesis. 1936. Page 142.
>M.R. June 26th

St. Bernulf
>A.S. March 24th
>B.S. Bernolfo

St. Lambert of Saragossa
>Baring-Gould, Sabine. The Lives of the Saints. Volume 14. John Hodges. 1880. Page 209.
>B.S. Lamberto di Saragozza

M.R. April 16th

Martyrs of Cardeña
    A.S. August 6th
    B.S. Martiri di Cardena
    C.E. under Burgos
    Croiset, Jean. Suplemento a la Ultima Edición del Año Christiano del Padre Juan Croiset. Vol II. Madrid. 1753. Pages 156-160.
    Florez, Enrique. España Sagrada: Contiene las Iglesias Colegiales, Monasterios, y Santos de la Diocese de Burgos. Vol XXVII. Madrid. 1772. Pages 224-234.
    M.R. August 6th

Sts. Atilan and Froilan
    A.S. October 5th
    B.S. Attilano
    B.S. Froilano
    de Masdeu, Juan Francisco. Historia Critica de España de la Cultura Española. Vol XIII. Book II. Madrid. 1794. Pages 361-363.
    Piferrer, Nicholas. Compendio Historico de la Iglesia de España. Vol I. Madrid. 1781. Pages 294-297.

St. Olivia
    A.S. June 10th
    B.S. Olivia di Palermo
    Dunbar, Agnes Baillie Cunninghame. A Dictionary of Saintly Women. Volume I. London. 1904. Page 120.

St. Theoctiste of Lesbos
    B.S. <u>Teoctista di Lesbo</u>
    Delehaye, H. <u>La Vie de Sainte Theotiste de Lesbos</u>. Byzantion Journal. Vol. I. 1924. Pages 191-200.
    M.R. <u>November 10th</u>

Sts. Arsenius, Pelagius, and Silva of Arlanza
    B.S. <u>Pelagio, Arsenio, e Silviano</u>
    Florez, Enrique. <u>España Sagrada: Contiene las Iglesias Colegiales, Monasterios, y Santos de la Diocese de Burgos</u>. Vol XXVII. Madrid. 1772. Pages 110-130

St. Majolus
    A.S. <u>May 11th</u>
    B.S. <u>Maiulo</u>
    M.R. <u>May 11th</u>

Sts. Calixte and Mercurial of Osca
    A.S. <u>October 14th</u>
    B.S. <u>Callisto de Huesca</u>

St. Rudesind
    A.S. <u>March 1st</u>
    B.S. <u>Rudesindo</u>

St. Dominic of Silos
    B.S. <u>Domenico di Silos</u>
    Florez, Enrique. <u>España Sagrada: Contiene las Iglesias Colegiales, Monasterios, y Santos de la Diocese de Burgos.</u> Vol XXVII. Madrid. 1772. Pages 392-484.
    M.R. <u>December 20th</u>

N.C.E. St. Dominic of Silos

St. John of Gorze
    A.S. February 27th
    B.S. Giovanni di Gorze
    O'Callaghan, Joseph F. A History of Medieval Spain. Cornell University Press. Ithaca. 1975. Pages 117-120.

Sts. Argentea and Vulfura
    B.S. Argentea e Vulfura
    de Feria, Bartolome Sánchez. Palestra Sagrada o Memorial de los Santos de Córdoba. Vol I. Córdoba. 1772. Pages 294-307.
    de Nenclares, Eustaquio Maria. Santoral Español: Collección de Biografias de Todos Santos Nacidos en España. Vol. II. Madrid. 1864. Pages 557-558.

St. Madruina
    B.S. Madruyna
    de Argaiz, Gregorio. La Perla de Cataluña: Historia de Nuestra Señora de Monseratte. Madrid. 1674. Page 47.
    de San Nicolas, Pablo. Siglos Geronymianos: Historia General, Ecclesiastica, Monastica y Secular. Vol 14. Madrid. 1739. Page 458.
    Tiron, Rene. Historia y Trages de las Ordenes Religiosas. Barcelona. 1846. Page 286

St. Casilda
    A.S. April 9th
    B.S. Casilda di Toledo

Florez, Enrique. España Sagrada: Contiene las Iglesias Colegiales, Monasterios, y Santos de la Diocese de Burgos. Vol XXVII. Madrid. 1772. Pages 754-784.

Samuel, a.k.a. 'Umar ibn Hafsun

Almansa, Manuel Acien. Entre el Feudalism y el Islam: 'Umar Ibn Hafsun en los Historiadores, en las Fuentes y en la Historia. Universidad de Jaén. Jaén. 1997.

Fernandez, Fidel. Omar Ben Hafsun: Un Reino Cristiano Andaluz en Pleno Imperio Islamico Español. Editorial Juventud. Barcelona. 1942.

Marin-Guzman, Roberto. The Causes of the Revolt of 'Umar Ibn Hafsun in Al-Andalus 880-928. Arabica. 1995. Pages 180-221.

'Umar b. Hafsun. Encyclopedia of Islam. Version II. volume X. 2000. page 823.

Section II: The Crusades

St Matthew of Beauvais
    Baring-Gould, Sabine. The Lives of the Saints. Volume 14. John Hodges. 1880. Page 488.
    B.S. Matteo di Massaccio

St. Thiemo
    A.S. October 26th
    B.S. Thiemone
    Huber, Nikolaus. Fromme Sagen und Legenden aus Salzburg. Mittermuller. Salzburg. 1880. Pages 51-54.
    Schuster, Franz Xavier. Augsburger Dioezesen-Legende. 1904. Pages 132-133.
    Zauner, Judas Thaddaeus. Chronik von Salzburg. Salzburg. 1796. Pages 113-121.

St. Adjutor
    A.S. April 30th
    Bordeaux, Raymond. La Vie et l'Office de Saint Adjuteur. Ed. Jean Theroude. Originally published 1638, republished 1864.
    B.S. Adiutore di Vernon
    Dunbar, Agnes Baillie Cunninghame. A Dictionary of Saintly Women. Volume 1. London. 1904. Page 195. Under entry for his mother, St. Rosamond.
    Meyer, Edmond. Histoire de la Ville de Vernon et de son Ancienne Chatellenie. Vol I. 1875. Pages 89-92.

St. Aleaunie
    A.S. January 30th
    B.S. Adelelmo di Burgos

Bl. Gerard Thom

Blessed Gerard Tonque and his Everlasting Brotherhood: The Order of St. John of Jerusalem. Originally printed and published as Die Ordensregel der Johanniter/Malteser, but translated through the order's website in English. St. Ottilien Archabbey. Emming, Bavaria, Germany. 1983. Chapter 3.

Migne, Jacques-Paul. Encyclopedia Theologique ou, Serie de Dictionnaires sur toutes le Parties de la Science Religieuse. Vol II. 1851. Page 375.

Ollivier, Joseph. Discours Contenant une Notice sur la Vie de Gerard Tenque: Fondateur de l'Ordre des Hospitaliers de Saint-Jean de Jerusalem. Aix. 1868.

Porter, Whitworth. A History of the Knights of Malta or the Order of St. John of Jerusalem. London. 1883. Pages 1-15.

Villeneueve, Louis François. Monumens des Grands-Maitres de l'Ordre de Saint Jean de Jerusalem. Vol I. Paris. 1829. Pages 1-6.

Bl. Raymond du Puy

Blessed Gerard Tonque and his Everlasting Brotherhood: The order of St. John of Jerusalem. Originally printed and published as Die Ordensregel der Johanniter/Malteser, but translated through the order's website in English. St. Ottilien Archabbey. Emming, Bavaria, Germany. 1983. Chapter 4.

Porter, Whitworth. A History of the Knights of Malta or the Order of St. John of Jerusalem. London. 1883. Pages 15-45.

Villeneueve, Louis François. Monumens des Grands-Maitres de l'Ordre de Saint Jean de Jerusalem. Vol I. Paris. 1829. Pages 7-14.

Pope Bl. Urban II
    B.S. <u>Papa Urbano II</u>
    C.E. <u>Pope Bl. Urban II</u>
    M.R. <u>July 29th</u>

Our Lady of Almudeña
    de Villafane, Fr. Juan. <u>Compendio Historico en que se da Noticia de las Miligrosas y Devotas Imagenes de la Reina de Cielos y Tierra Maria Santissima.</u> 1740. Pages 14-29.
    Ossorio y Gallardo, Carlos and Bremon, Jose Fernandez. <u>Cronicas Madrileñas.</u> Madrid. 1983. Pages 79-85.
    Perez, Francisco. <u>Dos Mil Años de Santos</u>. Vol II. Madrid. 2001. Pages 1368-1370.

St. Cosmas of Aphrodisia
    A.S. <u>September 10th</u>
    B.S. <u>Cosma di Palermo</u>

St. Ernest
    A.S. <u>November 7th</u>
    B.S. <u>Ernesto di Zwiefalen</u>
    von Rommel, Dietrich Christoph. <u>Geschichte von Hessen</u>. Vol VI. Hamburg. 1836. Pages 346-348.

St. Olegarius
    B.S. <u>Ollegario</u>
    de Caralps, Juan García. <u>Breve Resume de la Historia y Vida de San Olegario</u>. Barcelona. 1817.
    de Ribadeneyra, Pedro. <u>Flos Sanctorum de las Vidas de los Santos</u>. Vol I. Madrid. 1761. Pages 424-427.

Florez, Henrique. España Sagrada: Teatro-Geografico-Historico de la Iglesia de España. Vol. XXIX. 1775. Pages 251-280.

St. Raymond of Roda
    A.S. June 21st
    B.S. Raimondo di Roda-Barbastro
de la Fuente, Vincente and Alzo, Johannes Baptist. Historia Ecclesiastica de España. Vol IV. Madrid. 1873. Pages 81-84.
    Gonzalez, Jose Fernandez. Crónica de la Provincial de Huesca. Madrid. 1866. Pages 62-63.

Bl. Raymond of Fitero
    A.S. listed under February 1st
    Baring-Gould, Sabine. The Lives of the Saints. Volume II. 1880. Pages 29-31.
    B.S. Raimondo di Fitero
    N.C.E. Bl. Raymond of Fitero

St. Julian of Cuenca
    A.S. January 28th
    B.S. Giuliano di Cuenca
    C.E. under Palencia and Burgos
    M.R. January 28th

Pope Bl. Eugene III
    A.S. July 8th
    B.S. Papa Eugenio III
    C.E. Pope Blessed Eugene III
    M.R. July 8th

St. Bernard of Clairvaux
    A.S. August 20th
    B.S. Bernardo di Chiaravalle
    C.E. St. Bernard of Clairvaux
    M.R. August 20th

St. Bertold
    A.S. March 29th
    B.S. Bertoldo, Priore Generale dei Carmelitani
    C.E. under The Carmelite Order

St. Brocard
    A.S. September 2nd
    B.S. Brocardo
    C.E. under The Carmelite Order

Bl. Peter the Venerable
    Baring-Gould, Sabine. The Lives of the Saints. Volume 12: December. John Hodges. 1877. Pages 280-290.
    B.S. Pietro II Venerabile
    C.E. Blessed Peter of Montbossier
    Kritzeck, J. Peter the Venerable and Islam. Princeton. Princeton University Press. 1964.
    Constable, Giles. Letters of Peter the Venerable. Vols I & II. Cambridge, MA. Harvard University Press. 1967.
    Peter the Venerable. Pope Benedict XVI. Given at St. Peter's Square, October 14th, 2009.

Sts. Bernard, Grace, and Maria
    A.S. August 21st
    B.S. Bernardo di Alzira, Grazia e Maria

de Blemur, Jacqueline Bouette. Anno Benedettino. Vol VI. 1727. Pages 444-447.

de Monsalvo, Jose Finestres y. Historia de el Real Monasterio de Poblet. Vol. IV. 1756. Page 98.

de Yepes, Antonio. Crónica de la Orden de San Benito. Vol VII. Salamanca. 1609. Page 4.

Our Lady of Fatima and the tale of Sir Goncalo Hermigues and Princess Fatima

de Andrada, Miguel. Miscellanea. 1629. Reprinted in 1867. by Imprensa Nacional. Lisbon. Page 35.

dos Remedios, Joaquim Mendes. Historia da Literatura Portuguesa desde as Origens ate a Actualidade. Coimbra. 1902. Pages 346-349.

Leal, Augusto Soares d'Azevedo Barbosa de Pinho. Portugal Antigo e Moderno. 1874. Vol. III. Page 152.

The original story of Our Lady of Fatima as told by the Cistercian Order comes from a Cistercian monk, Fr. João de Brito, in his Crónica da Ordem de Cister, Vol. VI, Chapter I, Page 370, published in 1602 and printed in Lisbon. A copy was not locally accessible. The book can be found in the Portuguese National Library.

Martim Moniz

Brandao, Antonio. Terceira Parte da Monarchia Lusitana. Lisbon. 1632. Page 146.

de Macedo, Joaquim Antonio. A Guide to Lisbon and its Environs. London. 1874. Pages 237-239.

Inchbold, A. Cunnick. Lisbon & Cintra. London. 1807. Page 30.

Gerald the Fearless
   Bishko, Charles. <u>The Spanish and Portuguese Reconquest: 1095-1492.</u> From <u>A History of the Crusades.</u> Vol. 3. Ed. Harry Hazard. University of Wisconsin Press. Madison. 1975. Pages 414-415.
   da Silva, Theodoro Jose. <u>Miscellanea Historico-Biographia</u>. Lisbon. 1877. Page 115.
   Link, Heinrich. <u>Voyage en Portugal depuis 1797 jusu'en 1799</u>. Vol II. Paris. 1803. Pages 176-179.

Order of Avíz
   C.E. <u>Order of Aviz</u>
   Currier, Charles. <u>History of Religious Orders.</u> New York. 1898. Page 217.
   Woodhouse, Frederick. <u>The Military Religious Orders of the Middle Ages.</u> Society for Promoting Christian Knowledge. London. 1879. Pages 295-296.

Order of Calatrava
   C.E. <u>Order of Calatrava</u>
   Currier, Charles. <u>History of Religious Orders.</u> New York. 1898. Pages 216-217.
   Woodhouse, Frederick. <u>The Military Religious Orders of the Middle Ages.</u> Society for Promoting Christian Knowledge. London. 1879. Pages 297-301.

Order of St. James of the Sword (also called the Order of Santiago)
   Blanco, Enrique Gallego. <u>The Rule of the Spanish Military Order of St. James.</u> Brill. Leiden. 1971.
   Lomax, Derek W. <u>The Order of Santiago.</u> Oxford University Press. Oxford. 1975.

Woodhouse, Frederick. The Military Religious Orders of the Middle Ages. Society for Promoting Christian Knowledge. London. 1879. Page 325.

Order of Alcántara
    C.E. Alcántara, Order of
    Torres y Tapia, Alonso. Crónica de la Orden de Alcántara. Vols I & II. Madrid. 1763.
    Woodhouse, Frederick. The Military Religious Orders of the Middle Ages. Society for Promoting Christian Knowledge. London. 1879. Pages 301-305.

Order of Mountjoy
    Dambreville, C.A. Abrege Chronologique de l'Histoire des Ordres de Chevalerie. Paris. 1807. Pages 74-76.
    Forey, A.J. The Order of Mountjoy. Speculum. Vol. 46. No. 2. April 1971. Pages 250-266.

Order of Monfragüe
    de San Pedro, Miguel Muñoz. La Desaparecida Orden de Caballeros de Monfragüe. Madrid. 1953.
    King, Georgina. A Brief Account of the Military Orders of Spain. Hispanic Society of America. New York. 1921. Page 159.
    Riley-Smith, Jonathan. The Oxford History of the Crusades. Oxford University Press. Oxford. 2002. Pages 180 and 195.

Knights of St. George of Alfama
    C.E. under Orders of St. George
    Ulick, Ralph. A History of Spain from the Earliest Times to the Death of Ferdinand the Catholic. Vol I. Longmans, Green & Co. London. 1895. Page 227.

Knights Templar
Addison, Charles. The History of the Knights Templar. London. 1842.
C.E. The Knights Templar
Dupuy, Pierre. Histoire de l'Ordre Militaire des Templiers. Brussels. 1751.
Frale, Barbara. The Chinon Chart: Papal Absolution to the Last Templar, Master Jacques de Molay. Journal of Medieval History. Vol. XXX. 2004. Page 127.
Martin, Sean. The Knights Templar: The History & Myths of the Legendary Military Order. Thunder's Mouth Press. New York. 2005.

Knights Hospitaller
C.E. Hospitallers of St. John of Jerusalem
Nicholson, Helen J. The Knights Hospitaller. 2001.
Nicolle, David. Knights of Jerusalem: The Crusading Order of Hospitallers 1100-1565. Osprey Publishing. Oxford. 2008.
Sire, H.J.A. The Knights of Malta. Yale University Press. New Haven. 1996.

Teutonic Knights or the German order of St. Mary in Jerusalem
C.E. Teutonic Order
Currier, Charles. History of Religious Orders. New York. 1898. Pages 213-215.
Urban, William. The Teutonic Knights: A Military History. Greenhill books. London. 2003.

The Order of St. Lazarus
C.E. under Order of St. Lazarus of Jerusalem
Currier, Charles. History of Religious Orders. New York. 1896. Page 218.

Hanson, Levitt. <u>An Accurate Historical Account of all the Orders of Knighthood.</u> Vol. II. London. 1802. Pages 124-126.

St. Nicasius of Sicily
<u>Archivio Storico Siciliano: Pubblicazione Periodica</u>. Year III. Vol I. Palermo. 1878. Pages 474-475.
Venuti, Vincenzo.<u> Dell-Esistenza Professione e Culto di S. Nicasio Martire</u>. Pietro Bentivegna. 1782.

Bl. Gerard Mecatti of Villamagna
A.S Appendix for <u>May 23rd</u>
B.S. <u>Gerardo Mecatti</u>
Bosio, Giacomo. <u>Le Imagini dei Beati e Santi</u>. Rome. 1860. Pages 47-52.
Brochi, Guiseppe. <u>Vita de Santi e Beati Fiorentini.</u> Florence. 1742. Page 557.
Riccardi, Fulgence-Marie. <u>L'Anno Francescano.</u> Vol II. Turin. 1789. Pages 85-86.
Richa, Giuseppe. <u>Notizie Istoriche delle Chiese Fiorentine</u>. Vol. I. 1755. Pages 296-298.

Richard the Lionheart.
Abbott, Jacob. <u>History of King Richard the First of England.</u> Harper & Brothers. New York. 1877.
C.E. <u>Richard I King of England</u>
de Visnauf, Geoffrey. <u>Interarium Peregrinorum et Gesta Regis Ricardi</u>. Translated and published by Helen Nicholson. 1997.
Flori, Jean. <u>Richard the Lionheart: Knight and King.</u> Edinburgh University Press. Edinburgh. 1999.
Gibbon, Edward. <u>Decline and Fall of the Roman Empire.</u> Vol VI. A. Strahan. London. 1788. Pages 102-110.

Bl. Albert Avogadro
    B.S. Alberto , Patriarca di Gerusalemme
    C.E. Blessed Albert
St. Berard of Carbio and Companions (Accursius, Adjutus, Otho, Peter, and Votalis)
    A.S. January 16th
    B.S. Berardo, Pietro, Ottone, Acursio, e Adiuto
    C.E. Berard of Carbio
    Chalippe, Candide. The Life of St. Francis of Assisi. New York. 1889. Pages 189-190.
    M.R. January 16th

St. Daniel and Companions (Agnellus, Donulus, Hugolinus, Nicholas, and Samuel)
    A.S. October 13th
    B.S. Daniele e Compagni a Ceuta
    C.E. Daniel and Companions
    M.R. October 10th

Sts. John of Perugia and Peter of Sassoferrato
    A.S. August 6th
    B.S. Giovanni da Perugia e Pietro da Sassoferrato
    Emidus, Fr. Manual of the Third Order of St. Francis of Assisi. Vol I. Burns, Oates, and Co. London. 1869. Pages 230-231.
    Ranise, Pietro. Storia Universale delle Missione Francescane. Vol I. Rome. 1857. Pages 183-187.

Bl. Raymond of Blanes
    Garí y Siumell, José Antonio . La Orden Redentora de la Merced. Barcelona. 1873. Pages 35-36.
    Lalau, Jose. La Leyenda de Oro. Madrid. 1844. Vol I. page 277.
    M.H.S. Page 58.

St. Diego de Soto
    A.S. January 29th
    M.H.S. Page 58.

St. Serapion
    A.S. January 29th
    B.S. Serapio
    Garí y Siumell, José Antonio. La Orden Redentora de la Merced. Barcelona. 1873. Pages 47-49.
    M.H.S. Pages 60-61.
    M.R. November 14th

St. Peter Rodriguez and Companions.
    Amado, Jose de Sousa. Historia da Igreja Catolica em Portugal. Vol IV. Lisbon. 1872. Page 207.

Sts. Raymond of St. Victor and William of St. Leonard
    Garí y Siumell, José Antonio. La Orden Redentora de la Merced. Barcelona. 1873. Pages 49-52.
    M.H.S. Page 58.

Sts. Peter of St. Denis and Bl. Bernard of Prades
    Garí y Siumell, José Antonio. La Orden Redentora de la Merced. Barcelona. 1873. Pages 55-58.
    Ribera, Manuel Maria. Centuria Primera del Real y Militar Instituto de la Inclita Religion de Nuestra Señora de la Merced. Part I. Barcelona. 1726. Pages 569-570.

Sts. Ferdinand Perez and Louis Blanc
    de la Pena y Farell, Narciso Feliu. Annales de Cataluña. Vol II. Barcelona. 1709. Page 53

Garí y Siumell, José Antonio . La Orden Redentora de la Merced. Barcelona. 1873. Pages 59-60.
M.H.S. Page 58.

Bls. Raymond and William of Granada
Ribera, Manuel Maria. Centuria Primera del Real y Militar Instituto de la Inclita Religion de Nuestra Señora de la Merced. Part I. Barcelona. 1726. Page 512.

Bl. Theobald of Narbonne and St. Ferdinand of Portalegre
de la Pena y Farell, Narciso Feliu. Annales de Cataluña. Vol II. Barcelona. 1709. Page 180.
Garí y Siumell, José Antonio . La Orden Redentora de la Merced. Barcelona. 1873. Pages 61-63.
M.H.S. Page 58.

Sts. Ferdinand of Portalegre and Eleutherius of Platea
de la Pena y Farell, Narciso Feliu. Annales de Cataluña. Vol II. Barcelona. 1709. Page 180.
Garí y Siumell, José Antonio . La Orden Redentora de la Merced. Barcelona. 1873. Pages 63-66.
M.H.S. Page 58.

Bl. Luis Gallo
Garí y Siumell, José Antonio . La Orden Redentora de la Merced. Barcelona. 1873. Page 45.
M.H.S. Page 58.

St. William the Wise
  Ribera, Manuel Maria. <u>Centuria Primera del Real y Militar Instituto de la Inclita Religion de Nuestra Señora de la Merced</u>. Part I. Barcelona. 1726. Page 580.
  Spreti, Vittorio. <u>Enciclopedia Storico-Nobiliare Italiana</u>. Arnaldo Forni. 1981. Vol. VII. Page 38.

Bl. Sancho of Aragón
  Abarca, Pedro. <u>Los Reyes de Aragón en Anales Historicos</u>. Madrid. 1682. Pages 289-291.
  Garí y Siumell, José Antonio. <u>Biblioteca Mercedaria</u>. Barcelona. 1875. Pages 23-24.

Bl. Peter of Cadireta
  de Lanuza, Vincensio Blasco. <u>Historias Ecclesiasticas Seculares de Aragón</u>. Vol. II. Zaragoza. 1622. Page 176.
  de Sarabia y Lezana, Joseph. <u>Annales de la Sagrada Religion de Santo Domingo</u>. Vol II. Madrid. 1709. Pages 329-331.
  Diago, Francisco. <u>Historia de la Provincia de Aragón de la Orden de Predicadores</u>. Barcelona. 1599. Pages 11-12.
  M.S. <u>Pietro de la Cadiretta</u>
  Mulcahey, M. Michele. <u>First the Bow is Bent in Study: Dominican Education before 1350</u>. Pontifical Institute of Mediaeval Studies. Toronto. 1998. Page 345.

Sts. Mark Matthias and Anthony Valesio
  Garí y Siumell, José Antonio . <u>La Orden Redentora de la Merced</u>. Barcelona. 1873. Pages 104-108.
  M.H.S. Page 58.

St. Peter Pascual
  B.S. <u>Pietro Pascasio</u>

C.E. under <u>Granada</u>
M.H.S. Pages 61-62.
M.R. <u>December 6th</u>

St. Peter Armengol
    A.S. under <u>January 29th</u>
    B.S. <u>Pietro Armengol</u>
    Garí y Siumell, José Antonio. <u>La Orden Redentora de la Merced</u>. Barcelona. 1873. Pages 77-80.
    M.R. <u>April 27th</u>
    M.H.S. Pages 62-63.

Bls. Monaldo of Ancona, Francis Petriolo, and Antonio Cantonio
    A.S. March 15th
    B.S. <u>Monaldo da Ancona, Francesco da Petriolo e Cantoni, Antonio da Milláno</u>
    da Civezza, Marcellino. <u>Storia Universale delle Missioni Francescane</u>. Vol. II. Rome 1858. Pages 360-375.

Bl. Raymond Lull
    A.S. Listed in text as <u>June 30th</u>
    Barber, William. <u>Raymond Lull, the Illuminated Doctor</u>. London. 1903.
    B.S. <u>Raimondo Lullo</u>
    C.E. <u>Raymond Lully</u>
    Zwemer, Samuel. <u>Raymond Lull: First Missionary to the Muslims</u>. Funk & Wagnalls. London. 1902.

Bls. James and Adolph
    Garí y Siumell, José Antonio. <u>La Orden Redentora de la Merced</u>. Barcelona. 1873. Page 127.
    M.H.S. Page 59.

St. Alexander of Sicily
  Garí y Siumell, José Antonio. <u>La Orden Redentora de la Merced</u>. Barcelona. 1873. Page 130-134.
  M.H.S. Page 59.
  Ribera, Manuel Maria. <u>Centuria Primera del Real y Militar Instituto de la Inclita Religion de Nuestra Señora de la Merced</u>. Part I. Barcelona. 1726. Page 580.

Bl. Arnaud Amalric
  B.S. <u>Arnaldo Amalrico</u>
  Cooper, Thompson. <u>Biographical Dictionary</u>. Vol I. George Bell & Sons. London. 1890. Page 45.
  Klawinski, Ron. <u>Chasing Heretics: A Modern Journey through the Medieval Languedoc</u>. Hungry Mind Press. 1999. Pages 86-88.
  Strayer, Joseph. <u>The Albigensian Crusades</u>. University of Michigan Press. Ann Arbor. 1992. Pages 89-104.

Bl. Berengar, the German of Bellpuig
  Ribera, Manuel Maria. <u>Centuria Primera del Real y Militar Instituto de la Inclita Religion de Nuestra Señora de la Merced</u>. Part I. Barcelona. 1726. Page 456.

St. Ugo Canefri
  B.S. <u>Ugo di San Giovanni</u>
  Cibrario, Luigi. <u>Descrizione Storica della Ordini Religiosi</u>. Vol II. Turin. 1845. Pages 352-353.

St. Raymond Nonnatus
  C.E. <u>St. Raymond Nonnatus</u>
  M.H.S. Pages 59-60.
  M.R. <u>August 31st</u>

Bl. Tancred of Siena
  A.S. August 21st
  Drane, Augusta. The Life of St. Dominic with a Sketch of the Dominican Order. London. 1857. Pages 181-183
  O'Daniel, Victor. The First Disciples of Saint Dominic: Adapted and Enlarged from Father Anthony Touron's Histoire Abrégée des Premiers Disciples de Saint Dominique. Rosary Press. Somerset, OH. 1928. Chapter 12.

St. Bernard Calbó
  de Broca, Andreu de Bofarull i. Annales Historicos de Reus. Reus. 1866. Pages 625-626.
  de Luna, Francisco Martorell y. Historia de la Santa Cinta. Barcelona. 1627. Page 146.
  Morera y Llaurado, Emilio. Tarragona Antigua y Moderna. Tarragona. 1894. Page 208.

King St. Ferdinand III of Castile
  A.S. May 30th
  B.S. Ferdinando III Re de León
  C.E. St. Ferdinand III
  M.R. May 30th

Bl. Agnus of Zaragoza
  de Hebrera y Esmir, Jose Antonia. Crónica Serafica de la Santa Provincial de Aragón de la Regular Observancia de Nuestro Padre San Francisco. Part I. Zaragoza. 1703. Page 243-313.

King St. Louis IX of France
  A.S. August 25th
  B.S. Luigi IX Re di Francis

C.E. St. Louis IX
M.R. August 25th

St. Raymond of Peñafort
    A.S. January 7th
    B.S. Raimondo di Penyafort
    C.E. St. Raymond of Peñafort
    M.R. lists as January 23rd, but has been moved back to the original date of January 7th as of 1970

Pope Bl. Gregory X
    B.S. Papa Gregorio X
    C.E. Pope Gregory X

Bl. Conrad of Ascoli
    C.E. Blessed Conrad of Ascoli
    Emidus, Fr. Manual of the Third Order of St. Francis of Assisi. Vol I. London. 1869. Page 198.

St. Maria de Cervellón the Helper
    A.S. September 25th
    B.S. Maria de Cervellón
    C.E. Mary of Cervillione
    de Ribadeneyra, Pedro. Flos Sanctorum de las Vidas de los Santos. Madrid. 1761. Pages 101-116.
    M.H.S. Page 63-64.
    M.R. September 19th

Bl. Arnold of Queralt
>Ribera, Manuel Maria. Centuria Primera del Real y Militar Instituto de la Inclita Religion de Nuestra Señora de la Merced. Part I. Barcelona. 1726. Page 416.
>Miret y Sans, Joaquin. Les Cases de Templers y Hospitalers en Catalunya. Barcelona. 1910. Pages 356-358.

Bl. Arnold of Rossinol
>Bover, J.M. Varones Ilustres de Mallorca. Palma. 1847. Pages 679-686.

Sts. John de Matha and St. Felix of Valois, founders of the Trinitarians'
>A.S. Listed in a discussion on August 20th about St. Bernard of Clairvaux
>>B.S. Felice di Valois
>>B.S. Giovanni di Matha
>>C.E. St. Felix of Valois and under Slavery and Christianity
>>C.E. under Order of Trinitarians
>de la Providence, Calixte. Vie de Saint Jean de Matha. Paris. 1867
>>M.R. February 8th (Matha) and November 4th (Valois)

St. Francis of Assisi
>A.S. October 4th
>St. Bonaventure. The Little Flowers of St. Francis. Reprinted by E.P. Dutton and Company. New York. 1951. Pages 55-57.
>>B.S. Francesco da Assisi
>>C.E. St. Francis of Assisi
>>M.R. October 4th

St. Anthony of Padua
    A.S. June 13th
    B.S. Antonio di Padova
    C.E. St. Anthony of Padua
    M.R. June 13th

Our Lady of Puig
    Balaguer, Victor. Historia de Cataluña y de la Corona de Aragón. Vol II. Barcelona. 1860. Pages 343-351.
    Flandro, Joan Mey. Crónica o Commentario del Gloriosissim e Invictissim Rey en Lacme. Valencia. 1557. Chapter LX.
    Lafuente, Modesto. Historia General de España. Vol V. Madrid. 1851. Pages 419-423.

St. Peter Nolasco, founder of the Mercedarians
    A.S. January 29TH
    B.S. Pietro Nolasco
    C.E. St. Peter Nolasco
    M.H.S. Pages 22-24.
    M.R. December 25th

Our Lady of Ransom or Our Lady of Mercy
    Ave Maria. Congregation of the Holy Cross. Notre Dame University. 1880. Pages 801-802.
    M.R. mentioned on August 10th, but celebrated on September 24th

Bl. William of Bas
    Garí y Siumell, José Antonio. La Orden Redentora de la Merced. Barcelona. 1873. Pages 66-70.
    M.H.S. Pages 47-48.

Ribera, Manuel Maria. <u>Centura Primera del Real y Militar Instituto de la Inclita Religion de Nuestra Señora de la Merced</u>. Part I. Barcelona. 1726. Pages 293-296.

St. Peter of Amer
  Garí y Siumell, José Antonio. <u>Biblioteca Mercedaria</u>. Barcelona. 1875. Pages 12-13.
  Garí y Siumell, José Antonio. <u>La Orden Redentora de la Merced</u>. Barcelona. 1873.
  M.H.S. Page 50.
  Ribera, Manuel Maria. <u>Centura Primera del Real y Militar Instituto de la Inclita Religion de Nuestra Señora de la Merced</u>. Part I. Barcelona. 1726.

St. Thomas Aquinas
  A.S. <u>March 7th</u>
  B.S. <u>Tommaso di Aquino</u>
  C.E. <u>St. Thomas Aquinas</u>
  M.R. <u>March 7th</u>

Bl. Ambrose of Siena
  A.S. <u>March 20th</u>
  Baring-Gould, Sabine. <u>Lives of the Saints</u>. Vol. III. March. John Hodges. 1872. Pages 386-387.
  B.S. <u>Ambrogio Sansedoni</u>
  C.E. under <u>Society of the Holy Name</u>
  M.R. <u>March 20th</u>

Our Lady of Loreto
    C.E. Santa Casa di Loreto
    Falkner, George. A Pilgrimage to the Shrine of Our Lady of Loreto. Manchester. 1882.
    M.R. December 10th
    Shapcote, Emily. Among the Lilies and Other Tales with a Sketch of the Holy House of Nazareth and Loreto. London. 1881.

John of Plano Carpini, Benedict of Poland, and William of Rubruck.
    B.S. Giovanni di Montepiano
    C.E. Giovanni da Piano Carpine
    C.E. William Rubruck
    The Texts and Versions of John de Plano Carpini and William de Reubruquis. Ed. C. Raymond Beazley. The Hakluyt Society. London. 1903.
    The Journey of William of Rubruck to the Eastern Parts of the World. Ed. W. Woodville Rockhill. The Hakluyt Society. London. 1900.

Fr. Raymond Martí
    Amat, Felix Torres. Memorias para Ayudar a Formar un Diccionario Critico de Escritores Catalanes. Barcelona. 1836. Pages 392-396.
    C.E. Preachers, Order of
    Getino, Luis and Palacios, Miguel. La Summa Contra Gentiles y el Pugio Fidei. Vergara. 1905.

The Forgotten Knights of Ru'ad Island
    Barber, Malcolm. The Trial of the Templars. Cambridge University Press. Cambridge. 2006. Pages 22-23.

Edbury, Peter. The Kingdom of Cyprus and the Crusades, 1191-1374. Cambridge University Press. Cambridge. 1991. Pages 105-107.

Fr. Riccoldo da Monte di Croce
    C.E. Ricoldo da Monte di Croce
    da Monte di Croce, Riccoldo. Viaggio in Terra Santa. Reprinted by Bibiloteca Imperiale. Siena. 1864.
    Ranise, Pietro. Storia Universale delle Missione Francescane. Vol VI. Prato. 1881. Pages 337-339.
    Studi Biografici e Bibliografici sulla Storia della Geografia i Internazionale. Vol I. Societa Geografica Italiana. Rome. 1882. Pages 687-690.

Section III: The Expansion

Bl. William of Castellammare
    B.S. Guglielmo da Castellammare di Stabia.
Wadding, Luke and Sbaralea, Joannes. Supplementum et Castigation ad Scriptores Trium Ordinum S. Francisci. Rome. 1936. Pages 346.

St. Nikola Tavelić and Companions (Adeodat of Rodez, Peter of Narbonne and Stephen of Cuneo), or the Franciscan Martyrs of Jerusalem
    Angelus Domini. Pope Paul VI. Sunday, June 21st, 1970.
    Canonizzazione dei Martiri Nicola Tavelic, Deodato da Rodez, Stefano da Cuneo e Pietro da Narbonne. Omelia del Santo Padre Paolo VI. Pope Paul VI. Sunday, June 21st, 1970.
    Ciccarelli, Diego. Francescanesimo e Cultura a Noto. Officina di Studi Medievali. Palermo. 2003. Pages 177-187.
    Mandic, Dominik. Documenta martyrii B. Nicolai Tavelic. Pontifical Gregorian University. Rome. 1958.

Bls. John of Cetina and Peter de Dueñas
    A.S. Mentioned in May 19th under the section Praetermissi et in Alios Dies Reiecti.
    B.S. Giovanni da Cetina e Pietro de Dueñas
    de Hebrera y Esmir, Jose Antonia. Crónica Serafica de la Santa Provincial de Aragón de la Regular Observancia de Nuestro Padre San Francisco. Part I. Zaragoza. 1703. Pages 384-409.
    de la Pena y Farell, Narciso Feliu. Annales de Cataluña. Vol II. Barcelona. 1709. Page 348.
    de la Torr y Angulo, Manuel Barbado. Compendio Historico Lego-Seraphico. 1745. Pages 353-356.

St. Venturino of Bergamo
    B.S. Venturino di Bergamo
    C.E. Venturino of Bergamo
    Hocedez, E. La Legende Latine du B. Venturino da Bergame. Analecta Bollandiana. Vol. 25. 1906. Pages. 298-303.
    Lea, Henry Charles. A History of the Inquisition of the Middle Ages. Vol II. New York. 1888. Pages 380-382.

John of Montecorvino
    B.S. Giovanni da Montecorvino
    C.E. John of Montecorvino
    Dawson, Christopher. Mission to Asia. Medieval Academy of America. New York. 1980. Pages 31-39.
    Maclear, George Frederick. A History of Christian Missions during the Middle Ages. Macmillan and Co. London. 1863. Pages 375-377.
    Robson, Michael. The Franciscans in the Middle Ages. Boydell Press. Woodbridge. 2006. Pages 108-118.

Bl. Bartholomew of Bologna
    B.S. Bartolomeo da Bologna
    C.E. Bartholomew "Apostle of Armenia"
    Drane, Augusta Theodosia. The Life of St. Dominic. New York. 1892. Pages 329-330.

Our Lady of Guadalupe (Extremadura, Spain)
    Altamirano, Ignacio Manuel. Paisajes y Leyendas. Mexico. 1884. Pages 309-313.
    Diaz y Perez, Nicholas. Extremadura: Badajoz y Caceres. Barcelona. 1887.
    Icazbalceta, Joaquin García. Carta acerca del Origen de la Imagen de Nuestra Señora de Guadalupe de Mexico. Mexico. 1896. Page 7.

Pope Bl. Urban V
    B.S. Papa Urbano V
    C.E. Pope Bl. Urban V
    M.R. December 19th

Marco Polo
    C.E. Marco Polo
    C.E. under Prester John
    Polo, Marco. Travels of Marco Polo. Trans. William Marsden revised by Thomas Wright. London. 1854.
    Towle, George Makepeace. Marco Polo: His Travels and Adventures. New York. 1880.

King Louis I of Hungary
    Engel, Pal. The Realm of St. Stephen: A history of Medieval Hungary, 895-1526. I.B. Taurus. New York. 2001. Pages 157-199.
    Louis the Great: King of Hungary and Poland. Ed. S.B. Vardy, et al. East European Monographs. Dis. Columbia University Press. New York. 1986.

Bl. James of Tahust
    Ribera, Manuel Mariano. Real Patronato de los Serenissimos Señores Reyes de España en el Real y Militar Orden de Nuestra Señora de la Merced. Barcelona 1725. Pages 157 and 443.

Sts. Peter Malasanc and John of Granada
    M.H.R. Page 98.
    Ribera, Manuel Mariano. Real Patronato de los Serenissimos Señores Reyes de España en el Real y Militar

Orden de Nuestra Señora de la Merced. Barcelona 1725. Page 616.

Bl. Ferdinand, the Holy Prince of Portugal
    A.S. June 5th
    B.S. Ferdinando del Portogallo
    McMurdo, Edward. The History of Portugal. Sampson, Low, Marston, Searle, & Rivington. London. 1888. 384-413.
    Owen, Robert. Sanctorale Catholicum. C. Kegan Paul & Co. London. 1880. Pages 274-276.

Bl. Anthony Neyrot
    A.S. August 6th
    B.S. Antonio Neyrot
    N.C.E. Bl. Anthony Neyrot
    Procter, John. Short Lives of the Dominican Saints. London. 1901. Pages 87-90.

Bls. Antonio Primaldo, Bishop Stefano Argercolo de Pendinellis, and the 800 Martyrs of Otranto
    A.S. August 14th
    B.S. Martiri di Otranto
    C.E. under Otranto
    Pastor, Ludwig. The History of the Popes. Volume IV. Kegan, Paul, Trench, Truebner, & Co. London. 1894. Pages 333-347.

Bl. Arnold Serra and Companions.
    Garí y Siumell, José Antonio. La Orden Redentora de la Merced. Barcelona. 1873. Page 442.

Ribera, Manuel Maria. Centuria Primera del Real y Militar Instituto de la Inclita Religion de Nuestra Señora de la Merced. Part I. Barcelona. 1726. Page 574.

John Hunyadi
    C.E. Janos Hunyady
    Fejer, Georgius. Genus, Incunabula et Virtus Joannis Corvini de Hunyad Regni Hungariae. Buda. 1844.
    Held, Joseph. Hunyadi: Legend and Reality. Columbia University Press. 1985.
    Muresanu, Camil. John Hunyadi: Defender of Christendom. Translated by Laura Treptow. Center for Romanian Studies. Oxford. 2000.

St. John Capistrano
    A.S. Lists as October 23rd
    B.S. Giovanni da Capestrano
    C.E. St. John Capistran
    M.R. mentioned on October 23rd, but also celebrated on March 28th

Skanderbeg
    Babinger, Frans. Mehmed the Conqueror and his Time. Princeton University Press. 1992. Pages 152-153.
    Barletius, Marinus. Historia de Vita et Gestis Scanderbegi Epirotarum Principis. Rome. 1508.
    C.E. under the articles Pope Callistus III, Crusades, and Constantinople
    Hodgkinson, Harry. Scanderbeg: From Ottoman Captive to Albanian Hero. Center for Albanian Studies. 1999.
    Moore, Clement. George Castriot, Surnamed Scanderbeg, King of Albania. New York. 1850.

Bl. Catherine of Bosnia
    Babinger, Frans. Mehmed the Conqueror and his Time. Princeton University Press. 1992. Page 383.
    Bralic, Stefano. Monografia Storica sulle Crudelta Musulmane in Bosnia-Erzegovina. Rome. 1898. Pages 35-37.
    B.S. Caterina, Regina di Bosnia

Bl. Angelo Carletti di Chivasso
    A.S. refers to him on November 17th
    B.S. Angelo da Chivasso
    C.E. Bl. Angelo Carletti di Chivasso

Bl. Pacificus of Cerano
    A.S. June 16th
    B.S. Pacifico da Cerano
    C.E. Bl. Pacificus of Cerano
    Du Monstier, Arthur. Martyrologium Franciscanum. Paris. 1638. Page 33.

Our Lady of Europe
    Carreres Joan. Santuarios Marianos de Andalucia Occidental. Ediciónes Encuentro. Madrid. 1992. Page 63.
    Rayon, Jose León Sancho. Collecion de Documentos Ineditos para la Historia de España. Vol CVI. Madrid. 1893. Pages 365-415.

King Alfonso V of Aragón
    C.E. under Pope Callistus III
    de Capmany, Antonio. Compendio Cronologico-Historico de los Soberanos de Europa. Vol I. Don Blas Roman. Madrid. 1792.Page 413.

La Fuente, Modesto. <u>Historia General de España</u>. Vol VIII. Madrid. 1852. Pages 273-355.

Miron, E.L. <u>The Queens of Aragón: Their Lives and Times</u>. New York. 1913. Pages 265-286.

Henry the Navigator

Beazley, Raymond. <u>Prince Henry the Navigator: The Hero of Portugal and of Modern Discovery</u>. London. 1894.

C.E. <u>Prince Henry the Navigator</u>

Martins, J. P. Oliveira. <u>The Golden Age of Prince Henry the Navigator</u>. London. 1914.

Russell, Peter. <u>Prince Henry the Navigator: A Life</u>. Yale University Press. New Haven. 2000.

The Order of St. George

Boulton, D'Arcy Jonathan D'Acre. <u>The Knights of the Crown: The Monarchical Orders of Knighthood in Later Medieval Europe, 1325-1520</u>. Boydell Press. Woodbridge. 2000. Pages 39-44.

N.C.E. <u>Order of St. George</u>

The history and foundation document of the Order of St. George is courtesy of the Order of St. George online.

Order of the Dragon

Ashmole, Elias. <u>The History of the Most Noble Order of the Garter</u>. England. 1717. Page 65.

Organe de la Societe Suisse d'Heraldique. <u>Archivum Heraldicum</u>. Vols 17-19. Imprimerie Schulthess & Co. Zurich. 1903. Pages 55-59.

Rezachevici, Constantin. <u>From the Order of the Dragon to Dracula</u>. Journal of Dracula Studies. 1999. Pages 3-7.

Order of Saints Lazarus and Maurice
	Boulton, D'Arcy Jonathan D'Acre. <u>The Knights of the Crown: The Monarchical orders of Knighthood in Later Medieval Europe, 1325-1520</u>. Boydell Press. Woodbridge. 2000. Pages 256-260.
	C.E. <u>Order of Saint Lazarus of Jerusalem</u>
	Ferrari, Alessandro<u>. L'Ordine dei Santi Maurizio e Lazzaro</u>. Rivista Araldica. 1955. Pages 117-122.

Order of Our Lady of Bethlehem
	C.E. under <u>The Military Orders</u>
	Palmieri, Vincenzo<u>. L'Ordine Militare e Ospitaliere di S. Maria di Betlemme : il Centro Clandestino Orbet</u>. Oficine Grafiche Confalonieri. Milano. 1949.

Bl. James of St. Peter
	Ribera, Manuel Maria<u>. Centuria Primera del Real y Militar Instituto de la Inclita Religion de Nuestra Señora de la Merced</u>. Part I. Barcelona. 1726. Page 562.

Bl. Marc Criado
	B.S. <u>Marco Criado di Andujar</u>
	de Prado, Antonio Ventura. <u>El Apostol de las Alpujarras: Vida, Martirio y Culto de Fr. Marcos Criado, del Orden del la S.S. Trinidad, Redempcion de Cautivos</u>. 1738.
	de la Providence, Calixte. <u>Vie de Saint Jean de Matha</u>. Paris. 1867. Pages 332-333.
	de Sancto Antonio, Bernardinus. <u>Epitom Generalium Redemptionum Captiurum Quae a Fratribus Ordinis S. Triniatis Sunt Factae</u>. 1623. Page 91.

St. Jerome of Werden
    A.S. July 9th
    B.S. Martiri di Gorcum
    M.R. July 9th

Servant of God Bishop John Andrew Carga
    A.S. mentioned under August 2nd under Praetermissi et in Alios Dies Reiecti
    Pinzani, Francesco. Vita del Venerabile Monsignore Giovanni Andrea Cargade Sandaniele. San Daniele. 1855.

Bls. Denis of the Nativity and Redemptus
    Guenin, Eugene. La Route de l'Inde. Paris. 1903. Pages 249-253.
    M.R. October 17th

St. Ketevan of Mukhrani, Queen of Georgia
    Harding, Luke. Georgians Seek Buried Bones of Martyred Queen. The Guardian. London. June 25th, 2000.
    Rayfield, Donald. The Literature of Georgia- A History. Clarendon Press. Oxford. 1994. Pages 105-106.
    Suny, Ronald. The Making of the Georgian Nation. Indiana University Press. 1994. Pages 50-51.

Bl. Giovanni da Prado
    B.S. Giovanni di Prado
    C.E. Morocco
    da Latera, Flamino Annibali. Manual de'Fratri Minori. Rome. 1776. Page 263.
    di Venezia Pietro. Legendario Francescano. Vol I. Venice. 1721.

King St. Stephen III of Moldavia
> Bevan, Wilson. The World's Leading Conquerors. New York. 1913. Pages 269-271.
> Pastor, Ludwig. The History of the Popes from the Close of the Middle Ages. Vol. IV. 1894. Pages 284-286.
> Sadoveanu, Mihail. The Hatchet: The Life of Stephen the Great. Eastern European Monographs. Columbia University Press. New York. 1991.

St. Francis Xavier
> Bartoli, Daniello et al. The Life of St. Francis of Xavier: Apostle of the Indies and Japan. New York. 1889.
> B.S. Francesco Saverio
> C.E. St. Francis Xavier
> Coleridge, Henry. The Life and Letters of St. Francis Xavier. Vol I. London. 1872.
> M.R. December 3rd

St. Joseph of Leonessa
> B.S. Giuseppe da Leonessa
> C.E. St. Joseph of Leonessa
> M.R. February 4th

Bl. Mark of Aviano
> Beatification of Six New Servants of God. Pope Bl. John Paul II. Sunday, April 27th, 2003.
> B.S. Marco d'Aviano
> de Montor, Artaud. The Life and Times of the Popes. Vol VI. Catholic Publication Society of America. New York. 1910. Page 138.
> N.C.E. Bl. Mark of Aviano

Our Lady of Guadalupe, Patroness of the Americas
    Johnston, Francis. The Wonder of Guadalupe. TAN Publishers. 1981.
    La Virgin del Tepeyac. Published by the Jesuits. Revista Catolica. Las Vegas, New Mexico. 1885.
    N.C.E. Our Lady of Guadalupe
    Vera, Fortino. Tesoro Guadalupano. Vols I & II. Amecameca. 1887.

Our Lady of Victory
    Kellner, Karl. Heortology: A History of Christian Festivals from their Origin to the Present Day. London. 1908. Pages 270-271.
    M.R. October 7th

Mary Help of Christians
    See Our Lady of Victory

Pope St. Pius V
    Anderson, Robin. St. Pius V. TAN Publishers. 1973.
    B.S. Papa Pio V
    C.E. Pope St. Pius V
    Mendham, Fr. Joseph. The Life and Pontificate of Saint Pius the Fifth. London. 1832.

St. John of Ribera
    B.S. Giovanni de Ribera
    Canonizacion del Beato Juan de Ribera. Pope Bl. John XXIII. Sunday, June 12th, 1960.
    Ximenez, Juan. Vida del Beato Juan de Ribera. Joseph de Orga. Valencia. 1798.

Ven. Carlo Carafa
    B.S. Carlo Carafa
    N.C.E Carafa (Caraffa)

Pope Bl. Innocent XI
    B.S. Papa Innocenzo XI
    C.E. Pope Innocent XI

Holy Name of Mary
    C.E. Feast of the Holy Name of Mary
    M.R. September 12th
    See also Pope Bl. Innocent XI and King John Sobieski III

Queen Isabella and King Ferdinand
    C.E. Isabella I
    del Pulgar, Fernando. Crónica de los Señores Reyes Católicos Don Fernando y Doña Isabella de Castilla y de Aragón. Valencia. Benito Monfort. Written in the 16th century, reproduced from a manuscript copied in 1780.
    de Mariana, Juan. Historia General de España. Vol V. Barcelona. 1839. Chapter 10.
    N.C.E. Isabella I, Queen of Castile
    Plunkett, Ierne. Isabel of Castile. Knickerbocker Press. 1915.
    Prescott, William. History of the Reign of Ferdinand and Isabella the Catholic. 1860.
    Walsh, W.T. Isabella of Spain: The Last Crusader. TAN Books. Rockford, IL. 1987.

Don Alfonso de Albuquerque
    C.E. Afonzo de Albuquerque
    Danvers, Frederick. The Portuguese in India. London. 1894.
    de Albuquerque, Braz. Commentarios do Grande Afonso de Albuquerque. Lisbon. 1774.
    Diffie, Bailey and Winius, George. Foundations of the Portuguese Empire: 1415-1580. University of Minneapolis Press. Minneapolis. 1977.

Cardinal Francisco Jimenez de Cisneros
    C.E. Francisco Ximenez de Cisneros
    de la Fuente, Vincente. Cartas de los Secretarios del Cardinal D. Fr. Francisco Jimenez de Cisneros. Madrid. 1875.
    Lea, Henry. The Moriscos of Spain: Their Conversion and Expulsion. Philadelphia. 1901. Pages 25-56.
    Lyell, James. Cardinal Ximenes: Statesman, Ecclesiastic, Soldier and Man of Letters. London. 1917.
    Rummel, Erika. Jimenez de Cisneros: On the Threshold of Spain's Golden Age. Arizona Center for Medieval and Renaissance Studies. 1999.
    Walsh, W.T. Characters of the Inquisition. TAN Books. Rockford, IL. 1987. Pages 181-213.

Pál Tomori
    Fodor, Pal and David, Geza. Ottomans, Hungarians, and Habsburgs in Central Europe. Brill. Leiden. 2000. Pages 103-126.
    Molnar, Miklos. A Concise History of Hungary. Cambridge University Press. Cambridge. 2001. Page 85.

The Habsburg Family and the Habsburg-Ottoman wars
 C.E. Rudolph of Habsburg
 Colquhoun, Archibald and Ethel. The Whirlpool of Europe: Austria-Hungary and the Habsburgs. Dodd, Mead & Co. New York. 1907.
 Fodor, Pal and David, Geza. Ottomans, Hungarians, and Habsburgs in Central Europe. Brill. Leiden. 2000.
 Wheatcroft, Andrew. The Habsburgs: Embodying Empire. Penguin. 1996.
 Whitman, Sidney. The Realm of the Habsburgs. Leipzig. 1893.

Christovão da Gama
 Lobo, Jeronimo. The *Itinerario* of Jeronimo Lobo. Trans. Don Lockhart. Hakluyt Society. London. 1984. Pages 64-70.
 Newitt, M.D. A History of Portuguese Exploration Overseas: 1400-1668. Routledge Park. New York. 2005. Pages 112-132.
 Whiteway, R.S. The Portuguese Expedition to Abyssinia in 1441-1543. Nendeln. 1902.

Order of St. Stephen
 Engel, Pal. The Realm of St. Stephen: A History of Medieval Hungary 895-1526. I.B. Taurus & Co. London. 2005. Pages 81-90.
 Woodhouse, Frederick. The Military Religious Orders of the Middle Ages. Society for Promoting Christian Knowledge. London. 1879. Page 338.

Holy League
 C.E. Lepanto and Feast of Our Lady, Help of Christians
 Cook, M., A History of the Ottoman Empire to 1730. Cambridge University Press. London. 1976. Pages 99-132.

Dyer, Thomas. <u>Modern Europe from the Fall of Constantinople to the Establishment of the German Empire</u>. Vol. II. London. 1877. Pages 313-324.

Maxwell, William and Cox, George. <u>Don John of Austria: Or Passages from the History of the Sixteenth Century 1547-1578</u>. London. 1883. Pages 345-513.

Stephens, Henry. <u>The Story of Portugal</u>. London. 1903. Page 352.

Sultan Yahya

Bongi, Salvatore. <u>Sopra Una Missione Di Gaspare Scioppo A Lucca Come Ambasciatore Del Sultano Iachia</u>. Giornale Storico Degli Archivi Toscani. Vol. VI. Firenze. 1860. Pages 211-221.

Catualdi, Vittorio. <u>Sultan Jahja dell'Imperial Casa Ottomana od Altrimenti Alessandro, Conte Di Montenegro Ed I Suoi Discendenti In Italia</u>. Triese. 1889.

Jaitner, Klaus. <u>Autobiographische Texte und Briefe</u>. Part I. Vol. II. C.H. Beck. Munich. 2004. Pages 1071-1074.

Sforza, Giovanni. <u>Il Falso Sultano Jachia</u>. Atti Della R. Accademia Delle Scienze Di Torino. Vol. XLIII. Turin. 1907-1908. Pages 627-644.

King John Sobieski III

C.E. <u>John Sobieski</u>

Slocombe, George. <u>Poland.</u> New York. 1916. Pages 138-166.

Sobieski, John. <u>The Life of King John Sobieski: John the Third of Poland</u>. Boston. 1915.

Tatham, Edward. <u>John Sobieski</u>. Oxford. 1881.

Section IV: Modern Times

Bl. Gomidas Keumurgian
    Agagianian, F. L. Un Martire dell'unita della Chiesa di Dio. Rome. 1929.
    Crown of Martyrdom. Apostolic Letter of Pope Pius XI. Sunday, June 23rd, 1929.
    M.R. November 5th

Bl. Martyrs of Damascus ((Franciscan friars) Nicholas Alberga, Engelbert Kolland, Ascanio Nicanore, Emmanuel Ruiz, Peter Soler, and Carmelo Volta, (Postulants) John Fernandez, and Francis Pinazo, (Lay Franciscans) 'Abd Al-Mu'ti Massabki, Francis Massabki, and Raphael Massabki)
    M.S. Beati Martiri di Damasco
    N.C.E. Martyrs of Damascus
    Salotti, Carlo. L'Eroismo di Tre Martiri Maroniti: Franceso, Mooti, e Raffaele Massabki, nella Gloria della Beatificazione. Rome. 1926.
    Santa Missa per la Proclamazione di Nove Beati. Pope Bl. John Paul II. Sunday, October 3rd, 1982.

Bl. Salvatore Lilli and Companions
    N.C.E. Blessed Martyrs of Armenia
    Salvatore Lilli, Holy Land Martyr. Written and published by the Franciscan Mission Commissariat of the Holy Land. Washington, D.C. 1983.
    Santa Missa per la Proclamazione di Nove Beati. Pope Bl. John Paul II. Sunday, October 3rd, 1982.

Bl. Archbishop Ignatius Maloyan and 447 Companions
Beatification of Seven Servants of God. Pope Bl. John Paul II. Sunday homily of October 7th, 2001.
Uğur, Üngör. When Persecution Bleeds into Mass Murder: The Progressive Nature of Genocide. Genocide Studies and Prevention Journal. University of Toronto Press. Vol. 1. No.2. September 2006. Pages 173-196.

Servant of God Bishop Flavianus Michael Malke
Jamil, Metropolitan Michael. Salasil At-Tarikh. Beirut. 2003. Page 171.
Opening of the Cause for Metropolitan Martyr Michael Malke. Syrian Catholic Patriarch. April 8th, 2008.

Bl. Mariam Baouardy, a.k.a. Blessed Mary of Jesus Crucified
Brunot, Amédée. Mariam the Little Arab: Sister Mary of Jesus Crucified. 1846-1878. Reprinted by Carmel of Maria Regina, Eugene, OR. 2000.
Neger, Doris C. The Little Arab. Sophia Magazine. Vol. 31. No. 1. Jan-Feb 2001.

St. Daniel Comboni
Canonization of Three Blesseds. Pope Bl. John Paul II. Sunday homily of October 5th, 2003.
Gaiga, Lorenzo. Daniele Comboni, La Missione Continua. Bologna. 1995.
Romanato, Gianpaolo. L'Africa Nera Fra Cristianesimo e Islam. L'Esperanza di Daniele Comboni. Corbaccio. 2003.
Zungliani, Domenico. San Daniele Comboni: Biografia a partire dagli scritti. EMI. 2009.

Our Lady of Tekije
Finkel, Caroline. Osman's Dream: The Story of the Ottoman Empire. Basic Books. New York. 2005. Pages 335-337.
Kellner, Karl. Heortology: A History of Christian Festivals from their Origin to the Present Day. London. 1908. Pages 270-271.
Leger, Louis. A History of Austro-Hungary from the Earliest Time to the Year 1889. London. 1889. Pages 341-343.
Thanks to Our Lady of Tekije Church, Novi Sad, Vojvodina, Serbia.

St. Charbel Makhlouf
Beatification of the Maronite Monk Charbel Makhlouf. Pope Paul VI. Friday, December 3rd, 1965.
Canonisation de Charbel Makhlouf. Sunday. Pope Paul VI. October 9th, 1977.
Daher, Paul. A Cedar of Lebanon. St. Paul Publications. London. 1956.

Marian Shrine of Mariamabad
Bishop Hopes Mariamabad Shrine will Become the Lourdes of Pakistan. UCA News. February 7th, 1991.
Catholics Pray for Persecutors during Marian festival. UCA News. September 8th, 2009.
Felix, Qaiser. Converts from Islam on Pilgrimage to Mariamabad, Asia's "Lourdes". Asia News. September 12th, 2006.
Piara, Margaret. Pilgrims Spontaneous Devotion in Mariamabad. September 9th, 2008.

St. Josephine Bakhita
   Beatification of Sr. Josephine Bakhita. Pope Bl. John Paul II. Monday, May 18th, 1992.
   Canonization of 123 New Saints. Pope Bl. John Paul II. Sunday Homily of October 1st, 2000.
   Dagnino, Maria. Bakhita Tells Her story. Canossian Figlie della Carita. Rome. 1993.
   N.C.E. St. Giuseppina (Josephine) Bakhita)

The Shihab Family
   Bashir Shihab II. Encyclopedia of Islam. Edition II. Vol. I. Page 1078.
   Firro, Kais. A History of the Druzes. Brill. Leiden. 1992. Pages 26-56.
   Rustum, A. J. Bechir II: Entre le Sultan et le Khedive. Beirut. 1956-1957.

Joanna Nobilis Reinhardt, a.k.a. Begum Sumru and Farzana Khan
   Grey, C. and Garrett, H.L.O. European Adventurers of Northern India: 1785 - 1849. Reprinted by Asian Educational Services. New Delhi. 1993.
   Seth, M. Jacob. History of the Armenians in India from the Earliest Times to the Present Day. Calcutta. 1895. Pages 76-77.
   Sharma, Raj. History of Christian Missions: North Indian Perspective. Mittal Publications. New Delhi. 2005. Pages 5-15.
   White, William. Notes and Queries. Vol 91. John C. Francis. London. 1895. Pages 309-310
   Keene, H.G. The Fall of the Mogul Empire of Hindustan. Oxford. 1887.

   Thanks to the Church of Our Lady of Graces
   in Sardhana, Uttar Pradesh, India.

Fr. François Bourgade
    C.E. Francois Bourgade
    Lorcin, Patricia. Algeria & France 1800-2000: Identity, Memory, Nostalgia. Syracuse University Press. Syracuse. 2006. Pages 15-16.
    Neckebrouck, Valeer and Cornille, Catherine. A Universal Faith? Peoples, Cultures, Religions, and the Christ. Peeters Press. Louvain. 1992. Pages 73-88.

Fr. Carlos Cuarterón
    Crowned with the Stars: The Life and Times of Don Carlos Cuarterón, First Prefect of Borneo, 1816-1880. Diocese of Kota Kinabalu. 2005.
    Cuarterón, Carlos. Exposizione di una Nuova Missione Apostolica Nell'Oceania Occidentale. 1855.
    N.C.E. under The Catholic Church in Malaysia

Br. Marie-Clement Rodier
    Charrier, Rene. Les Frères Courage. Memoire Spiritain, Etudes et Documents 1. Paris. 1994. Pages 62-69.
    Dugo, Giovanni and Di Giacomo, Angelo. Citrus: The Genius Citrus. Taylor & Francis. 2002. Page 15.
    Reuther, Walter and Webber, Herber. The Citrus Industry. Vol. 1. University of California Division of Agricultural Sciences. 1967. Page 510.

Bishop Philippe-Jacques Abraham
    Mando, Nouri Isho. Bazibdai Archdiocese of Ancient Assyria in the History of the Chaldean Church. Published on chaldeaneurope.com. October 1st, 2011.
    Rhétoré, Jacques. Les Chrétiens aux Bêtes. Les Éditions du Cerf. Paris. 2005. Pages 316-322.

Msgr. Addai Scher
  Kitab Sayyar Ashhar Shuhada Al-Mashriq Al-Qadisin. Published by the Dominican Order. Mosul. 1900. Page 425.
  Naayem, Joseph and Oussani, Gabriel. Shall This Nation Die?. Reprinted courtesy of AINA. 1921. Pages 125-168.

Bishop Mar Toma Audo
  Baum, Wilhelm and Winkler, Dietmar. The Church of the East: A Concise History. RoutledgeCurzon. London. 2003. Page 165.

Filippo Dormeyer
  Martirologio Cistercense. Roman Curia. Pontifical Academy Culturum Martyrum.

Fr. Franciscus Georgius Josephus van Lith
  Aritonang, Jan. and Steenbrink, Karel. A History of Christianity in Indonesia. Brill. Leiden. 2008. Pages 170-172.
  Meeting with the Bishops, Priests, Men and Women Religious of Indonesia. Pope Bl. John Paul II. Tuesday, October 10th, 1989.

Fr. Paul Mulla
  Basetti-Sani, Fr. Julius. Dialogue between Christians and Muslims. Muslim World Journal. Hartford Seminary. Hartford. Vol. 57. Issue 2. Pages 126-137.
  Jarrett-Kerr. Martin. Patterns of Christian Acceptance: Individual Response to the Missionary Impact, 1550-1950. Oxford University Press. 1972. Pages 196- 201.

Fr. Nelson Javellana
    Carino, Fr. Alfonso. Fr. Nelson Javellana, OMI: 1941-1971. Oblates of Mary Immaculate Philippine Province. Cotabato City. November 9th, 2006.
    The List of Priests Killed in 40 Years of Mission in Mindanao. Agenzia Fidea. Vatican City. October 29th, 2011.

Br. Sean Devereux
    Delmer, Michael. Sean Devereux: A Life Given for Africa, 1964-1993. Don Bosco Publications. New Rochelle. 2004.
    Devereux, Dermot. While My Heart Beats: The Sean Devereux Story: 1964-1993. Pen Press. 2001.

Thanks to the Sean Devereux Children's Fund, Hampshire, UK.

The Proto-Atlas Martyrs and the Martyrs of Atlas
(This section includes all of the martyrs of this period)
    Kiser, John. The Monks of Tibhirine: Faith, Love and Terror in Algeria. St. Martin's Press. New York. 2002.
    McGee, Martin. Christian Martyrs for a Muslim People. Paulist Press. 2008.
    Perennes, Jean. A Life Poured Out: Pierre Claverie of Algeria. Orbis Books. Maryknoll. 2007.

Bishop Benjamin de Jesus
    Carino, Fr. Alfonso. Fr. Nelson Javellana, OMI: 1941-1971. Oblates of Mary Immaculate Philippine Province. Cotabato City. November 9th, 2006.
    Evangelista, Sonny. Enhance the Positive: In a Land of Hope and Unity. Vol XVI. No. 8. September 2004.
    Parker, J, Michael. Filipino Bishop's Murder Stuns San Antonio Oblates. San Antonio Express-News. February 5th, 1997.

Servant of God Fr. Rhoel Gallardo and the Claret School Martyrs
Cervantes, Ding. Priest's Family wants Sayyaf Head Captured. Philippine Star. May 5th, 2000.

Communities Mark Priest's Terror Death. UCA News. May 3rd, 2011

Torres, Jose. Into the Mountain: Hostages by the Abu Sayyaf. Claretian Publications. Quezon City. 2001.

Appendices

Appendix A

List of Feast Days by Calendar Date

January

Day	Person	Death year	Notes
6th	Bl. Raymond of Blanes	1235	Venerated in the Mercedarian Order
6th	St. John of Ribera	1611	Expelled the Moriscos from Spain
7th	St. Raymond of Peñafort	1275	
7th	Skanderbeg	1468	Not a saint, but an Athleta Christi
8th	St. Abu of Tbilisi	786	
13th	Sts. Gumesindus and Servus-Dei	852	Martyrs of Córdoba
15th	St. Diego de Soto	1237	Venerated in the Mercedarian Order
16th	St. Berard of Carbio and Companions	1220	
28th	St. Julian of Cuenca	1208	
28th	St. Peter Nolasco	1256	Founder of the Mercedarian Order
29th	St. Ashot I of Iberia	830	
30th	St. Aleaunie	1097	

February

Day	Person	Death year	Notes
1st	St. Elias of Heliopolis	779	
4th	St. Joseph of Leonessa	1612	
6th	Sts. Peter of St. Denis and Bl. Bernard of Prades	1247	Venerated in the Mercedarian Order
8th	St. John de Matha	1213	Founder of the Trinitarian Order
8th	St. Josephine Bakhita	1947	Patroness of the Sudan
16th	Pope Bl. Gregory X	1276	
19th	St. Beatus of Liébana	800	
21st	St. Peter Mavimenus	743	
26th	St. Torcatus and 27 Martyrs	715	
27th	St. John of Gorze	974	

March

Day	Person	Death year	Notes
1st	St. Rudesind	977	
6th	Forty-two Martyrs of Amorion	848	
6th	St. Olegarius	1137	
7th	St. Thomas Aquinas	1274	"The Angelic Doctor"
9th	St. 'Abd Al-Masih	Circa 7th c.	Existence questionable
11th	St. Sophronius	638	Helped craft the Pact of 'Umar
11th	St. Eulogius of Córdoba	859	Martyrs of Córdoba
13th	Sts. Roderick and Salomon	857	
13th	Sts. Argentea and Vulfura	931	St. Argentea was the daughter of 'Umar ibn Hafsun
14th	Bl. Agnus of Zaragoza	1260	
15th	St. Leocritia	859	Martyrs of Córdoba
15th	St. Raymond of Fitero	1163	
15th	Bls. Monaldo of Ancona, Francis Petriolo, and Antonio Cantoni	1314	Catholics but are also venerated in the Armenian Apostolic Church
20th	Bl. Ambrose of Siena	1286	
24th	St. Bernulf	836	
27th	St. Matthew of Beauvais	1098	Knight of the First Crusade

March, continued

Day	Person	Death Year	Notes
28th	St. Venturino of Bergamo	1344	
28th	St. John Capistrano	1456	"The Warrior Priest"; also celebrated on October 23rd
29th	St. Bertold	1195	Founder of the Carmelite Order

April

Day	Person	Death Year	Notes
1st	St. Alexander of Sicily	1317	Venerated in the Mercedarian Order
9th	St. Casilda	1050	
10th	Sts. Mark Matthias and Anthony Valesio	1293	Venerated in the Mercedarian Order
12th	Sts. Ferdinand of Portalegre and Eleutherius of Platea	1257	Venerated in the Mercedarian Order
12th	Bl. Angelo Carletti di Chivasso	1495	
16th	St. Lambert of Saragossa	900	
17th	Sts. Elias, Isidore, and Paul	856	Martyrs of Córdoba
18th	St. Perfectus	850	Martyrs of Córdoba
19th	Bl. Conrad of Ascoli	1371	Incorruptible
27th	St. Peter of Armengol	1304	
30th	Sts. Amator, Louis, and Peter	855	Martyrs of Córdoba
30th	St. Adjutor	1131	
30th	Pope St. Pius V	1572	Organized the Holy League for Lepanto

May

Day	Person	Death Year	Notes
3rd	Bl. Arnold of Rossinol	1317	Venerated in the Mercedarian Order
10th	Bl. Anthony Neyrot	1460	Apostatized to Islam but reconverted to the Faith
11th	St. Majolus	994	
13rd	Bl. Gerard Mecatti of Villamagna	1230	Only Crusader knight with a church dedicated to him
15th	St. Witesindus	856	Martyrs of Córdoba
20th	Bl. Arnold Serra and Companions	1492	Venerated in the Mercedarian Order
22nd	Bls. John of Cetina and Peter de Dueñas	1397	
24th	Bl. Giovanni da Prado	1631	
25th	Sts. Peter Malasanc and John of Granada	1428	Venerated in the Mercedarian Order
28th	St. William of Gellone	755	Grandson of Charles Martel
30th	King St. Ferdinand III of Castile	1252	

June

Day	Person	Death Year	Notes
3rd	St. Isaac of Córdoba	851	Martyrs of Córdoba
4th	Bl. Pacificus of Cerano	1481	
5th	St. Sancho the Soldier	851	Martyrs of Córdoba
5th	Bl. Ferdinand, the Holy Prince of Portugal	1443	
7th	Sts. Habenitus, Jeremiah, Peter, Sabinian, Walabonsus and Wistremundus	851	Martyrs of Córdoba
8th	St. Peter of Amer	1301	Venerated in the Mercedarian Order
10th	St. Olivia	Circa 9th c.	Existence questionable
11th	St. Peter Rodriguez and Companions	1242	
11th	Bls. Ignatius Maloyan and 447 Companions	1915	First beatified martyrs of the Armenian Genocide
12th	St. Peter of Mt. Athos	Circa 8th c.	
13th	St. Fandilas	853	Martyrs of Córdoba
13th	St. Anthony of Padua	1231	
14th	Sts. Anastasius, Digna, and Felix	853	Martyrs of Córdoba
15th	St. Benildus	853	Martyrs of Córdoba
21st	St. Raymond of Roda	1126	

June, continued

Day	Person	Death Year	Notes
25th	St. Eurosia	714	
26th	Sts. Pelagius the Boy Martyr of Córdoba and Hermogius	926	
28th	St. Argymirus	856	Martyrs of Córdoba
29th	Bl. Raymond Lull	1315	"The Illuminated Doctor"

July

Day	Person	Death Year	Notes
1st	St. Nicasius of Sicily	1187	Knights Templar executed by Saladin after Hattin massacre
2nd	King St. Stephen III of Moldavia	1504	Eastern Orthodox Saint, but recognized by the Church as an Athleta Christi
4th	St. Archil of Kakheti	787	
8th	Pope Bl. Eugene III	1153	Close friend of St. Bernard of Clairvaux
9th	St. Theodore of Edessa	857	Converted Caliph Al-Mu'eiyyad
9th	St. Jerome of Werden	1572	
10th	Bl. Franciscan Martyrs of Damascus	1860	
11th	St. Abundius	854	Martyrs of Córdoba
16th	St. Sisenandus	851	Martyrs of Córdoba
17th	St. Charbel Makhlouf	1898	Incorruptible
19th	St. Aurea	856	Martyrs of Córdoba
19th	Bl. Peter of Cadireta	1279	
20th	St. Paul of St. Zoilus	851	Martyrs of Córdoba
25th	St. James the Greater	44	Patron of Spain; known as "Matamoros" ("Muslim killer")
25th	St. Theodemir	851	Martyrs of Córdoba

July, continued

Day	Person	Death Year	Notes
27th	Sts. Aurelius, Felix, George, Liliosa, and Natalia	852	Martyrs of Córdoba
29th	Pope Bl. Urban II	1099	Called for the Crusades
30th	Bl. Arnaud Amalric	1225	

August

Day	Person	Death Year	Notes
6th	Martyrs of Cardeña	953	
8th	Bl. William of Castellammare	1364	Venerated in the Mercedarian Order
11th	John Hunyadi	1456	Not a saint, but Athleta Christi
12th	St. Porcarius and Companions	732	
12th	Pope Bl. Innocent XI	1689	Called for Holy League to protect Vienna against Ottoman invasion
13th	Bl. Mark of Aviano	1699	
14th	800 Martyrs of Otranto	1480	
20th	Sts. Christopher and Leoviglid	852	Martyrs of Córdoba
20th	St. Bernard of Clairvaux	1153	"Doctor Mellifluus"; Friend of Pope Bl. Eugene III
21st	Sts. Bernard, Grace, and Maria of Alcira	1181	Converts from Islam
25th	King St. Louis IX of France	1270	Only Saint among the French kings
25th	Bl. Mariam Baouardy	1878	Martyred by Muslims but miraculously came back to life

August, continued

Day	Person	Death Year	Notes
26th	St. Victor of Cerezo	850	Beheaded by Muslims but picked up his own head after execution
26th	St. Mercurial	1003	
27th	St. Ebbo	740	
28th	Bl. James of Tahust	1405	Venerated in the Mercedarian Order
30th	Sts. Arsenius, Pelagius, and Silva of Arlanza	950	
31st	St. Raymond Nonnatus	1240	

September

Day	Person	Death Year	Notes
1st	St. Daniel of Arles	888	Venerated locally in Gerona, Spain
2nd	St. Brocard	1231	
3rd	St Sandilia	855	Martyrs of Córdoba
3rd	Bl. Gerard Thom	1120	
3rd	Sts. John of Perugia and Peter of Sassoferrato	1231	
5th	St. Madruina of Barcelona	999	Venerated locally in Barcelona, Spain
9th	Bl. Tancred of Siena	1241	
10th	St. Cosmas of Aphrodisia	1160	
15th	Sts. Emilias and Jeremiah	852	Martyrs of Córdoba
16th	Sts. Rogelius and Servus-Dei	852	Martyrs of Córdoba
17th	St. Columba	853	Martyrs of Córdoba
18th	Ven. Carlo Carafa	1633	
19th	St. Pomposa	853	Martyrs of Córdoba
19th	St. Maria de Cervellón	1290	Incorruptible; known as "The helper"
20th	St. Eusebia and Companions	731	
23rd	Sts. Andrew, Anthony, John, and Peter	900	

September, continued

Day	Person	Death Year	Notes
24th	Bl. Marc Criado	1569	Trinitarian Order
25th	Bl. Albert Avogadro of Jerusalem	1215	Helped found Carmelite Order
26th	St. Ketevan of Mukhrani, Queen of Georgia	1614	Eastern Orthodox Saint, but relics venerated by Augustinian monks in Goa, India
27th	Sts. Adulphus and John	822	Martyrs of Córdoba
28th	St. Thiemo	1102	Never formally canonized, but recognized by the Church as a saint

October

Day	Person	Death Year	Notes
4th	St. Peter of Damascus	743	
4th	St. Francis of Assisi	1226	Converted the Sultan of Egypt who was Saladin's nephew, Al-Kamil
5th	Sts. Atilan and Froilan	916/ 905	
8th	St. Ugo Canefri	1233	
10th	Bl. James of St. Peter	1516	
10th	St. Daniel Comboni	1881	
10th	St. Daniel and Companions	1227	
15th	Sts. Constantine and David	740	
15th	St. Calixte	1003	
16th	Sts. Ferdinand Perez and Louis Blanc	1250	Venerated in the Mercedarian Order
17th	Servant of God Bishop John Andrew Carga	1617	
18th	Bl. Theobald of Narbonne	1253	Venerated in the Mercedarian Order
19th	St. Laura	864	Martyrs of Córdoba
20th	Bl. Berenger, the German of Bellpuig	1250	Venerated in the Mercedarian Order

October, continued

Day	Person	Death Year	Notes
21st	Bls. Raymond and William of Granada	1250	Venerated in the Mercedarian Order
21st	Bl. Sancho of Aragón	1275	Venerated in the Mercedarian Order
22nd	Sts. Alodia and Nunilo	851	Martyrs of Córdoba
23rd	Bl. Catherine of Bosnia	1478	
25th	St. Fructus and his brothers	715	
25th	St. Bernard Calbó	1243	
26th	Bl. Arnold of Queralt	1308	Venerated in the Mercedarian Order

November

Day	Person	Death Year	Notes
4th	St. Felix of Valois	1212	Founder of the Trinitarian Order
5th	Bl. Gomidas Keumurgian	1707	
7th	St. Ernest	1148	
10th	St. Theoctiste of Lesbos	Circa 9th c.	
12th	St. Emilian of Cogolla	5th c.	Co-Patron of Spain with St. James
12th	Bl. Raymond du Puy	1160	
14th	St. Serapion	1240	
14th	Franciscan Martyrs of Jerusalem	1391	
18th	St. Theofrid of Orange	732	Feast day sometimes celebrated on October 19th
19th	Bl. Salvatore Lilli and Companions	1895	
24th	Sts. Flora and Maria	851	Martyrs of Córdoba
29th	Bl. John of Montecorvino	1328	Apostle to the Far East
29th	Bls. Denis of the Nativity and Redemptus	1638	

December

Day	Person	Death Year	Notes
3rd	Bl. Luis Gallo	1268	Venerated in the Mercedarian Order
3rd	Bl. William of Bas	1260	Venerated in the Mercedarian Order
3rd	St. Francis Xavier	1552	
4th	St. John of Damascus	749	Feast was previously March 27th
4th	Sts. Raymond of St. Victor and William of St. Leonard	1242	Venerated in the Mercedarian Order
5th	St. William the Wise	1270	Venerated in the Mercedarian Order
6th	St. Peter Pascual	1300	
15th	St. Bacchus Dahhat	787	
15th	St. Urbicius	802	
16th	Bls. James and Adolph	1314	Venerated in the Mercedarian Order
17th	Sts. Florian, Calcanicus, and the 56 Martyrs of Eleutheropolis	637	
19th	Pope Bl. Urban V	1370	
20th	St. Dominic of Silos	1073	
25th	St. Anthony Ruwah	799	
25th	Bl. Peter the Venerable of Montbossier	1156	Founder of Islamic Studies in the West

Feast Days and Revelations of Our Lady

Month	Day	Feast	Year	Notes
April	7th	Our Lady of Puig	1238	Intercession for victory in capturing city of Valencia
May	5th	Our Lady of Europe	1468	Feast day was moved several times
May	13th	Our Lady of Fatima	1917	Connected to the siege of Alcácer do Sal in 1158 and the tale of Princess Fatima
May	24th	Mary Help of Christians	1571	Instituted following Lepanto
August	5th	Our Lady of Tekije/Snowy Mary	1716	Church and celebration shared by Catholics and Orthodox
September	8th	Our Lady of Covadonga	718	Beginning of the Reconquista
September	8th	Our Lady of Guadalupe, Extremadura	1326	Original Our Lady of Guadalupe
September	8th	Celebration for the Marian Shrine of Mariamabad	1892	Marian Shrine in Pakistan
September	12th	Holy Name of Mary	1684	Victory for Battle of Vienna

Feast Days and Revelations of Our Lady, continued

Month	Day	Feast	Year	Notes
September	24th	Our Lady of Ransom	1218	Connected to St. Peter Nolasco and the Mercedarian Order
October	7th	Our Lady of Victory	1571	Instituted after Lepanto; Also known as "Our Lady of the Rosary"
November	9th	Our Lady of Almudeña	1085	Rediscovery of the statue of St. Mary in Madrid
December	10th	Our Lady of Loreto	1291	Miracle of the Loreto house
December	12th	Our Lady of Guadalupe	1531	Patroness of the Americas

Appendix B

The Pact of 'Umar[1]

There are several versions of the Pact of 'Umar, which was drawn up between St. Sophronius and the Caliph 'Umar in 637. It governed relations between Christians, Jews, and Muslims for centuries. It continues to serve as an important guide for governing relations between Christians and Muslims in Muslim majority societies. This version dates from the 10th century and was written by the Spanish Muslim historian At-Turtushi in his book, the <u>Lantern of Kings.</u>

One will note that St. Sophronius, who would likely have been present when the pact was being drawn up, was not mentioned. This is probably because the text At-Turtushi supplied here was not the original text St. Sophronius consented to. Nevertheless, it is of great theological and historical importance because the information it transmits communicates the conditions which Islam did and continues to impose on Christians since the seventh century.

On Ruling the Ahl Adh-Dhimma

'Abd Ar-Rahman bin Ghanam said: We wrote to 'Umar bin Al-Khattab the time he made peace with the Christians of Syria:

In the name of Allah, the Beneficent, the Merciful.

This is the letter of Allah's slave 'Umar, the commander of the believers, from the Christians of such-and-such a city. When you came to us asking us for protection of ourselves, our children, our wealth, and the people of our sect, we made conditional upon ourselves for you that:

We shall not renew in our cities or surrounding areas monasteries, churches, convents, or monastic cells.

We shall not repair what falls apart, and nor what is in the quarters of the Muslims, by night or by day.

We shall open our doors to passerby and wayfarers. If they are from the Muslims, three nights shall we provide for them.

We shall not house a spy in our churches or residences, and we shall not conceal them from the Muslims.

We shall not teach our children the Quran.

We shall not appear in our streets and shall not evangelize anybody.

We shall not hinder anybody from our relatives to enter into Islam if he wishes.

We shall honor the Muslims and we shall stand for them when sitting if they wish to sit.

We shall not impersonate them in anything of our clothes, the qalnaswa[2], turban, sandals, or parting of the hair.

We shall not speak their language.

We shall not adopt their honorific names.

We shall not ride on saddles.

We shall not brandish swords and we shall not take any weapon, nor shall we carry one.

We shall not print our seals using the designs of the Arabs.

We shall not sell alcoholic drinks.

We shall cut the hair on our foreheads, dress in the same clothing wherever we are, and fasten the zunar[3] around our waists.

We shall not display crosses on our books in any way or on the roads of the Muslims or their markets.

We shall not strike our cymbals in our churches, except quietly, and we shall not raise our voices during reading in our churches among Muslim areas. We shall not raise our voices with our dead.

We shall not display light in any way on the roads of the Muslims or their markets.

We are not to allow them (i.e. Christians to be buried) with our (i.e. Muslim) dead.

We shall not take a slave that has been designated for the Muslims.

We shall not build upon their (i.e. the Muslims) houses.

When the letter came to 'Umar, he added in it: We shall not strike a Muslim.

We make this conditional upon ourselves and the people of our sect, and we accept said protection. If we abandon in any way what we have made conditional for you and protection for ourselves, the pact is forfeit for us and it will be incurred for us what is incurred for rebels and deviants.

'Umar wrote that "Sign off on what they ask, and affix two conditions upon them in addition to what they have imposed upon themselves- that they sell no young male slave from the Muslims, and whomever strikes a Muslim intentionally has broken this agreement."

The document also notes in the same chapter:

Nafia' said from Aslam the Mawli of 'Umar bin Al-Khattab that 'Umar bin Al-Khattab wrote to the Christians of Syria: They will separate their riders, ride on one side, when riding stay to one side, and wear a different style of clothing in order that they can be identified by the Muslims.

and

As for the churches, 'Umar bin Al-Khattab commanded that all churches build after Islam be destroyed, and he prohibited the renovation of churches, and forbade high steeples or a cross outside the church, except on the front side. 'Urwa bin Muhammad destroyed it with the idolaters, and this is the madhhab[4] of the ulema[5] of all the Muslims. 'Umar bin Al-'Aziz strengthened this in that he forbade the building or renovation of a synagogue or church in the Dar Al-Islam.[6] Hasan Al-Basri said: It was from the Sunna[7] that they destroyed the churches which were new and old in the land, and forbade the Ahl Adh-Dhimma from rebuilding what was destroyed. Al-Astakhri said:

If they destroyed the outside of a wall they forbade (its rebuilding), and if they destroyed the inside which was next to them (i.e. a side facing a Muslim area) they forbade (fixing it). They forbade that it be over the Muslims in building height. Making it of equal height was permitted, but it was not allowed.[8]

Appendix C

The Treaty of Tudmir

The Treaty of Tudmir was contracted between Musa ibn Nusayr's son, 'Abd Al-'Aziz, and Tudmir, also written as Theodemir, who was the Visigoth Governor of Murcia. It mirrors in many ways the stipulations of the Pact of 'Umar. However, the difference here is that the Treaty's stipulations applied specifically to the Catholics living along the eastern coast of what was at the time recently-conquered Spain by Islamic armies. This is because it took at least until the Battle of Guadalete in 718 for Islamic armies to completely overwhelm the Spanish countryside and take full control over the Iberian Peninsula.

This document dates from the late 12th century and was recorded by the Muslim historian Ad-Dabbi in his <u>Desire of the Inquirer into the History of the People of Andalusia</u>. According to the document, the agreement was made on Tuesday, April 11th, 713.

Treaty of Tudmir[1]

In the name of Allah, the Beneficent, the Merciful.

This is the letter of 'Abd Al-'Aziz bin Musa bin Nusayr to Tudmir bin Ghabdush. He has accepted a peace treaty that Allah has made for him, his *dhimma*, and the *dhimma* of his prophet. (The Muslims) will not approach him, nor any one of his followers, nor bother him, nor take away his property, nor kill them, nor enslave them, nor separate between their children and women.[2] (The Muslims) will not hate their religion,[3] nor burn their churches, nor confiscate their places of worship or sacred spaces as long as (the treaty) is followed. These conditions will be in seven cities: Orihuela, Valentilla, Alicante, Mula, Bigastro, Bello,[4] Lorca.[5]

(The Christians) will not:[6]

Give residence or shelter any of our enemies.

Promote fear of our religion.

Conceal information of our enemies from our knowledge.

It is incumbent upon him and his companions that they pay each year:

One Dinar.[7]

Four measures[8] of wheat.

Four measures of barley.

Four liquid measures of concentrated fruit juice.

Four measures of vinegar.

Two liquid measures[9] of honey.

Two liquid measures of olive oil.

Half shall be required for slaves.

Witnessed by 'Uthman bin 'Abd 'Abda Al-Qurayshi, Habib bin Abu 'Ubayda bin Maysara Al-Fihri, and Abu Qa'im Al-Hadhli.

Written in 11 rajab, 94 hijra.

Appendix D

The Decree of Al-Mutawakkil

This decree was crafted by the 'Abbasid Caliph Al-Mutawakkil 'Ali Allah Ja'far bin Al-Mu'tasim, known as Al-Mutawakkil. He became Caliph in 847 while the Muslim world was in the midst of a theological crisis between orthodox Islamic theology and the heretical Mu'tazilite movement. Al-Mutawakkil ended the crisis by siding with the orthodox and ordering the destruction of all Mu'tazilite works and the conversion or death of Mu'tazilite intellectuals. His staunch dedication to Islamic orthodoxy defined his reign, and this translated into his relationship with non-Muslims.

The decree given here is directed at Christians and Jews. As evidenced by the language, it is modeled on the Pact of 'Umar. It is more intense than the Pact, but this was common in the Muslim world, as the enforcement of Islamic teaching depended on the will of the ruler in a particular area. The general trend was and remains that the more inclined to Islamic orthodoxy a ruler is, the more aggressive is his enforcement of the Pact's provisions. Al-Mutawakkil's repression of the Christians, particularly in Syria, was what moved St. Theodore to visit him in an attempt to stop the mistreatment.

It is of interesting note that in addition to the fact that Al-Mutawakkil's son Al-Mu'eiyyad converted to the Faith, he also met with St. Cyril while he was still working as an ambassador for the Byzantine Empire. St. Cyril and his brother, St. Methodius, later converted the Slavic peoples in Eastern Europe and created the Cyrillic Alphabet, thus earning them the title of "Apostle of the Slavs."

Al-Mutwakkil was murdered by a Turkish slave in 861.

The Decree of Al-Mutawakkil
From Tabari's History[1]

In that year,[2] Al-Mutawakkil commanded that the Christians and the Dhimmis[3] all wear yellow hoods and zunar belts, ride on saddles with wooden stirrups, install two pommels on the rear of their saddles, and affix two buttons on their hats from a cloth different than their hat's color, in order that the Muslims might distinguish them.

(He ordered) that (the Dhimmis) affix two patches to all that they wear of a different color, and that the patches would be on the front of the chest and on the back, and that each patch be four finger spans in width and of a yellow color. To those who wore turbans, as such they were to be of a yellow color. Those of their women who went out had to wear a yellow wrap. He ordered that their slaves wear zunar belts and he forbade them from wearing those with decorations.

He commanded the destruction of (the Dhimmis') renovated places of worship[4] and that 1/10th of their residences be taken. If the area was spacious enough, it was turned into a mosque, but if it could not be transformed into a mosque, then it was made into open land.[5]

He commanded that the doors of (the Dhimmis') houses have images of wooden devils nailed to them in order to differentiate their residences from those residences of the Muslims.

He ended the employment (of Dhimmis) in civil positions and government work which would give them authority over Muslims.

He prohibited children (of the Dhimmis) from studying in Muslim schools or studying with Muslims. He ceased permitting (the Christians) to display the cross during their Palm Sundays, and from processing in the streets. He ordered that their graves be made level with the ground, so that (none) would stand higher than the graves of the Muslims.

Thus (Al-Mutawakkil) wrote:

In the name of Allah, the Compassionate, the Merciful.

    Allah, may he be blessed and exalted in his glory, who cannot be disputed in his power to do what he wills, has chosen Islam for himself and favored it. He has through (Islam) honored his angels, propagated it by his messengers, and assisted his servants. He embraced it with righteousness, surrounded it with help, and protected it from error. He made it present notable virtues by distinguishing it from (other) laws[6] through making it pure and virtuous, within its laws through charity and nobility, and by their execution with beauty and confidence. He has honored those who propagated it through what he has permitted and prohibited for them. He explained his laws and statues, bound (the Muslims) to (them), and prepared for them great rewards and recompense. He said in (the Quran), by which he commands, prohibits, urges, and counsels:

Verily Allah commands justice and goodness, and giving to ones relatives, and so he forbids indecency, falsehood, and bad behavior, and he admonishes you, that you might remember[7]

He says, prohibiting his people from participating in improper food, drink, and marital relations, and making them superior over the people of the world:

Forbidden from you are carrion, blood, pork, and what name other than Allah has been pronounced over it, that which has been killed by strangulation, beating, crushing or goring, and that which has been eaten by animals, excepting what you have made legal by proper slaughter, and what has been offered to idols. Additionally, divination by arrows is forbidden. [8]

After this, he then concludes with what he forbade for them to participate in. Thus by this verse, he protects his religion and completes his blessing upon his chosen and purified people. Allah, great and exalted, said:

Today I have rejected those who disbelieve from your religion. Fear them not, but fear me. This day I have perfected your religion; I have chosen Islam as your religion. [9]

Allah, the great and exalted, said:

Forbidden to you are your mothers, daughters, sisters, maternal and paternal aunts, nieces, mothers whom have suckled you, siblings by suckling, [10] *mother-in-laws, step-daughters who are under your care whose mothers you have entered into. But if you have not entered into them, there is no blame for you, and permitted are your sons' wives from your own loins, and that you have two sisters among them, except what has already passed, and Allah is forgiving, merciful.*

All married women except those whom your right hand possesses Allah decrees to you, and he makes (all women) permissible for you except the aforementioned, provided that you desire them with your wealth- taking them is without culpability. As for those whom you seek benefit, give them their prescribed dowries, and there is no guilt about what you agree upon after what is prescribed. Verily Allah is knowing and wise.

He who is unable to marry freely may marry a believing woman of those whom you right hand possesses, from your young believing (slave) girls. Allah knows your faith. Some of you are from some (of the same), and so marry them with the permission of their people, and give them their dowries righteously, being chaste women and not fornicating. When they are married, if they fornicate, then punish them with half of what is prescribed for free women. This is for those who fear committing sin among you. That you have patience is better for you, and Allah is forgiving, merciful.

Allah desires that he explains to you and guides you by the traditions of those who were before you, and turns you to repentance, and Allah is knowing, wise.

Verily Allah desires repentance unto him, and he desires those who seek lusts to go greatly astray.[11]

Allah says:

O ye who believe! Verily alcoholic drinks, idols, and divining arrows are the works of Satan. Shun them, in order that you might be successful.

Verily Satan desires that hatred and enmity arise among you through alcoholic beverages, and that he hinder you from remembrance of Allah and prayer. Will you cease?

So obey Allah, the messenger, and beware! If you turn back, know that it is (only) for our messenger to proclaim clearly.[12]

He thereby forbids the Muslims from eating the most impure and dirty (foods) among the people of the world, and from drinking that which arouses enmity, hatred, and hinders remembrance of Allah's name and prayers.[13] He also forbids illicit marriage, for those who understand.

He gives (the Muslims) good qualities and noble virtues. He makes the people of faith faithful, virtuous, merciful, confident, and truthful. He sows neither division nor resistance, nor arrogance, nor boastful pride, nor betrayal, nor perfidy, nor oppression, nor wrongdoing, but he commands the former and forbids the latter, promising paradise and hell-fire as a (respective) reward and punishment.

Allah has specifically chosen and favored the Muslims from his honor. He has made them superior by the religion which he has bestowed upon them, distinguished them from other religions by their laws of charity, upright statutes, and clear proofs. Allah has purified their religion by what he has permitted and forbidden from them. This is by decree from Allah, great and exalted, to strengthen his religion, his will to decisively show his truth, and his desire to complete his blessing upon his people," so that those who perished might perish in order that Allah would place victory and fortune to the pious and disgrace in this life and the afterlife to the infidels."[14]

(The Decree)

The Commander of the Faithful, may Allah grant him success, decided that the Dhimmis in all his provinces, far and near, of all classes, were to wear hoods- which their merchants, their secretaries, and their young and old wear- of a yellow color. None will be permitted to avoid this.

To those who are unable to buy such hoods will take two same-colored cloth pieces to their clothing. They shall have a complete circumference, and be affixed on the outside of the garments in the front and the back.

They shall all fasten buttons on their caps which have a different color than those of caps. They shall stick out when fastened, so not as to adhere and be hidden, or so that which is plaited on may not be hidden.

Likewise, they must take wooden stirrups to their saddles and install pommels on the rear of their saddle bows.

They will not be allowed to remove the pommels from the saddle bows and place them on the sides further back. What they do will be inspected so that the orders of the Commander of the Faithful are compliantly executed. The inspector will spot compliance, as it will be readily visible.

Their male and female slaves who wear girdles must fasten zunar belts and a *kustij* in place of the girdles which were on their waists.[15]

You will instruct your workers in what they are ordered from the Commander of the Faithful. In this way, you will motivate them to execute (the examinations as stated). You shall warn them about circumventing and deviating, and about punishment of Dhimmis who deviate from this way, if by opposition, apathy, or something else, in order that all of them and cling to the path which the Commander of the Faithful has placed upon them, Allah willing.

So know, ye who consider the order of the Commander of the Faithful- dispatch the letter of the Commander of the Faithful to your officers in their respective regions, concerning what will be done, Allah willing.

The Commander of the Believers asks Allah, his lord and master, to bless his slave and messenger Muhammad, his angels, and to sustain him, having made him Caliph and (given) him command of his religion. May he execute Allah's command, which he has done only by Allah's help, and fulfill what he has been appointed to do, and gain a reward and a better recompense. For (Allah) is the Noble, the Merciful.

Written by Ibrahim bin Al-'Abbas in Shawwal, 235 Hijra.[16]

Appendix E

1504 Fatwa to the Moriscos

This fatwa was issued in 1504 as a response to the expulsion of the Mudéjars at the recommendation of Francisco Cardinal Jiménez de Cisneros. The reason for the expulsions was that after the Reconquista finished, there were constant uprisings from the Muslim population in Spain that threatened the nation's ability to survive. Cardinal Cisneros attempted to fix this problem by ordering that Muslims who wanted to stay in Spain would have to convert to the Catholic Faith.

The expulsions did not work as planned. Many converted nominally to the Catholic Faith, but secretly remained Muslims and continued their rebellions throughout the 16th century. The rebellions did not end until 1609 with the expulsion of the Moriscos.

This fatwa is of particular interest because the Grand Mufti of Oran, Ahmad bin Boujam'ah, implores the Moriscos to live as Catholics publicly but to practice Islam in secret and continue their rebellions. This is known as *taqiyya*, by which Muslims are permitted and allowed in Islam to lie to non-Muslims so long as it furthers the spread of Islam. In this case, it was the re-Islamization of Spain. However, since taqiyya is a part of Islamic theology, this fatwa is simply a practical application of Islamic religious teachings that are as relevant today as they were in the days of Cardinal Cisneros and the Reconquista.

Fatwa of Ahmad bin Boujam'ah
Mufti of Oran
To the Moriscos
December 8th, 1504[1]

Praise be to Allah, prayers and peace upon our lord Muhammad, his family, and his companions.

Our brothers were arrested for their faith, as though they were bound over hot coals. For the sake of Allah, they received their reward just the same. Souls and children strove in pleasing him, close strangers, Allah willing, from a neighboring place in the highest heaven of heavens. They mourned the way of the righteous ancestors in bearing hardships. When the souls blossomed into youth, we asked Allah that he would ingratiate us and that he would help us and you to observe the right in good faith and sincerity, and that he would place success among us and you, and a way out from all difficulties. So the peace of his book[2] upon you, and from the lowest of Allah's slaves and who is in the greatest need of forgiveness and blessing, the slave of Allah the great Ahmad bin Boujam'ah of Oran.

As Allah was to all in his goodness and protection, (we were) asking from your loyalty and exile the goodness of supplication as to bring about the goodness of the end (of the current situation) and salvation from the horrors of that land, and gathered with those upon whom Allah has blessed on account of piety, and assuredly upon you in the necessity of the religion of Islam. Amen, upon what came from your children, that they do not fear committing evil against you, who know your enemies in your innermost thoughts, and goodness to the strangers which were pious when the people became corrupted. Verily Allah remembers between the neglectful ones as between life and death.

Know that the hewn wooden idols and carved rocks neither harm nor benefit, and the possessor of all is Allah.[3] Allah does not take a son, and there is nothing with him from god. So worship him and remain steadfast in worship. Pray, (even) if by gesture, give zakat, (even) if it is gestured to your poor or done in hypocrisy, because Allah does not see your outward impression, but your hearts. Perform washing after sexual relations, even if by swimming in rivers. If it is not possible to do prayers, then follow up in the daytime. To dunk is as good as purification in the water.

It is for you to perform tayammum,[4] even if wiped with a hand against the wall. If it cannot be seen, go down for prayer and stay as such, regardless if in water or land, except if it is possible to motion by hand and face to clean dirt or a rock or a tree from which to perform tayammum. So intend to gesture, moving as a secret friend in explaining the letter for his speech (the prayers of Allah be upon him), and come to what you obeyed.

If they make you prostrate to idols in prayer or during the time they gather to pray, forbid by intention and intend that your prayers are legitimate, and show what they show when worshipping idols. Allah has your intentions. If you are unable to face the Qibla[5], in truth it is like the prayer of fear when in battle.[6]

If they make you drink wine, then drink it, for there is no intention of doing it. If they force pork upon you, then eat it as one who denies (eating it), for your hearts intend it is forbidden. The same holds if they make you do something (else) forbidden. If their daughters marry you, it is permissible because they are People of the Book. If they make you marry your daughter to them, then regard this as forbidden except for coercion, for you are married, but in your hearts if you found the power to change it, you would. Likewise if they make you perform usury or that which is forbidden, then do it (while) denying (it) in your hearts.

Then you do not have to (commit usury) except for the heads of your wealth, and intend with the rest, if you confess to Allah the great. If they make you accept words of infidelity, if it is possible for you penance (later) and speak in riddles, then do so. Otherwise be guardians of the hearts with the faith that you uttered and are bound to.

If they say "Curse Muhammad", than curse him saying "Mumad!",[7] for they curse saying "Mumad," intending that he is Satan or an accursed Jew, for many slander his name. If they say "Jesus died on the cross" and they intend (he rose) from the dead, and is perfect and arisen, and his death and his crucifixion and sing his memory openly, repeat what the people do. For Allah made him die and raised him up on high. He did not oppress you, so report what is in it to us, for we advise you, Allah willing, regarding what you wrote in it.

I ask Allah that he guide the world to Islam in order that you worship Allah openly, by Allah's power, without persecution or trials, indeed by the victory of the noble Turks.[8] We testify to you at our hands (before) Allah, (for) you believed in Allah and you are truthful. Your response was necessary. Peace upon you all.

Date: The first of Rajab, year 910 A.H., Allah knows all. May this message reach them, Allah the Great willing.

Appendix F

Sultan Murad III's letter to the "Lutherans" of Flanders and Spain

This letter was written by Sultan Murad III during the late 16th century. It is particularly interesting because of Sultan Murad III's words concerning the Catholic Church and the Papacy. He was an intelligent man, and like previous sultans, he based his attempts at conquest on a divide-and-conquer strategy. He was an avid Muslim, and had no interest in the Protestant movement's religious aspects other than it as being a means to conquer Europe and the Church. As such, he wrote using inflammatory language to appease and draw support from Calvinist revolutionaries fighting against the Church in Europe. Thus while the letter is addressed to the "Lutherans" in Flanders and Spain, the persons he was addressing were actually Calvinists.

The Protestant sentiment towards the Ottoman assistance was mixed. While some Protestants embraced it, many were uncomfortable because they viewed Sultan Murad III's actions as an attempt to exploit the Protestant movement in order to advance his own religious and political ambitions. The Sultan alludes to this at the end of this letter in a veiled threat against those who would reject his offer.

The Calvinists overall accepted the most help from the Ottomans, and at times even assisted in leading military forces alongside the Ottomans against the Catholic Spanish and Habsburgs. Queen Elizabeth engaged in direct correspondence with Sultan Murad III, and for a time it appeared that a strong alliance was growing. However, eventually all of the Protestant-Muslim alliances failed, often because the Ottomans would turn against their Protestant allies.

In addition to the Calvinists, the rebellious elements among the Spanish Moriscos also accepted much fiscal and military assistance from the Ottomans. But this had been taking place since the end of the Reconquista and was confirmed through Grand Mufti Ahmad bin Boujam'ah's 1504 fatwa calling for the Turks to assist the Moriscos in their rebellions. While the Ottoman help was sporadic on account of their numerous military engagements during the 16th century, the help they gave to both the Calvinists and Moriscos nearly caused Spain to collapse from within. This was one of several important factors that prompted St. John of Ribera to push for the expulsion of the Moriscos in 1609.

It is likely that Sultan Murad III's words about the Catholic Faith reflect his own feelings based on his family history. His grandmother[1] was an apostate from Eastern Orthodoxy to Islam, and his mother and wife[2] were Italian apostates from the Catholic Faith. When St. Joseph of Leonessa went to visit and evangelize him, he unsuccessfully attempted to have St. Joseph tortured to death. While he was a Turk in language and culture, he was fully half Italian with the rest of his heritage being a mix of Ukrainian and Turkish.

Perhaps the greatest lesson which can be learned from this letter is that the Ottomans did not care about the religious beliefs or impact of the Protestant movement. Rather, the Sultan viewed his alliances with Protestants as a means to realizing Islam's expansion. This directly mirrored the Ottoman pattern of alliances with and against the Byzantines, Serbians, Ukrainian Cossacks, Venetians, and any other political or religious group during the conquest of the Balkan Peninsula. This strategy was very old, as it had already been applied during the Islamic conquest of Spain and Portugal under Musa ibn Nusayr and his general, Tariq ibn Ziyad in the 8th century.

Author's Note: I do not speak Ottoman Turkish. However, between my command of the Arabic language, a basic knowledge of Turkish grammar and vocabulary, and some careful research using Ottoman dictionaries and texts, I was able to give a general rendering of Sultan Murad III's letter into English. I do not consider it to be a complete translation. Additionally, I also concede there are likely numerous errors on account of the aforementioned reasons. While I was aware of these issues, I chose to render into English and include this document in the text because of its significance to the infamous "Turco-Calvinist" alliance against the Catholic Church during the 16th and 17th centuries and since I had yet to find a complete translation of the text into English.

A copy of the royal letter of the Sultan to the nobles of the followers of the Lutheran school in Flanders and Spain.[3]

To the esteemed nobles of the Christian milla.[4]

To the great leaders of the sect of Jesus in Flanders[5] and Spain who belong to the Lutheran division, and to the Counts,[6] Chiefs,[7] Princes[8], and heads of the Lutherans' noblemen. May Allah realize their intended goals through the (Sultan's) good letter of friendship, which he foremost reached out and commenced.

First, let it be known that the great sultans first prostrate to the ground, that among kings,[9] his majesty rules by the truth of the Messiah. May (the Messiah's) name be blessed, made peaceful, honored, and exalted by the grace of Allah, and Allah's peace and blessings be upon his beloved messenger, our lord Muhammad Al-Mustafa. Gentlemen, may Allah's power and abundant blessings be with you.

First and foremost is this; the fateful, majestic, powerful, omnipotent decree of Allah that his children fight for Allah's righteous majesty and the greatest of Princes, Muhammad Al-Mustafa, Allah's peace and blessings be upon him.

Gentlemen, the truth of our messenger is to the world of the Muslim people, who you believe in and speak by those who profess among you. This hidden and overlooked good, and your truth of your Princes' belief in casting aside doubt is (the means) by which they bring your counts[10] crushing military victories. We with your truthful ones overthrew and destroyed (the Catholics') altars. Your Christians have attacked the altars,[11] the images, the bells, and have renounced the idols. The Almighty has shown his truth by the renunciation (of the idols), and Master Jesus his messenger, and by (renouncing slavery to) belief in idols. And now, my dear, you desire to have the truth of his religion by asking and desiring it (over falsehood). But the faithless Pope and his created religion has misled speech about Lord Jesus, peace be upon him, and made (his followers) cling to idols of gods with their making, altars, and idolatrous images. Your Lord doubts that your princes commit harm to your truth. (But) how many of those who profess (your faith) follow the way of (the Pope's) error, he who conjures up the teachings of Satan in order to seduce and misguide. How much blood of yours is spilled on account of the Pope's unsheathed sword and (his followers) tendency to kill every last one (they meet)![12]

This is our reason for the sultan's mercy, the royal commiseration of every one of us, and struggling in your cause's expenses by land and sea every time with your princely assistance coming forth. First is the tyranny of the (Catholic) religion to us. Your salvation and truth of your religion is compelled to be assisted by necessity, especially in Flanders and Spain. How many of your Chiefs and Princes are so helpful! (But) the Pope, (the Catholic) Faith,[13] and (the Catholics') misguidance hate that which your truthful speech knowingly confesses; the truth of religion and the Source,[14] or that which is enlightened beauty. Oh, the tyranny of (the Catholic) oppression, death, and persistent fear of them, who first caused the affliction!

Live and celebrate your first friendship, your affection, and your official declaration of kindness as our most dear friends, and the intent of his royal majesty the Sultan who first planned it. But this of our first attempts failed, for nobody had believed (us regarding) the first official declaration (of friendship).

But (for) this matter we will support you, being in order that the good faith of the Sultan's official declaration to those who are in charge fight for your cause, (as there was) delay (to) those in charge who had not heard currently (from) the Capitol.[15] Your esteemed speakers, whose names we have not spoken, or to (whom) sided with begrudgingly- the conditions of (the agreement) will not be known. Trust the sacred bond[16] of our communications. You are foremost beloved, befriended, and ingratiated (by) our commiseration, (having) formally opened (relations), dispatched (speakers), pledged (allegiance), and arrived (in Istanbul). This (action) has strength.

If (there is) grief on account of all your faith by rendering and loudly vocalizing[17] (it), Chiefs of the Lutheran's princes and nobles, your friendship surely establishes knowledge (that) this good agreement does not speak with deliberation. For the deliberation is communicated by your mouth, as does paper with knowledge, of which all words are a blessed deliberation, emanating first as having been like one who confesses knowledge.

Additionally, whatever transpired during the time of agreement, the Pope with your religion's military victories and battles renders a desire of assistance. Eight have been informed accordingly, having been faithful, worthy men of Istanbul. Our rod (of leadership) worries not (about) this matter. They do not speak jointly about conditions, knowing what is your appointed time, and gradually (acquiring) military victory. Our rod (of leadership) knows, if that you first seek assistance, (the Sultan) extends himself foremost, knowing the good preparations and sensitive agreement, (lest he) lose the opportunity for aiding your religion's followers in overcoming a grave struggle and striving best.

First then, (let) your and our people speak not of your great honor, (as that would be) superficial. His next meeting- may it aid your steps, take heed of his wounds, accordingly to instill desire of the name of the Imperial letter. Lastly, to those among you who would cheat and deceive- first know the benefits of friendship, the treasure of right guidance, and the desires that it might be. Peace (unto you).

Index

'Abbas, Shah, 225
'Abd Al-'Aziz, 14
'Abd Ar-Rahman Al-Ghafiqi, 30
'Abd Ar-Rahman II, 49
'Abdullah ibn 'Amir Al-Hajib Al-Mansur. *See* Almanzor
'Asma Ad-Din Khatun, 125
'Umar ibn Hafsun, 78
A Refutation of the Saracen's Sect or Heresy. *See* Peter the Venerable of Montbossier, Bl.
Abu 'Abd Ar-Rahman Al-Amin. *See* Jamal Zaytuni
Abu 'Abdullah Muhammad XII. *See* Boabdil
Abu of Tbilisi, St., 38
Abundius, St., 58
Addai Scher, Bishop, 280
Adhemar of Puy, Bishop, 83
Adjutor, St., 86
Adulphus and John, Sts., 51
Agnus of Zaragoza, Bl., 155
Ahmad ibn Ibrahim Al-Ghazi, 253
Al-'Adid Li-Din Allah Abu Muhammad 'Abdullah bin Yusuf Al-Hafiz Li-Din Allah, 125
Albert Avogadro of Jerusalem, Bl., 139
Albertus Magnus, Bl. *See* Thomas Aquinas, St.
Aleaunie, St., 86
Alexander of Sicily, St., 149
Alexander VI, Pope, 242
Alexandrian Crusade, 190

Al-Fa'iz Bi-Din Allah, 125
Alfonso I of Aragón, King, 96
Alfonso I of Portugal, King, 93
Alfonso IV of Portugal, King, 189
Alfonso IX, King, 153
Alfonso the Catholic, King, 15
Alfonso V of Aragón, King, 213
Alfonso VII of Castile, King, 88, 112
Alfonso XI, King, 189
Alhambra Declaration, 244
Al-Kamil, 162
Al-Layth ibn Sa'd ibn 'Abd Ar-Rahman, 37
Almanzor, 73
Almohads, 92
Al-Mu'eiyyad. *See* Theodore of Edessa, St.
Al-Muwahhidun. *See* Almohads
Alodia and Nunilo, Sts., 54
Al-Qama, Islamic Governor of Asturias, 15
Alvarus Paulus, 61
Al-Walid I, 45
Amadeus VI of Savoy, Count, 190
Amator, Louis, and Peter, St., 59
Ambrose of Siena, Bl., 168
Anastasius, Digna, and Felix, St., 57
Andrew, Anthony, John, and Peter, Sts., 64
Angelo Carletti di Chivasso, Bl., 211

Anthony Neyrot, Bl., 198
Anthony of Padua, St., 165
Anthony Ruwah, St., 39
Antoninus of Florence, St. *See* Anthony Neyrot, Bl.
Antonio Primaldo, Bl. *See* Martyrs of Otranto
Apology of Al-Kindi. *See* Peter the Venerable of Montbossier, Bl.
Archbishop Ignatius Maloyan and 447 Companions, Bl., 268
Archil of Kakheti, St., 39
Argentea and Vulfura, Sts., 73
Argymirus, St., 59
Armenian Genocide, 268
Arnaud Amalric, Bl., 151
Arnold of Queralt, Bl., 160
Arnold of Rossinol, Bl., 160
Arnold Serra and Companions, Bl., 201
Ars Magna, 149
Arsenius, Pelagius, and Silva of Arlanza, St., 69
Asad Ad-Din Shirkuh bin Shadhi. *See* Shirkuh
Ashot I of Iberia, St., 40
As-Salih Ismail bin Nur Ad-Din Mahmoud bin 'Ammad Ad-Din bin Aq Sanqar, 125
Asteria, 27
Atilan and Froilan, Sts., 67
Aurea, St., 60
Aurelius, Felix, George, Liliosa, and Natalia, Sts., 55
Bacchus Dahhat, St., 39
Baha' Ad-Din, 127
Bairam, 183

Baldwin II of Jerusalem, King, 117
Baldwin IV of Jerusalem, King, 126
Baphomet, 119
Bartholomew of Bologna, Bl., 187
Bashir bin Qasim Shihab II, Prince, 276
Battle of
 Alarcos, 112
 Ankara, 195
 Arsuf, 118
 Bacente, 253
 Cresson, 126
 Dorylaeum, 85
 Écija, 145
 Guadalete, 14
 'Inab, 104
 Las Navas de Tolosa, 112
 Lepanto, 255
 Marjayoun, 126
 Matapan, 256
 Mohács, 202, 219
 Montisgard, 126
 Niš, 202
 Petrovaradin, 273
 Ramla, 85
 Río Salado, 189
 Simancas, 69
 St. Gotthard, 251
 Valdejunquera, 65
 Valea Alba, 229
 Vaslui, 228
 Vienna, 259
 Wayna Daga, 254
 Wofla, 253
Bayezid II, 202, 210
Beatus of Liébana, St., 29

Begum Sumru. *See* Joanna Nobilis Reinhardt
Benedict of Poland, 171
Benildus, St., 58
Benjamin de Jesus, Bishop, 290
Berard of Carbio and Companions, St., 139
Berengar, the German of Bellpuig, Bl., 151
Berengaria of Navarre, 132
Berlabei, 201
Bernard Calbó, St., 153
Bernard of Clairvaux, St., 98
Bernard of Prades, Bl., 142
Bernard, Grace, and Maria of Alcira, Sts., 95
Bernulf, St., 63
Bertold, St., 104
Better a Turk than a Papist, 220
Bishop Flavianus Michael Malke, Servant of God, 269
Bishop John Andrew Carga, Servant of God, 224
Bl. Eugene III, Pope, 98
Bl. Gregory X, Pope, 157
Bl. Innocent XI, Pope, 240
Bl. Urban II, Pope, 88
Bl. Urban V, Pope, 190
Boabdil, 244
Bobastro, 78
Br. Henry Vergès, 286
Br. Marie-Clement Rodier, 279
Br. Sean Devereux, 286
Brocard, St., 105
Caliph 'Abd Ar-Rahman III, 65
Calixte and Mercurial of Osca, Sts., 73
Callixtus III, Pope, 205, 208

Carlo Carafa, Ven., 239
Casilda, St., 77
Cathedral of
 Oviedo, 16
 St. Mary in Valencia, 18
Catherine of Bosnia, Bl., 209
Cerezo del Río Turón, 63
Ceuta, 326
Charbel Makhlouf, St., 273
Charles Dominic Cristofori. *See* Mark of Aviano, Bl.
Charles Martel, 30
Christopher and Leoviglid, Sts., 56
Christovão da Gama, 253
Church of
 Our Lady of Grace, 247
 Our Lady of Graces, 279
 St. Acislus, 51, 53, 57
 St. Catherine, 272
 St. Christopher in Labruge, 65
 St. James at Compostela, 17
 St. John the Baptist, 7
 St. Mary of the Altar of Heaven in Rome, 211
 St. Peter in Córdoba, 56
 St. Theodore, 40
 St. Vincent, 77
 St. Zoilus, 52, 53
 the Holy Sepulcher, 11
Columba, St., 58
Confutatio Alcorani. *See* Fr. Riccoldo di Monte da Croce
Congregation of Pious Rural Workers, 239
Conrad of Ascoli, Bl., 158
Constantine and David, Princes of Georgia, Sts., 36

Contra Legem Saracenorum.
    See Fr. Riccoldo di Monte
    da Croce
Conversion of the Banu Habib, 47
Cosimo di Medici, Duke, 217
Cosmas of Aphrodisia, St., 94
Daniel and Companions, St., 140
Daniel Comboni, St., 272
Daniel of Arles, St., 64
De Rationibus Fidei contra Saracenos, Graecos, et Armenos ad Cantorem Antiochenum. *See* Thomas Aquinas, St.
Denis of the Nativity and Redemptus, Bls., 226
devşirme, 207
dhow, 69
Diego de Soto, St., 141
Dominic of Silos, St., 76
Don Alfonso De Albuquerque, 245
Dracula. *See* Vladimir III Ţepeş, Prince
Ebbo, St., 26
Egliona, 14
Eighth Crusade, 136
El Cid, 106
Elena. *See* Sultan Yahya
Elias of Heliopolis, St., 36
Elias, Isidore, and Paul, St., 59
Emilian of Cogolla, St., 18
Emilias and Jeremiah, St., 57
Ernest, St., 94
Eugene of Savoy, Prince, 273
Eugenius IV, Pope, 197
Eulogius of Córdoba, St., 61
Europa Point, 212

Eurosia, St., 23
Eusebia and Companions, St., 24
Expulsion of the mudéjars, 248
Fandilas, St., 57
Farzana Khan. *See* Joanna Nobilis Reinhardt
Fatima, Princess, 101
Fatimid Caliphate, 91
Fatwa to the Moriscos, 403
Favila, 16
Ferdinand González of Castile, Count, 69
Ferdinand of Aragón, King, 242
Ferdinand of Portalegre and Eleutherius of Platea, Sts., 144
Ferdinand Perez and Louis Blanc, Sts., 143
Ferdinand, the Holy Prince of Portugal, Bl., 197
Fernando Martins de Bulhões. *See* Anthony of Padua, St.
Fifth Crusade, 135
Filippo Dormeyer, 281
First Crusade, 83
Flora and Maria, Sts., 54
Florian, Calcanicus, and the 56 Martyrs of Eleutheropolis. Sts., 9
Fortún of Pamplona, King, 23
Forty-two Martyrs of Amorion, 41
Fourth Crusade, 135
Fr. Antonio de Gouvea, 226
Fr. Carlos Cuarterón, 279
Fr. Franciscus Georgius Josephus van Lith, 282
Fr. François Bourgade, 279
Fr. Nelson Javellana, 286

Fr. Paul Mulla, 285
Fr. Raymond Martí, 172
Fr. Rhoel Gallardo and the Claret School Martyrs, Servant of God, 290
Fr. Riccoldo di Monte da Croce, 173
Francis of Assisi, St., 162
Francis Xavier, St., 229
Franciscan Martyrs of Damascus, 265
Franciscan Martyrs of Jerusalem. *See* Nikola Tavelić, Adeodat of Rodez, Peter of Narbonne, and Stephen of Cuneo, Sts.
Francisco Cardinal Jiménez de Cisneros, 247
Fraxinetum, 70
Fructus and his brothers, St., 23
García Sánchez I, King, 69
Garnier de Nablus, 132
Gelawdewos, Emperor, 253
George Kastrioti. *See* Skanderbeg
Gerald the Fearless, 106
Gerard Mecatti of Villamagna, Bl., 130
Gerard Thom, Bl., 86
German order of St. Mary in Jerusalem. *See* Order of the Teutonic Knights
Gil Cordero, 188
Giovanni da Prado, Bl., 226
Godfrey of Bullion, 83
Gomidas Keumurgian, Bl., 265
Gonçalo Hermigues, Count, 101
Gonzalo Padilla, 114

Grand Mufti of Oran, 248, *See* Appendix E
Gregory VIII, Pope, 127
Gumesindus and Servus-Dei, Sts., 55
Guy de Lusignan, 127
Habenitus, Jeremiah, Peter, Sabinian, Walabonsus and Wistremundus, Sts., 52
Habsburg Family, 250
Habsburg-Ottoman wars. *See* Habsburg family
Henry the Navigator, 213
Heresy of the Ishmaelites. *See* John Damascene, St.
Hermogius, St., 65
Herod Agrippa I, 17
Hersekzade Ahmed Pasha. *See* Catherine of Bosnia, Bl.
Hoces del Río Duratón Natural Park, 23
Holy League, 254
Holy Name of Mary, 241
Hongwu, Emperor, 186
Hrotsvitha, 65
Ibn Khaldun, 6
ibn Tumart, Abu 'Abdullah Muhammad, 92
Imre Thököly, 259
Iñiga Fortúnez, 23
Innocent III, Pope, 112
Innocent IV, Pope, 171
Isaac Komnenos, 131
Isaac of Córdoba, St., 52
Isabella of Castile, Queen, 242
Ishak-Bey Kraloğlu. *See* Catherine of Bosnia, Bl.
Iskandar Thani, 227
Jabalah ibn Al-Aiham, 19
Jamal Zaytuni, 289

James and Adolph, Sts., 148
James of St. Peter, Bl., 223
James of Tahust, Bl., 212
James the Greater, St., 17
Jerome of Werden, St., 223
Joan of Aza, Bl., 76
Joanna Nobilis Reinhardt, 276
John Capistrano, St., 204
John Damascene, St., 44
John de Matha and Felix of Valois, Sts., 161
John Hunyadi, 202
John I of Portugal, King, 197
John of Cetina and Peter de Dueñas, Bls., 184
John of Gorze, St., 74
John of Montecorvino, Bl., 186
John of Perugia and Peter of Sassoferrato, Sts., 140
John of Plano Carpini, 171
John of Ribera, St., 238
John Sobieski III, King, 258
John VI Kantakouzenos, Emperor, 179
Joseph of Leonessa, St., 230
Josephine Bakhita, St., 274
Juan de Zumarrága, Bishop, 234
Julian of Ceuta, Count, 13
Julian of Cuenca, St., 97
Justus and Pastor, Sts. *See* Urbicius, St.
Ketevan of Mukhrani, Queen of Georgia, St., 224
Khazaria, 38
King Ferdinand I of León, 76
King Louis I of Hungary, 193
King Philip III of Spain, 239
Knights Hospitaller. *See* Order of the Knights of Malta

Knights of Ru'ad Island, 172
Knights of St. George of Alfama. *See* Order of the Knights of St. George
Krujë, 208
Kublai, 158
Lambert of Saragossa, St., 64
Laura, St., 62
Leocritia, St., 61
Leopold I, Emperor, 232
Liber Iudiciorum. *See* King Ferdinand III of Castile, St.
Liber Peregrinacionis. *See* Fr. Riccoldo di Monte da Croce
Los Reyes Católicos. *See* Ferdinand of Aragón, King and Isabella of Castile, Queen
Luis Gallo, Bl., 144
Madruina of Barcelona, St., 75
Majolus, St., 70
Majuma, 35
Mamduh Beğ, 268
Mansur ibn Sarjun At-Taghlabi. *See* John Damascene, St.
Manzikert, Battle of, 71
Mar Toma Audo, Blshop, 281
Mar Yaballaha, 173
Marc Criado, Bl., 223
Marco Bragadin, 236
Marco Polo, 192
Margaret of Province, 155
Maria de Cervellón, St., 159
Mariam Baouardy, Bl., 271
Mark Matthias and Anthony Valesio, Sts., 147
Mark of Aviano, Bl., 232
Marsilius, 94
Martim Moniz, 106
Martyrs of Cardeña, 66

Martyrs of Otranto, 200
Martyrs of Our Lady of the Atlas, 288
Martyrs of the Missionaries of Africa, 287
Martyrs of Tibhirine. See Martyrs of Atlas
Mary, Help of Christians, 237
Matamoros. See James the Greater, St.
Matthew of Beauvais, St., 85
Mehmet Ali Mullazade. See Fr. Paul Mulla
Mehmet Reshid, Dr., 268
Memoriale Sanctorum. See Eulogius of Córdoba, St.
Miguel de Cervantes, 162
Minor Crusade of 1101, 85
Monaldo of Ancona, Francis Petriolo, and Antonio Cantoni, Bls., 146
Monastery of
    Alcobaça, 102
    Cluny, 70
    Gorze in Metz, 74
    San Pedro de Cardeña, 66
    St. Christopher, 52
    St. Emilian de Cogolla, 76
    St. John the Baptist in Burgos, 86
    St. Martín en la Rojana, 56
    St. Mary of Poblet, 95
    St. Peter in Barcelona, 75
    St. Pierre le Vif, 26
    St. Sabas, 19, 45, 55
    St. Salvador en Pinna Mellaría, 58
    St. Sebastian of Silos, 76
    St. Victor in Marseille, 24
    Sts. Justus and Pastor, 56

Tábanos, 52, 55, 57, 58
Zwiefalen, 94
Moussais, 29
Mu'awiya ibn Abu Sufyan, 6
Mu'in Ad-Din Unur Al-Atabeği, 91
Muhammad I, 49
Murad III, 231
Musa ibn Nusayr, 13
Nerses of Iberia, 38
Nicasius of Sicily, St., 129
Nikola Tavelić, Adeodat of Rodez, Peter of Narbonne, and Stephen of Cuneo, Sts., 183
Ninth Crusade, 136
Nur Ad-Din, 91, 125
Odo the Great, 31
Olegarius, St., 96
Olivia, St., 68
On the New Knighthood. See Bernard of Clairvaux, St., See Bernard of Clairvaux, St.
Oppas, Bishop of Seville, 13
Order of
    Alcántara, 113
    Avíz, 111
    Christ. See Order of the Knights Templar
    Monfragüe, 114
    Montesa. See Order of the Knights Templar
    Mountjoy, 114
    Our Lady of Bethlehem, 217
    St. George, 215
    St. James of the Sword, 113
    St. Lazarus, 123
    St. Stephen, 217
    Sts. Lazarus and Maurice, 216

the Dragon, 215
the Knights of St. George, 115
the Knights Templar, 117
the Teutonic Knights, 122
Order of Calatrava, 112
Order of Santiago. *See* Order of St. James of the Sword
Ordoño I, King, 65
Ordoño III, King, 75
Orhan, 179
Orientalism, 178
Osman, Founder of the Ottoman Empire, 179
Our Lady of
   Almudeña, 88
   Covadonga, 13
   Czestochowa, 259
   Europe, 212
   Fatima, 101
   Guadalupe, Extremadura, 188
   Guadalupe, Patroness of the Americas, 234
   Loreto, 169
   Mariamabad, 274
   Mercy, 167
   Puig, 165
   Ransom, 167
   Tekije, 273
   the Rosary, 235
   Victory, 235
Pacificus of Cerano, Bl., 211
Pact of 'Umar. *See* Appendix B and Sophronius, St.
Pál Tomori, 249
Paschal II, Pope, 121
Paul of St. Zoilus, St., 53
Peasant's Crusade, 83
Pedro II of Aragón, King, 115

Pelagius of Asturias, 13
Pelagius the Boy Martyr of Córdoba, St., 65
Pelayo, 15
Perfectus, St., 51
Peter Abélard, 99
Peter Armengol, St., 159
Peter I of Cyprus, King, 190
Peter Malasanc and John of Granada, Sts., 197
Peter Mavimenus, St., 35
Peter Nolasco, St., 166
Peter of Amer, St., 170
Peter of Cadireta, Bl., 145
Peter of Damascus, St., 35
Peter of Mt. Athos, St., 46
Peter of St. Denis, St., 142
Peter Pascual, St., 147
Peter Rodriguez and Companions, St., 142
Peter the Venerable of Montbossier, Bl., 100
Philip IV of France, King, 119
Philip the Fair. *See* Philip IV of France, King
Philippa of Lancaster, 197
Philippe-Jacques Abraham, Bishop, 280
Pierre Claverie, Bishop, 289
Pomposa, St., 58
Porcarius and Companions, St., 24
Prince Lazar of Serbia, St. *See* Catherine of Bosnia, Bl.
Qays ibn Rabi'a Al-Ghassani. *See* 'Abd Al-Masih and Barbar, Sts.
<u>Quantum Praedecessores</u>. *See* Bl. Eugene III, Pope
Radbot, Count, 250

Ramiro II, King, 69
Rawh Al-Qurayshi. *See* Anthony Ruwah, St.
Raymond and William of Granada, Bls., 143
Raymond du Puy, Bl., 87
Raymond Lull, Bl., 148
Raymond Nonnatus, St., 152
Raymond of Blanes, Bl., 141
Raymond of Fitero, St., 97
Raymond of Peñafort, St., 156
Raymond of Roda, St., 96
Raymond of St. Victor and William of St. Leonard, Sts., 142
Raynald of Châtillon, 126
Recemundus of Córdoba, Bishop, 74
Religious Orders
 Carmelites, 104
 Cistercians, 98
 Dominicans, 76
 Mercedarians, 166
 Trinitarians, 161
Richard Plantagenet. *See* Richard the Lionheart
Richard the Lionheart, 131
Roderic, King, 13
Roderick and Salomon, Sts., 60
Rodrigo Álvarez, Count, 114
Rogelius and Servus-Dei, St., 57
Rudesind, St., 75
Saladin, 125
Saladin tax, 131
Salah Ad-Din Yusuf Al-Ayyubi. *See* Saladin
Salur people, 187
Salvatore Lilli and Companions, Bl., 267

Sancho of Aragón, Bl., 145
Sancho the Soldier, St., 52
Sandilia, St., 59
Santiago de Compostela. *See* Church of St. James at Compostela
Savoyard Crusade, 190
Second Crusade, 91
Sens, 26
Serapion, St., 141
Seventh Crusade, 135
Shawar bin Mujayr As-Sa'di, 125
Shihab Family, 276
Shirkuh, 125
Siege of
 Acre, 118
 Alcácer Do Sal., 102
 Antioch, 104
 Askalon, 118
 Belgrade, 205
 Cannanore, 246
 Granada, 244
 Jerusalem, 84
 Jiddah, 246
 Kerak, 126
 Ru'ad Island, 118
 Tangiers, 198
 the Castle of St. George, 106
Siege of Belgrade, 202
Sigismund, Holy Roman Emperor, 202
Simeon, St., 46
Sisenandus, St., 53
Sixth Crusade, 135
Sixtus IV, Pope, 228
Sixtus V, Pope, 247
Skanderbeg, 207
Smyrniote Crusade, 185

423

Sophronius. St., 11
Spanish Inquisition, 244
Spe Salvi. *See* Josephine Bakhita, St.
Speraindeo, 61
Sr. Odette Prevost, 288
Sr. Paul-Hélène Saint-Raymond, 286
Srs. Angele-Marie and Bibiane, 288
Srs. Caridad Álvarez-Mártin and Esther Paniagua-Alonso, 287
St. Bernard's Pass, 70
St. Ferdinand III of Castile, King, 153
St. Louis IX of France, King, 155
St. Pius V, Pope, 237
St. Stephen III of Moldavia, King, 228
Stefano Argercolo de Pendinellis, Bishop. *See* Martyrs of Otranto
Stephen Hercegovic. *See* Hersekzade Ahmed Pasha
Stephen of Blois, 83
Stjepan Vukčić. *See* Catherine of Bosnia, Bl.
Studia Linguarum, 156
Sultan John. *See* Sultan Yahya
Sultan Yahya, 256
Summa Contra Gentiles. *See* Thomas Aquinas, St.
Szymon of Lipnica, St. *See* John Capistrano, St.
Tamerlane, 187
Tancred of Siena, Bl., 152
Tarif ibn Malluk, 13
Tariq ibn Ziyad, 13
Temuraz, 225

The Summary of All the Saracen's Heresies. *See* Peter the Venerable of Montbossier, Bl.
The Words of the False Prophet Muhammad. *See* Peter the Venerable of Montbossier, Bl.
Theobald of Narbonne, Bl., 143
Theoctiste of Lesbos, St., 68
Theodemir, St., 54
Theodore of Edessa, St., 42
Theofrid of Orange, St., 25
Thiemo, St., 85
Third Crusade, 125
Thomas Aquinas, St., 167
Torcatus and Twenty-Seven Martyrs, Sts., 10
Treaty of Granada, 244
Treaty of Karlowitz, 252
Treaty of Żurawno, 258
Turco-Calvinism, 220
Ugo Canefri, St., 151
Umayyad Mosque of Damascus. *See* Church of St. John the Baptist
Urban III, Pope, 127
Urbicius, St., 27
Vasco da Gama. *See* Christovão da Gama
Venturino of Bergamo, St., 185
Victor of Cerezo, St., 63
Vladimir III Țepeș, Prince, 195
Walter Reinhardt, 277
William I of Provence, Count, 70
William of Bas, Bl., 167
William of Castellammare, Bl., 183

William of Gellone, St., 28
William of Rubruck, 171
William the Wise, St., 144
Witesindus, St., 59
Wittiza, King, 13

Yeshaq I of Ethiopia, Emperor, 213
Yusuf An-Nasir, 139
Yusuf ibn Tashfin, 71
Zahara de la Sierra, 243
Zengi, 91

Endnotes

Introduction

[1] Various spellings for Muhammad are used in classical and modern writing. They include Mohammed, Muhammed, Mohammad, Machomet, Mahomet, Mehmed, and Mehmet. For <u>Lions of the Faith</u>, the form Muhammad will be used.

[2] Gen 1:26

[3] For discussion about this issue, see the speeches of Pope Bl. John Paul II. <u>Biblical Account of Creation Analyzed</u>. September 12th, 1979, and <u>Creation as a Fundamental and Original Gift</u>. January 2nd, 1980. Further discussion about this issue can be found in Pope Bl. John Paul II. <u>Man and Woman He Created Them: A Theology of the Body</u>. Trans. Michael Waldstein. Pauline Books & Media. Boston. 2006

Section I

[1] Though the Oriental Orthodox and Assyrian Churches were in a state of schism with Rome, they were very different from heretical groups such as the Arians who denied Jesus' divinity.

[2] For an excellent discussion of the Christian, Jewish, and Pagan persecutions under Islam during the early conquests in classical and modern writings, see Hoyland, Peter. <u>Seeing Islam as Others Saw It</u>. Reprinted by Darwin Press. Princeton. 1997.

[3] "Caliphate" is sometimes written as "Khilafa." It refers to the governance of the temporal world under Islamic theology and law, as the two disciplines are inseparable.

[4] Ibn Khaldun. <u>The Muqaddimah: An Introduction to History</u>. Trans. Franz Rosenthal. Princeton University Press. Princeton. 2005. Page 188.

[5] As quoted by Tertullian in his Apologeticum.

[6] The word *jihad* comes from the Arabic form III verb *jaahada*, meaning "to struggle with somebody for something," and is understood in Islamic theology to mean first the temporal expansion of Islam by military means among non-Muslim peoples. The "spiritual struggle," as is emphasized by many modern Muslim apologists, is at best a secondary and far-less used meaning in Islamic theology. *Jihad* is often confused with the root verb from which it derives, *jahada*, which means "to struggle."

[7] Photo taken by Jan Smith on May 12th, 2010. Licensed under the Creative Commons Attribution/Share-alike Generic License 2.0.

[8] Yarmuk was the site of a great battle between the early Islamic armies and the Byzantines in 636. The Muslim victory there opened the way for Islam's rapid military expansion.

[9] Monothelitism taught that Christ has only one divine will and no human will. It is a heresy, as Christ possessed both as human and a divine will, being that he was both God and man.

[10] The keys of the Church of the Holy Sepulcher were given to an 'Abdullah ibn Nusaybah, who accompanied 'Umar on the early conquests. The Nusaybah family continues to remain as custodians of the church through today. The only time they did not serve as custodians was during the Crusades.

[11] See Appendix B for a translated copy of the Pact of 'Umar.

[12] Feast days also included September 7th and 9th among the sources.

[13] The Count Julian story has been questioned by many scholars. Some say that the story was wholly a legend, and that Julian was actually a Byzantine or a North African by the name of Urban, or perhaps another Gothic count whose name has been lost to history.

[14] Tudmir was the Visigoth governor of Murcia. This agreement was made with 'Abd Al-'Aziz, Musa ibn Nusayr's son. See Appendix C for the complete text.

[15] While there is no doubt from the historical record that Jews assisted the Islamic invasions, there has been question as to the extent of their participation. It seems that their assistance to the Muslims was a reaction to the mutually disagreeable relations they had with the Spanish Visigoth kings.

[16] Though the Vandals and Visigoths were different peoples, both came to Spain as part of the barbarian migrations during the fourth and fifth centuries.

[17] There is a legend that Pelagius was pressed into his rebellion on account of his sister Ormesina being abducted and forced to marry Muslim governor 'Uthman ibn Naissa, known as Munuza. Likewise, some have said that Pelagius sought a political alliance with the Muslims by marrying his sister off to Munuza, which eventually failed.

[18] Virgen de Covadonga. Photo taken by estudiooberon.com on March 2007. Licensed under the terms of the Creative Commons Attribution/Share-alike Unported License 3.0.

[19] St. James the Muslim-Killer. Photo taken by Conan on August 12th, 2009. Licensed under the terms of the Creative Commons Attribution/Share-alike Generic License 2.0.

[20] Pelayo. Photo taken by Luis Villa del Campo on August 6th, 2008. Licensed under the terms of the Creative Commons Attribution/Share-alike Generic License 2.0.

[21] Sometimes written as Onneca.

[22] Some sources list the day at October 19th.

[23] Taken from Steele, Joel and Esther. <u>A Brief History of Mediaeval and Modern</u> Peoples. American Book Company. New York. 1899. Page 23.

[24] Photo taken by Professor Tom Oberhot from his family website, http://home.eckerd.edu/~oberhot/moussais.htm. Used with permission.

[25] Wolf, Kenneth B. <u>Conquerors and Chroniclers of Early Medieval Spain</u>. Liverpool University Press. Liverpool. Second Edition. 1999. Page 145.

[26] THE ROCK OF GIBRALTAR. Photo taken by --=XEON=-- on August 19th, 2007. Licensed under the terms of the Creative Commons Attribution/Share-alike Unported License 3.0.

[27] Photo taken at the California Academy of Arts and Sciences by Tillman on January 18th, 2009. Licensed under the terms of the Creative Commons Attribution/Share-alike Unported License 3.0.

[28] The Roman Martyrology called the people who killed St. Peter of Damascus "Agarines." This is most likely a corruption of "Hagarines," or "sons of Hagar." This is another term for "Ishmaelites," as St. John Damascene uses, since Hagar was the mother of Ishmael.

[29] Quran 5:33. Under Islamic law disagreement with, preaching against, or apostasy from Islam is regarded as an act of war and merits swift, heinous punishment up to and including execution.

[30] Majuma refers to the classical city of Maioumas, known in modern times as the Port-of-Gaza, which is located in the Rimal district. It has been and continues to be the most prosperous area in Gaza, and originally was a port on the Silk Road. Prior to Christianity's arrival, it was a center of paganism until St. Porphyry in the 5th century Christianized the city and destroyed its pagan temples. Maioumas later became a geographic base for the Monophysite heresy, and eventually it was swallowed up around 633 by the Islamic conquests.

[31] See Appendix B for a discussion about the zunar and the Pact of 'Umar.

[32] Layth ibn Sa'd was born in 713 in Egypt. He exerted a great influence on Ahmad ibn Hanbal, who was at the center of the Mu'tazilite

controversy of the 9th century and who is regarded as one of the Islam's greatest thinkers. It is said that Layth was more knowledgeable and faithful than many of the more famous Muslim scholars. He died in 791.

[33] Byzantine Authors: Literary Activities and Preoccupations. Ed. John Nesbitt. Brill. Leiden, Netherlands. 2003. Page 101.

[34] The 'Abbasids usurped power from the Umayyads in 750.

[35] There is a similar story narrated in the Miracles of St. George about a monk named Pachomios which contains the same time and historical details with minor variations. It is speculated that the semi-legendary Pachomios is the same person as the real St. Anthony Ruwah.

[36] Location unknown.

[37] Harun Ar-Rashid is regarded as one of the greatest 'Abbasid Caliphs. He was very interested in theology, and was a central figure in the Mu'tazilite controversy about the question of whether or not the Quran was an uncreated or created document.

[38] See Appendix D.

[39] Some Muslims may argue that the Caliphate is passed by a general voting consensus, known as *ijma'*. This was practiced on occasion throughout history, and was an exception rather than a rule. The 'Abbasids passed power via father-to-son as did the Umayyads, Fatimids, Mamluks, Ottomans, and other Islamic empires.

[40] While Al-Mu'eiyyad is not a canonized saint, some sources say his memory is celebrated on May 3rd.

[41] St. Sabas monastery. Photo taken by Jean and Nathalie on May 4th, 2011. Licensed under the terms of the Creative Commons Attribution/Share-alike Generic License 2.0.

[42] This was part of the infamous "White Slave Trade" (An-Nukhaas) that did not stop until the early 19th century when American Marines

forced the end of Muslim piracy by destroying the armies of the Ottoman-controlled Beğ of Tripoli. This was the inspiration for the US Marines' hymn:

> "From the halls of Montezuma to the shores of Tripoli,"
> "We fight our country's battles, in the air, on land, and sea."

[43] This was an 8th century controversy involving the use of images in Christian worship. It arose in the east and was most likely influenced by the Islamic disdain of images in holy places.

[44] There is debate as to the veracity of this story. It has been suggested that St. John left because Al-Walid was attempting to divest Christians from his administration.

[45] The Ka'ba is a large, black box in the center of Mecca. Whenever Muslims pray, they pray in its direction. The focus of the Ka'ba is a black stone, known as *Al-Hajar Al-Aswad*, which Muhammad claimed was the first stone of the Ka'ba laid by Abraham and Ishmael. It is regarded as the holiest place in Islam. As far as Muhammad's claims are concerned, there is no proof to corroborate them other than his own assertions.

[46] See St. John of Damascus in The Fathers of the Church. Vol. 37. Translated by the Catholic University of America. CUA Press. 1958. Pages 153-160.

[47] While it is sometimes claimed that St. Peter of Mount Athos was one of the first settlers, there were Christian hermits who resided there centuries earlier than he.

[48] St. Nicholas, also called "The Wonderworker," was a 4th century Bishop of Myra and was the inspiration for the legend of Santa Claus. St. Simeon's story may be found in Luke 2:23-35.

[49] From the Arabic *mu'arraba*, meaning "one who is arabized."

[50] For a further discussion of the incident, see the Quran 33:37 and At-Tabari, Muhammad ibn Jarir. The History of Al-Tabari. Volume XXXIX. Trans. Ella Landau-Tasseron. SUNY Press. Albany. 1998. Pages 180-181.

[51] The monastery of Tábanos is better known as the "Monasterio de Tavana." Its location is not known, but circumstantial evidence suggests it was in the woods approximately six or seven miles north of Córdoba.

[52] Memoriale Sanctorum, Book I, Chapter IV, Paragraphs 44 and 45.

[53] The sources also refer to Natalia as Sabigoth.

[54] Memoriale Sanctorum, Book II, Chapter X, Paragraph 10.

[55] Relics of the Martyrs of Córdoba. Taken by Lancasterman88 on October 21st, 2009. Licensed under the terms of the Creative Commons Attribution/Share-alike Generic License 3.0.

[56] Some sources say it was boiling pitch.

[57] St. Eulogius of Cordoba. Cathedral of Cordoba. 17th century. Unknown artist. Library of the Diocese of Cordoba. Licensed under the terms of the Creative Commons Attribution/Share-alike Unported License 3.0.

[58] Some sources refer to Labruge as "Labrugia." This location is in the Vila do Conde district in northern Portugal. St. Christopher's church was eventually built next to the monastery around 1100. The church still exists but the monastery does not.

[59] For an interesting study about homosexuality among the Spanish Muslim Caliphs, and particularly St. Pelagius' case, see Olsen, Glenn. The Sodomitic Lions of Granada. Journal of the History of Sexuality. Vol. 13. No. 1. January 2004. Pages 1-25.

[60] The idea that Muslims worshipped idols was a common misconception among Catholics in central Europe, who were seldom exposed to Islam. This misconception was less found among the

Byzantines, Italians, Portuguese, or Spanish, as they were in frequent contact with Islam.

[61] From Güemes, Lucas. Historia de la Vida, Sepulchro, Reliquias y Congrecación del Inclito Martir San Vitores. Pascual Polo. Burgos. 1849.

[62] Cueva de San Millán de la Cogolla. Photo taken by aherrero on February 10th, 2008. Licensed under the terms of the Creative Commons Attribution/Share-alike Generic License 2.0.

[63] St. Olivia would have been placed in the martyr section, but there are questions as to her existence. Nevertheless, her story certainly parallels the experience of many young women kidnapped by Muslims and at the very least served as an inspiration to the faithful.

[64] It has been noted that her story may be based on that of the 4th century St. Mary of Egypt. However, her experiences with Islam are of notable mention, as with St. Olivia.

[65] Some accounts say it was St. Emilian of Cogolla.

[66] Dhow at Zanzibar. Photo taken by Harvey Barrison on June 4th, 2012. Licensed under the terms of the Creative Commons Attribution/Share-alike Generic License 2.0.

[67] Almoravid is the latinization of the phrase "al-Murabitun," meaning "those from Rabat."

[68] Via Great St. Bernard Pass. Photo taken by Tomislav Medak on July 30th, 2009. Licensed under the terms of the Creative Commons Attribution/Share-alike Generic License 2.0.

[69] Also known as St. Madrona or Matrull.

[70] Catedral de Burgos. Photo taken by Juan Ramon Rodriguez Sosa on September 2nd, 2010. Licensed under the terms of the Creative Commons Attribution/Share-alike Generic License 2.0.

Section II

[1] There are four accounts of Pope Bl. Urban II's speech at Clermont. Each one is slightly different than the others, but all emphasize this common theme. The most often referred to was given by the Frankish chronicler Fulcher of Chartres.

[2] When the Crusades are spoken about, they most often mean those to the Middle East. However, the support of the Reconquista eventually grew into becoming part of the crusader movement.

[3] One example was chronicled by the Muslim traveler Ibn Jubayr in the city of Tibnin in 1184. Notice that it is Ibn Jubayr who is critical of his fellow Muslims for being friendly with the French Crusaders-

"We moved from Tibnin- may Allah destroy it- at daybreak on Monday. Our way lay through continuous farms and ordered settlements, whose inhabitants were all Muslims, living comfortably with the Franks. Allah protect us from such temptation. They surrender half their crops to the Franks at harvest time, and pay as well a poll-tax of one dinar and five qirat for each person. Other than that, they are not interfered with, save for a light tax on the fruits of trees. Their houses and all their effects are left to their full possession. All the coastal cities occupied by the Franks are managed in this fashion, their rural districts, the villages and farms, belonging to the Muslims. But their hearts have been seduced, for they observe how unlike them in ease and comfort are their brethren in the Muslim regions under their Muslim governors. This is one of the misfortunes afflicting the Muslims. The Muslim community bewails the injustice of a landlord of its own faith, and applauds the conduct of its opponent and enemy, the Frankish landlord, and is accustomed to justice from him."

(Taken from Ibn Jubayr, The Travels of Ibn Jubayr, trans. Ronald Broadhurst. London. 1952. Page 315)

[4] There are accounts of Catholic soldiers in the Crusader States marrying Middle Eastern Christians and even Muslim women who converted to the Catholic Faith. However, the general trend was for

Crusader knights to return to Europe following completion of their pilgrimage. The exceptions to this were the Catholic Military Orders, who established long-term residency and also realized the greatest temporal and spiritual achievements during the Crusader period.

[5] In the Muslim world, the Crusades were a small episode because Islam's dominance was not permanently affected. This is reflected in that the first Muslim history of the Crusades was not written until 1899, entitled The Wars of the Cross. The post 20th century views of certain Muslim thinkers about the Crusades are a modern innovation based on promoting a specific vision of history rather than historical fact.

Islamic scholar James Kritzeck notes about the Muslim view on scholarship of not just the Crusades, but Medieval Europe compared to the work done by Christians and the Church among Muslims that:

Mediaeval Islam, in sum, appears to have paid Christian Europe the supreme insult of a virtually total disinterest. Distorted images (no single one, surely) there were, and information was scanty, always inadequate, and often false. But the Muslims lived in a complacent, ideologically seated world which was simply incurious about Europe. Proximity, rather than familiarity, bred contempt. Centuries later, after the struggles and storms whose effects are still felt in the Islamic world, they were forced to change. The parallels between their mediaeval situation and one which confronts and disturbs all of humanity today are, to say the least, striking. It is unfortunate that history here seems to suggest no solution.

(see Kritzeck, James. Moslem-Christian Understanding in Mediaeval Times: A Review Article. Comparative Studies in Society and History. Vol. 4. No.3. April 1962. Page 401.)

[6] Photo taken by seetheholyland.net on April 18th, 2010. Licensed under the terms of the Creative Commons Attribution/Share-alike Generic License 2.0.

[7] There were three battles at Ramla between 1101 and 1105. The first and third, respectively in 1101 and 1105, were Crusader victories.

[8] During the Crusades they were referred to as the Knights Hospitaller. However, they are also known as the Knights of Rhodes and the Knights of Malta, as they were stationed at both locations in the centuries following the Crusades. Since all three names are historically appropriate titles, they will be used in the context of their particular historical circumstances. Today, they are known as the Knights of Malta.

[9] There are other but less accepted accounts that St. Adjutor ran all night until he reached France.

[10] Public domain Image.

[11] The accounts are given by four chroniclers: Badric of Dol, Fulcher of Chartres, Guibert of Nogent, and Robert the Monk. All four versions may be found in Allen, S.J. and Amt, Emilie, editors. <u>The Crusades: A Reader</u>. University of Toronto Press. 2003. Pages 39-47. Fulcher of Chartres' chronicle is often the most referred to.

[12] Statue of Our Lady of Almudeña in the Almudeña Cathedral, Madrid, Spain. Photo taken by Bernard Gagnon on September 23rd, 2009. Licensed under the terms of the Creative Commons Attribution/Share-alike Unported License 3.0.

[13] Tawhid means "unification" in Arabic. It derives from the verb *wahhada*, meaning "to make something one" or "to unify." It refers to the Islamic concept of monotheism, which Islam often pits against what it claims to be the "polytheism" of Christianity. The irony of this term is that "unification" naturally means the making one from two or more separate parts, from which then follows the question of what elements are being united. However, this fact is often ignored by Islamic theologians.

[14] Statue of King Alfonso Henriques. Lisbon, Portugal. Photo taken by OsvaldoGago on May 21st, 2005. Licensed under the terms of the Creative Commons Attribution/Share-alike Unported License 3.0.

[15] Reproduction of an Almohad flag from the 11th through 13th c. by Ivan Sache. June 15th, 2003. Licensed under the terms of the Creative Commons Attribution/Share-alike Unported License 3.0.

[16] This is in contrast to the "Black Robes" which Benedictine monks wore.

[17] Peter Abélard was a theologian turned monk who had a love affair and out-of-wedlock child born to a fellow student turned nun, Heloise. He was a source of much controversy in the medieval world.

[18] See Sancti Bernardi Abbatis Clarae-Vallensis de Consideratione Libri Quinque ad Eugenium Tertium. Patrologia Latina. Vol. 182. Courtesy of Chadwyck-Healy Database via ProQuest.

[19] Pope Pius XII. Doctor Mellifluus. May 24th, 1953.

[20] Taken from Wishart, Alfred W. A Short History of Monks and Monasteries. Albert Brandt. Trenton. 1900. Page 193. Public Domain Image.

[21] Mary is called "Maryam" by Muslims.

[22] Castle of Alcácer do Sal. Alentejo, Portugal. Photo taken by Francisco Santos on March 23rd, 2007. Licensed under the terms of the Creative Commons Attribution/Share-alike Generic License 2.0.

[23] Sheen, Venerable Bishop Fulton J. The World's First Love. McGraw-Hill Book Company. New York. 1952. Page 208.

[24] Our Lady of Fatima Shrine. Photo taken by Beyond Forgetting on April 28th, 2005. Licensed under the terms of the Creative Commons Attribution/Share-alike Generic License 2.0.

[25] Castillo de Calatrava. Photo taken by zubitarra on April 7th, 2010. Licensed under the terms of the Creative Commons Attribution/Share-alike Generic License 2.0.

[26] The Castle was known as "Al-Ushbuna," which is the arabization of the word "Lisbon." However, as the Crusaders sought the intercession of St. George for victory, it was renamed the Castle of St. George.

[27] While El Cid is often portrayed as a hero, the historical record suggests otherwise. He played off the rivalry between the Kingdoms of Aragón and Castile to cement his own political rule. He consistently supported the Muslim ta'ifa ruling Banu Hud dynasty against the Catholics. El Cid's assistance he gave to the Muslims in the battles of Graus (1063), Cabra (1079), Piedra Pisada (1084) and Morella (1084) so weakened the Kingdom of Aragón that it found itself unable to defend its borders against the invading Almoravids. His actions did long-term and nearly irreparable damage to the Reconquista. He is a popular historical figure, but not one of positive notable mention to the Catholic Church's struggle with Islam.

[28] Beja is a city located in southwestern Portugal, and was hotly contested between the Catholics and the Muslims during the Portuguese Reconquista. It should not be confused with Bejaa, which is located in northern Tunisia and was a major slaving port during this same period.

[29] Mackay, Charles. Memoirs of Extraordinary Popular Delusions. Vol II. London. 1852. Page 23. Public domain Image.

[30] Rabbah may have been the name of a local Muslim lord.

[31] The reason for this was to prevent bringing Moriscos into the order who nominally converted to the Catholic Faith but who secretly still continued to practice Islam and work against the Church. This was a serious problem in Spain and Portugal and was a major reason that precipitated the Spanish and Portuguese Inquisitions.

[32] See the Knights Templar.

[33] Extremadura, Spain. Taken by Philip Capper on September 29th, 2005. Licensed under the terms of the Creative Commons Attribution/Share-alike Generic License 2.0.

[34] See St. Bernardi Abbatis De Laude Novae Militiae ad Milites Templi Liber. Patrologia Latina. Vol 182. Courtesy of Chadwyck-Healy Database via ProQuest.

[35] Baphomet is a corruption of the European "Mahomet," which comes from the Turkish word "Mehmet," meaning "Muhammad."

[36] From Archer, Thomas. The Crusades: The Story of the Latin Kingdom of Jerusalem. Putnam. New York. 1894. Page 176. Public domain image.

[37] The technical founding date is 1190, but their active military presence in the Holy Land did not begin until 1192.

[38] Luke 16:19-31

[39] Mackay, Charles. Memoirs of Extraordinary Popular Delusions. Vol II. London. 1852. Page 85. Public domain Image.

[40] Shirkuh was a very fat man, and the Islamic chroniclers note that he died of obesity.

[41] Saladin Statue. Taken by Graham van der Wielen on March 3rd, 2008. Licensed under the terms of the Creative Commons Attribution/Share-alike Generic License 2.0.

[42] Raynald of Châtillon. Taken by Richard Bolla on October 11th, 2008. Licensed under the terms of the Creative Commons Attribution/Share-alike Unported License 3.0.

[43] Sometimes celebrated on May 18th, 23rd, or 25th. The sources do not agree on which particular date his celebration takes place.

[44] He may have died in 1230. The dates are not specifically clear from the available sources.

[45] From Khalidi, Dr. Walid. All That Remains: The Palestinian Villages Occupied and Depopulated by Israel in 1948. Institute for Palestine

Studies. 2006 . Public domain Photo. The quote on the bottom of the photograph says "Hattin in 1934."

[46] Historians have noted this penance was connected at least twice with allusions to the "sin of Sodom." It is possible that Richard may have had bisexual or homosexual tendencies. Whatever sins he committed, it is of greater relevance that Richard piously sought forgiveness for these and his other sins through frequent confession and penance.

[47] John became the next King of England. The Magna Carta was written to curtail King John's attempts to seize absolute power. He was excommunicated by Pope Innocent III in 1209 for his attempts to suppress and seize Church assets. It is said that in response, John sent emissaries to the Spanish Almohad Emir Abu 'Abdullah Muhammad An-Nasir, saying that he would convert to Islam and give England to the Almohads if they assisted him. The Emir was said to have been so disgusted with John's behavior that he demanded the emissaries leave at once and that John was such a disgrace he was not worthy of an alliance with Islam. See Ronay, Gabriel. The Tartar Khan's Englishman. Cassel Publishing. London. 1978. Pages 28-34.

[48] Dickens, Charles. A Child's History of England. Henry Altemus. Philadelphia. 1897. Page 81. Public Domain Image.

[49] Mamluk comes from the Arabic "ma muluk," meaning "those owned by the kings." There were many of such persons throughout Islamic history, as slaves and slave armies played major roles in the Muslim world since Islam's inception. The Mamluks referred to here and in most historical Islamic documents were mostly Central Asians who were brought to Egypt as slaves and were converted to Islam. Under 'Izz Ad-Din Aybek At-Turkmani Al-Jashnakir As-Salihi, known as Aybek, he overthrew Saladin's Ayyubid Dynasty around 1249 and ushered in the Mamluk Bahri Dynasty.

[50] Finkel, Caroline. Osman's Dream: The Story of the Ottoman Empire. Basic Books. New York. 2005. Page 2. Osman is the Turkish form of the Arabic name 'Uthman, which traces its roots to the Third Caliph of the Islamic Empire who ruled from 644 to 656.

[51] Our Lady of Mercy. Taken by Antobeli on September 24th, 2009. Licensed under the terms of the Creative Commons Attribution/Sharealike Unported License 3.0.

[52] The Carmelite Order venerates him as a saint, while his formal recognition in the universal Church is as a beatified person.

[53] The Sultan may have been a local governor, although it is possible they may have been taken to Africa to see the Caliph himself. If it was the Caliph, it would have been Abu Zakarya Al-Mu'tasim Yahya bin An-Nasir. This Caliph recently ordered his father Abu Muhammad drowned so he could seize the Caliphate from him.

[54] He also may have been Irish.

[55] The Sultan is listed in the Catholic sources as a "Selin Banimarin," which likely means Salim of the Banu Marin tribe. At the time, there were a series of wars going on in Algeria between the Almohads, Hafsids, and Marinds. This Sultan in question may have been a local official or judge for the Marinids, but details are unclear.

[56] The name "Muhammad Alicur" does not appear as the ruler of Tunis at the time St. Peter was executed, as the Hafsid Caliph Abu Zakarya Yahya bin Hafs Al-Awwal was ruler. "Muhammad Alicur" may have been a judge or regent governor who sentenced St. Peter to death.

[57] The source uses the word "Turks" and not "Muslims." It should be noted that the Turks did not have a formidable naval presence in the Mediterranean until several centuries later under the Ottoman Empire. The only Muslim naval powers in the Mediterranean at this time were either the Hafsids in Tunis, the Almohads of Muslim Spain, or the Mamluks in Egypt.

[58] St. Ferdinand of Portalegre was martyred four years later when he was in route to North Africa on another mission of redemption.

[59] This was the Hafsid ruler Abu 'Abdullah Muhammad Al-Mustansir ibn Abu Zakarya bin 'Abdullah Abu Muhammad 'Abd Al-Wahid. He was

the same ruler under which King St. Louis IX of France unsuccessfully attacked Tunis during the Eighth Crusade in 1270.

[60] Burning a man to death in Islam is the most severe punishment because it is a sign of unquestionable damnation by Allah, as the pains caused by the fire burning a person alive are believed to continue into eternity. It is only given to those persons regarded by Islam as being destined for hell. This includes apostate Muslims as well as those who obstinately refuse to convert to Islam when pressured to. While Muhammad and his followers used this punishment during Islam's early days, even the Islamic historical record suggests this punishment was sparingly used because of the severe message it communicates.

[61] The Albigensian Crusades were similar to the Northern Crusades in that they were inspired by the Middle Eastern Crusades but did not involve Muslims.

[62] Some say the year was 1314, but 1286 seems to be the more likely date.

[63] The Catholic sources say the Sultan's name was Mahomet Alicut. However, there were only two potential Sultans of Tunis during this period. The first was the actual Hafsid ruler Abu Hafs 'Umar from 1293 to 1295. The other was his rival and after his death, the next actual ruler, Abu 'Asida Muhammad Al-Muntasir, from 1295 to 1309. It is more likely that Mahomet Alicut was a latinization of "Muhammad Al-Qadi," or Muhammad the judge, meaning that it may have been a local Muslim judge and not the Sultan who ordered the executions. However, the definitive answer has been lost to history.

[64] The castle in question was not specified in the sources, although it may have been the Sultan's palace.

[65] Ramon Llull. Taken by Miquel Cabot on April 15th, 2011. Licensed under the terms of the Creative Commons Attribution/Share-alike Unported License 3.0.

[66] The man who gave the order for execution is listed as a Moulay Mahomet. This may mean the Hafsid ruler of Tunis, Abu Darba

Muhammad Al-Mustansir Al-Lihyani. However, since the term Moulay is used, which is the Latinization of the Arabic *mawli*, meaning *lord*, it may have been a local official who gave the order for the execution.

[67] Bl. Arnaud is accused of saying the phrase "Kill them all, for the Lord knows his own" in reference to the massacres of the Cathars at Beziers, France in 1209. This accusation originated from the Cistercian monk and writer Caesar of Heisterbach who said that Bl. Arnaud allegedly said it. Speculations aside, it is definitively known that Bl. Arnaud wrote to Pope Innocent III about how the massacre of the Cathars was incited by persons of "low rank" and not by his or any other major Catholic leader's command:

"While discussions were still going on with the barons about the release of those in the city who were deemed to be Catholics, the servants and other persons of low rank and unarmed attacked the city without waiting for orders from their leaders. To our amazement, crying "to arms, to arms!", within the space of two or three hours they crossed the ditches and the walls and Beziers was taken. Our men spared no one, irrespective of rank, sex, or age, and put to the sword almost 20,000 people. After this great slaughter the whole city was despoiled and burnt."

See The History of the Albigensian Crusade: Peter of les Vaux-de-Cernay's Historia Albigensis. Trans. W.A. Sibly and M.D. Sibly. Boydell Press. Woodbridge. 2002. Page 142.

[68] St. Ferdinand III of Castile's statue in Madrid's Sabatini Gardens. Photo taken by Luis Garcia on July 1st, 2007. Licensed under the terms of the Creative Commons Attribution/Share-alike Generic License 2.0.

[69] King St. Louis IX of France Statue in Aigues-Mortes, Languedoc, France. Photo taken by Andy Hay on August 6th, 2006. Licensed under the terms of the Creative Commons Attribution/Share-alike License 2.0.

[70] St. Bonaventure. The Little Flowers of St. Francis. Reprinted by E.P. Dutton and Company. New York. 1951. Pages 55-57.

[71] St. Francis before the Sultan by Giotto di Bondone. Photo by Petrusbarbygere on April 1st, 2005. Licensed under the terms of the Creative Commons Attribution/Share-alike Unported License 3.0.

[72] January 31st in the pre-1969 calendar. His feast day has been moved several times.

[73] Also Our Lady of Mercy.

[74] Ibn Sina, a 10th century Persian Muslim philosopher.

[75] Ibn Rushd, a famous 12th century Spanish Muslim jurist.

[76] Muhammad Al-Ghazali, a 11th century Persian Muslim scholar and perhaps the greatest philosopher in Islamic history.

[77] This can be found in <u>Summa Contra Gentiles</u>, Book I, Chapter 6. English translation with a parallel Latin text by Joseph Kenny, O.P. Hanover House. New York. 1955-1957.

[78] This book can be found in translation by Fr. Damian Fehlner, edited by James Likoudis, and sold under the title <u>Aquinas on Reasons for Our Faith: Against the Muslims, Greeks, and Armenians</u>. Franciscans of the Immaculate. 2002.

[79] Tersatto is located in the modern city of Trsat, Rijeka, Croatia.

[80] It is interesting to note that on account of these miracles, Our Lady of Loreto is also known as the Patroness of pilots.

[81] Basilica of the Holy House. Taken by Massimo Roselli on July 26th, 2006. Licensed under the terms of the Creative Commons Attribution/Share-alike Unported License 3.0.

Section III

[1] This date is the reason why September 11th, 2001 was chosen for the attacks against the World Trade Center in New York City.

[2] Finkel, Caroline. Osman's Dream: The Story of the Ottoman Empire. Basic Books. New York. 2005. Page 2.

[3] For centuries, the Byzantines regarded Constantinople as the "Rome" of the East. The references to "Rum" ("Rome" in Arabic) refer to Constantinople, and were only used much later by Muslim writers to describe Rome, Italy.

[4] Bust of Osman I, founder of the Ottoman Empire in Söğüt, Turkey. Photo taken by Maderibeyza on December 22nd, 2007. Licensed under the terms of the Creative Commons Attribution/Share-alike Unported License 3.0.

[5] 'Eid Al-Adha is a four-day celebration, which begins on the 10th day of Dhu Al-Hijjah, which is the last month of the Islamic calendar.

[6] Jaffa Gate. Photo taken by Herwig Reidlinger on May 15th, 2005. Licensed under the terms of the Creative Commons Attribution/Share-alike Unported License 3.0.

[7] Mountains around Izmir. Photo taken by Ian W. Scott on May 9th, 2010. Licensed under the terms of the Creative Commons Attribution/Share-alike Generic License 2.0.

[8] Kublai, who Marco Polo met with, had recently died.

[9] Also known as Timur.

[10] Feast Day is unknown.

[11] Our Lady of Guadalupe, Extremadura. Photo taken by Emman on May 4th, 2006. Licensed under the terms of the Creative Commons Attribution/Share-alike Unported License 3.0.

[12] Monument to Count Amadeus VI of Savoy, Piazza Palazzo di Citta, Turin, Italy. Photo taken by Franco56 in March 2007. Licensed under the terms of the Creative Commons Attribution/Share-alike Unported License 3.0.

[13] The full name of Marco Polo's book was <u>The Book of the Marvels of the World</u>, and was transcribed by Rustichello da Pisa while Marco was imprisoned due to a conflict between Genoa and Venice following his return from the Far East.

[14] Bust of Marco Polo from Rouen, Haute-Normandie, France. Photo taken by Frederic Bisson on April 3rd, 2012. Licensed under the terms of the Creative Commons Attribution/Share-alike Generic License 2.0.

[15] Now in Romania.

[16] d. 1095.

[17] Prince Vladimir III Țepeș nominally converted to the Catholic Faith as a part of a conflict between him and *Athleta Christi* John Hunyadi's son, Matthias Corvinius. In spite of his conversion, Prince Vladimir's Catholicism seems to have been little more than a nominal means to secure his own power over conflicts with the Kingdom of Hungary. This combined with his merciless actions towards to the Muslim people, regardless of the immorality of the Ottoman invasions, are the reasons he is not included in this book.

[18] It is said that the unknown engineer name's was "Urban" or "Orban." The cannon he designed was the inspiration for the "Great Turkish Bombard," which was used by the Ottomans in future sieges. It is possible the engineer may have been a German.

[19] The day was May 22nd, 1453. It is also said that there was also a total lunar eclipse that happened then, which many people interpreted as another sign of the city's coming fall. See Mijatović, Čedomilij. <u>Constantine, the Last Emperor of the Greeks: or, the Conquest of Constantinople by the Turks</u>. Sampson Low, Marston, & Co. London. 1892. Pages 191-193. See also Guillermier, Pierre and Koutchmy, Serge. <u>Total Eclipses: Science, Observations, Myths, and Legends.</u>

Springer-Praxis Series in Astronomy and Astrophysics. Paris. 1999. Pages 85-86.

[20] It is likely the Caliph in question was the Hafsid ruler Abu 'Umar 'Uthman Bin Muhammad Al-Mansur. At the time, he was actively supporting the last Islamic resistance against the Spanish and Portuguese Reconquista.

[21] It is possible that "Berlabei" may have derived from the Turkish phrase "Beğlerbeğ," meaning "Lord of Lords," and was a term associated with high-ranking military officers or government officials. Thus, it may be that "Berlabei" was not an actual man's name, but a high-ranking officer present at Otranto who converted to the Catholic Faith and was likewise martyred.

[22] Matthew 10:39 and Luke 17:33.

[23] Sisa, Stephen. The Spirit of Hungary: A Panorama of Hungarian History and Culture. University of Michigan. 1990. Page 56.

[24] Statue of John Hunyadi at Heroes' square in Budapest, Hungary. Photo taken by Karelj on April 2009. Licensed under the terms of the Creative Commons Attribution/Share-alike Unported License 3.0.

[25] Also recognized feast day on October 23rd.

[26] Janissaries were made of Christian and Jewish boys who were abducted by the Ottomans at birth or a young age, castrated, and forced to serve as super-soldiers in the Ottoman army. This was part of the infamous devşirme, or "blood-tax" system.

[27] Statue of St. John Capistrano outside of St. Stephen's Church, Stefansplatz, Vienna, Austria. Photo taken by author in March 2004. Licensed under the terms of the Creative Commons Attribution/Share-alike Unported License 3.0.

[28] Sometimes written as Scanderbek or Skanderbeğ.

[29] Meaning "blood-tax." See Section III, note 26. Often times, boys taken as part of the blood-tax were castrated. However, since Skanderbeg was pledged by his father instead of being taken by force, he was not castrated. His descendants escaped to Italy after Albania's fall and carrying the Castriot family name, their bloodline and legacy continues today. One modern descendant is the Albanian-Italian author Giorgio Castriota.

[30] Beğ (pronounced "bay") means "Lord" in Turkish. Hence the name "Skanderbeg" means "Lord Alexander."

[31] Skanderbeg statue. Photo taken by Thomas Quine on May 12th, 2010. Licensed under the terms of the Creative Commons Attribution/Share-alike Generic License 2.0.

[32] Bl. Muhammad Abdalla's feast day is celebrated by the Mercedarian Order on February 22nd.

[33] At the time, Ethiopia was involved in heavy fighting against the Egyptian Mamluk Empire. Other Islamic rebellions in Somalia and other sections of East Africa were forming, and by the mid-16th century Ethiopia would have fallen to Islamic forces were it not for military intervention by the Portuguese.

[34] Some say Henry promoted his brother's sanctity in order to draw attention away from him. While this may be true, it is well-documented that Henry was deeply distraught by his brother's death.

[35] Boulton, D'Arcy. <u>The Knights of the Crown: The Monarchial Orders of Knighthood in Later Medieval Europe, 1325-1520.</u> Boydell Press. Woodbridge. 2000. Page 348.

[36] John Calvin called Islam the "other horn" of the Antichrist, with the former being the Pope.

[37] The saying in Dutch was "Liever Turks dan Paaps." For more information, see Schmidt, Benjamin. <u>Innocence Abroad: The Dutch Imagination and the New World, 1570-1670.</u> Cambridge University Press. Cambridge. 2001. Pages 103-105.

[38] For a copy of said letters in full text with a discussion about the circumstances of the times, see Rosedale, Rev. H.G. Queen Elizabeth and the Levant Company. London. 1904.

[39] There are many excellent writings about this. While there has been debate about the degree of collusion, there is no question that rebellious Moriscos and the Ottomans directly funded and colluded with leaders of the Protestant movements in the hopes of dividing the Church as to seek a means to invade and Islamize Europe. There are two studies of particular interest on this matter:

Barton, Edward and Pears, Edwin. The Spanish Armada and the Ottoman Porte. English Historical Review. Vol. 8. No. 31. July 1893. Pages 439-466.

Hess, Andrew. The Moriscos: an Ottoman Fifth Column in Sixteenth-Century Spain. The American Historical Review. Vol. 74. No. 1. October 1968. Pages 1-25.

[40] See Appendix E for a copy of the fatwa.

[41] His real name was Herman de Strijcker, but he is more popularly known as Herman Moded.

[42] Geuzenpenning from the Rijksmuseum, Amsterdam, Holland. Photo taken by Kees38 on July 7th, 2006. Licensed under the terms of the Creative Commons Attribution/Share-alike Unported License 3.0. Other similar copies of the metal can be found in the Stedelijk Museum de Lakenhal in Leiden as well as the Rijksmuseum in Amsterdam.

[43] Persia was gradually conquered by Islamic armies beginning in 633 through 644, and the country mass converted to Islam. After the Sunni-Shia split in 656, Persia remained a Sunni-Muslim majority nation and produced some of Islam's most renowned scholars such as Ahmad ibn Hanbal. During the late 15th century, Shiite Muslim missionaries from southern Lebanon began proselytizing in the areas of modern-day Azerbaijan, southeastern Turkey, and western Iran. In 1501 when Shah Ismail I established the Safavid Dynasty, he ordered

the mass conversion of Persia to Shia Islam from Sunnism, and the country has remained a Shia-majority since.

[44] Stephen the Great monument, Chisnau, Moldavia. Photo taken by Myrabella on August 3rd, 2012. Licensed under the terms of the Creative Commons Attribution/Share-alike Unported License 3.0.

[45] Her name was Cecilia Venier-Baffo. She was the daughter of Venetian nobleman Nicolo Venier and Violante Baffo. She was captured during an Ottoman raid on the island of Paros where Nicolo served as Lord. Upon her being placed into Sultan Selim II's harem and later being married to him, she was renamed Nurbanu Sultan.

[46] See Appendix F for a copy of Sultan Murad III's letter to the Calvinists, who he called "Lutherans," in Spain and Flanders.

[47] Our Lady of Guadalupe from the Basilica of Our Lady of Guadalupe, Mexico. Photo taken by Katsam on December 6th, 2006. Licensed under the terms of the Creative Commons Attribution/Share-alike License 3.0.

[48] For an interesting account of the events, see Hakluyt, Richard. The Principal Navigations, Voyages, Traffiques, and Discoveries of the English Nation. Vol V. Macmillan & Co. Glasgow. 1904. Pages 118.152.

[49] For a discussion about the Moriscos, see Hess, Andrew. The Moriscos: an Ottoman Fifth Column In Sixteenth-Century Spain. The American Historical review. Vol. 74. No. 1. October 1968. Pages 1-25.

[50] King Ferdinand and Queen Isabella statues from the Sabatini Gardens in Madrid. Photos taken by Luis Garcia on July 1st, 2007. Licensed under the terms of the Creative Commons Attribution/Share-alike Generic License 2.0.

[51] French painter Alfred Dehodencq's (1822 – 1882) painting, Les Adieux du Roi Boabdil a Grenade, has one of the most emotive expressions of "The Moor's last sigh."

[52] The Jews are most often spoken about with regard to the Inquisition. However, most of the persons the Inquisition focused on were the Moriscos. In all cases, the Inquisition was not directed at persons who openly professed to be Jews or Muslims, but rather at the Church in order to root out those who claimed to be Catholic converts from Islam or Judaism but in reality were not.

[53] It should be noted that the Alhambra Decree pertained to the expulsion of the Jews and did not address Muslims or Islam. However, it was the first step towards the expulsion of the Muslims because the Spanish government did not trust either group. The Muslims were not trusted because in addition to the eight centuries of fighting the Reconquista, the continual, systematic, and dangerous Islamic rebellions that began almost immediately after Granada's capitulation threatened to and nearly reestablished the Andalusian Caliphate within Spain. From the perspective of the Spanish government, crushing the Islamic rebellions included rooting out any rebel or potential rebel sympathizers. From their viewpoint, this included not just Muslims but also Jews and later Protestants. The situation with the Jews was particularly aggravated by poor contemporary relations within Spain and mistrust held from the historical assistance some Jews provided in facilitating the Islamic invasion of Spain in 711. Nevertheless, this does not change or minimize the scandal which the Alhambra Declaration caused. Pope Alexander VI, who was one of Queen Isabella and King Ferdinand's closest friends and supporters, was also one of the greatest vocal opponents in the Church against the Declaration and whose fervent protests were openly ignored by the Monarchs. These points are brought up as a reminder that the Alhambra Decree must be understood in its historical context. They do not ignore the practical problems and grave moral wrongs which were committed against Jews as well as Muslims because of the Alhambra Decree and the ensuing expulsion of the Mudéjars in 1500.

[54] Diu Island was a shipping point from the Far East. Part of Alfonso's goal was to trade directly with India and other Asian nations in order to economically paralyze the Muslim world. Since the Venetians made most of their income through purchasing and shipping goods carried by the Muslim traders, the newly-emerging Portuguese trade routes were a potential threat to Venice's economy.

[55] He was originally buried at Our Lady of the Hill church, but his body was moved a half century later.

[56] See Appendix E for a copy of the Fatwa.

[57] Memorial of Mohács. Photo taken by Antoine Sipos on October 23rd, 2009. Licensed under the terms of the Creative Commons Attribution/Share-alike Generic License 2.0.

[58] Technically, the first Holy League was established as part of the First Italian War from 1494 and 1498. The leagues are numbered and described here as they specifically relate to Islam.

[59] Known as Barbarossa because of his red beard, he was a Greek convert to Islam and one of the most infamous pirates in Islamic history.

[60] Also known as the Gulf of Corinth.

[61] His two elder brothers died before they could ascend to the Ottoman throne.

[62] The last Byzantine Emperor, Constantine XI and his father, Emperor John VIII, were both converts to the Catholic Faith along with many family members.

[63] Yahya means "John" in Arabic and Turkish.

[64] Under Islamic law, the Caliphate (or Sultanate) passes to the first-born son. There is a debate about legitimate versus illegitimate children in Islam and inheritance rights which has continued throughout the centuries. However, there is a strong consensus based on Quran 2:134, 2;141, 53:38-39, as well as other passages and Islamic sacred tradition that all children, legitimate or illegitimate, possess equal inheritance rights, with the only differentiations being made upon (a) order of birth and (b) gender as specified under Islamic law. Therefore, while Sultan Yahya is sometimes referred to as a false

sultan, a strong case based on Islamic law can be made for his claims of legitimacy to the Sultanate over those of his half-brother Ahmet.

[65] Dervishes were members of a sect of Sufi Islam based in Turkey and founded by the famed Sufi Muslim mystic and poet Jalal Ad-Din Rumi. They are sometimes called "Whirling Dervishes" because during various religious dances for worship they work themselves into religious ecstasy by whirling about.

[66] Some sources suggest he died in a monastery.

Section IV

[1] The city corresponds with the modern Kahramamarash, Turkey.

[2] Armenian Tigranakert/Diarbekir and Edessa/Urfa. ed. Richard Hovannisian. UCLA Armenian History and Culture Studies. Mazda Publishers. Costa Mesa. 2006. Page 359.

[3] In addition to the 447 that were martyred along with Bl. Archbishop Maloyan, a total of 862 Catholics were arrested. It is likely that they were martyred as well, but at a different location. In addition, there were also many other Christians who suffered terribly. These included the Eastern and Oriental Orthodox Greek and Armenian peoples, the Assyrian Church of the East, and the minority Protestant communities which had been established in the Ottoman Empire during the 19th century by English and American missionaries. As far as the Ottomans were concerned, the difference between the various Christian sects was irrelevant because it was their belief in Christ's divinity that justified their mass murder.

[4] While the Armenian Genocide targeted Armenians, it was not limited to just them. Many other peoples suffered, including the Pontic Greeks along the Black Sea coast and the Assyrian people. The real target of the genocide was not so much a racial extermination, but rather the forced Islamization of these peoples on account of their resistance to the Ottoman Empire after centuries of domination. It is probably more accurately described as a Christian genocide in that the

Ottoman Empire's goal was they systemic extermination of Christianity from Anatolia and its surrounding territories.

[5] Also known as "Limone San Giovanni."

[6] Sometimes written as "Peterwaredein."

[7] Keene, H.G. The Fall of the Mogul Empire of Hindustan. Oxford. 1887. Pages 70-71.

[8] "Begum" is the hinduized form of the Turkish word "Beğ," meaning "leader."

[9] Matthew 16:18.

[10] Photo taken in London on September 16th, 2006 by Reuters News Service. Photographer's name is unknown. Licensed under the terms of the Creative Commons Attribution/Share-alike Unported License 3.0.

[11] Mulla, Fr. Paul. Cheminemets Spirituels. Études Journal. Paris. October 1959. Pages 69-79.

[12] Matthew 10:33

[13] John 14:6

Appendix B

[1] Originally translated from At-Turtushi, Imam Abu Bakr bin Muhammad bin Al-Walid Al-Fihri. <u>Siraj Al-Muluk</u>. Chapter 51. Pages 109-110. Pact of 'Umar translation and notes copyrighted (©) by author. Used with permission.

[2] A kind of hat worn by Muslims during the Middle Ages.

[3] A brightly colored belt non-Muslims living Islamic societies were required to wear to distinguish them from Muslims. Removing it was a sign of conversion to Islam. St. Elias of Heliopolis was tricked into removing this by his employer to later accuse him of converting to Islam when he did not.

[4] Arabic for an Islamic school of thought or opinion.

[5] Arabic for scholars of Islam.

[6] Dar Al-Islam means "House of Islam," and is used to describe lands were Islam is dominant. This is in comparison to "Dar Al-Harb," meaning "House of War," which is the non-Muslim world. This comparison was most famously made in said terms by the 14th century Muslim theologian Ibn Taymiyya.

[7] Islamic sacred tradition.

[8] Meaning that while it was legally permissible by Islamic standards, it was frequently denied.

Appendix C

[1] Ad-Dabbi, Ahmad bin Yahya bin Ahmad bin 'Umayra Abu Ja'far. Bughiyah Al-Multamis fi Tarikh Rijal Ahl Al-Andalus. Madrid. 1885. Page 259. The version of Ad-Dabbi which I used was published by Dar Al-'Arabi in Cairo in 1967, and the text was located on Page 273. Translation and notes copyrighted (©) by author. Used with permission. For a comparative English translation, see the entry The Treaty of Tudmir in Reading the Middle Ages: Sources from Europe, Byzantium, and the Islamic World. ed. Barbara H. Rosenwein. Peterborough, Ontario. Broadview. 2006. Page 92.

[2] i.e. be forcibly taken and converted to Islam.

[3] Meaning forced conversions to Islam.

[4] Bello is written as "Ello" in the text.

[5] Alicante is both a municipality and a region in the Valencian community in southern Spain near Murcia. It includes the cities of Orihuela, Bigastro, and Lorca. Mula is found within Murcia. Valentilla likely refers to Valencia, which is just north of these cities with the exception of Bello. There are two regions named "Bello" in Spain, but the most likely is Bello in Jiloca County, as it is north of Valencia and likely followed in the path of Islamic armies as they marched up the eastern Spanish coastline.

[6] Compare these stipulations with those of the Pact of 'Umar.

[7] In classical times, the dinar was made of solid gold, and weighed approximately 4.25 grams. The weight of these coins has varied up to 4.5 grams, and is the equivalent of the Roman *solidus* coin.

[8] The term "measure" here is "amdud," which literally means "extensions" and refers to the amount that a man could give ("extend") to another in the palm of his hand. This has been subject to various interpretations by Islamic scholars, but equals approximately between 508 and 607 grams. Thus each person was expected to

provide the modern equivalent of between 14.88 and 17.6 ounces of each requested item per year, or approximately two cups.

[9] The term used here is "Aqsat." This is half of a "Sa'a," which is another traditional unit of measurement. As with the dinar, values change with culture and time. But under the Hanafi school of interpreting Islamic law it is equivalent to approximately 57 ounces of fluid, or approximately one cup short of a half-gallon.

Appendix D

[1] Taken from Tabari, Muhammad ibn Jarir. <u>The History of Al-Tabari</u>. Reprinted by Dar Al-Kotob Al-Ilmiya. Beirut. 1986. Vol V. Pages 303-305. Translation and notes copyrighted (©) by author. Used with permission.

For a comparative translation in English, see <u>The History of Al-Tabari Volume 34: Incipient Decline</u>. Trans. Joel L. Kraemer. SUNY Press. Albany. 1989. Pages 89-94.

[2] 850.

[3] By this, he is also referring to the Jews.

[4] The word used here can mean either a church or a synagogue, since the command applies to both Christians and Jews.

[5] i.e. destroyed.

[6] Meaning "religions."

[7] Quran 16:90.

[8] Quran 5:3.

[9] Quran 5:3.

[10] Meaning one who has nursed from the same woman or women. There is a concept in pre-Islamic Arab culture which passed into Islam that a filial relationship develops between babies who nurse from the same woman or women as well as the woman nursing. As such, any kind of intimate relationship between such persons at a later point during their lives would be regarded as incestuous.

[11] Quran 4:23-27.

[12] Quran 5:90-92.

[13] i.e. alcohol

[14] Compare with Quran 8:42-44.

[15] A kustij is a thick, colored rope which was worn by dhimmis under the zunar. It is similar to a girdle and is originally borrowed from Persian, as the kustij was traditionally used prior to Islam in Zoroastrianism as a ritual garment to signify the passage of youth into manhood.

[16] Between April 18th and May 17th of 850.

Appendix E

[1] Taken from the Arabic as narrated in Gaudeul, Jean-Marie. Encounters and Clashes: Texts. Pontifico Istituto di Studi Arabi e Islamici. Rome. 1984. Translation of the Arabic document and textual notes copyrighted (©) 2012 by author. Used with permission.

[2] The Quran.

[3] Many Muslims incorrectly believed that Christians worshipped idols. This was similar to how many European Catholics of the same period likewise incorrectly believed that Muslims worshipped idols.

[4] Ritual washing and ablution with dirt or dry matter as opposed to water.

[5] The direction of the Ka'ba, which Muslims face when they pray.

[6] Meaning that one can pray not facing the Ka'ba if he is unable to.

[7] It might be a Spanish language corruption of the Arabic word "mumit," meaning "dead," suggesting that Muhammad is a "dead" prophet as opposed to Jesus, who rose from the dead.

[8] Many Moriscos were in communication with the Ottomans, hoping that they would assist their rebellions. However much money and military aid they clandestinely shipped to Spain, the Ottomans were never able to fully come to the aid of the Moriscos because of other commitments they had in building their empire across the world.

Appendix F

[1] Her name was Roxelana, and she was a very famous woman in Ottoman history.

[2] Their names were Cecilia Venier-Baffo and Sofia Baffo respectively. Given the names, it is suspected they two may have been related. See Section III, note 45.

[3] Taken from the Mecmua-yı münşeat-i Feridun Bey by Feridun Bey. Reprinted by Darüttıbattil'âmire between 1848 and 1857 in Istanbul. Vol. II. Pages 450-452. (Sequences 1148-1150). Courtesy of Widener Library, Harvard University, Prince Alwaleed bin Talal Islamic Studies Program, Open Collections Program, Islamic Heritage Project. Cambridge, MA. Rendition of the Ottoman document and textual notes copyrighted (©) 2012 by author. Used with permission.

Since Feridun Bey died in 1583 and Sultan Murad III reigned from 1574 to 1595, the letter dates from before 1583. It was likely written between 1579 and 1580, as this was when Murad began his attempts to establish strong alliances with Protestants in Western Europe.

[4] Turkish "sect"

[5] Flanders in a region that encompasses parts of France, Belgium, and Holland.

[6] Turkish "Vizier"

[7] Turkish "Beğ"

[8] Turkish "Beğzade"

[9] Turkish "Khan"

[10] Turkish "Viziers"

[11] Turkish "crucible." This word probably derives from the Zoroastrian concept of an altar, as fire was central to worship. Zoroastrian temples

were known as "fire temples," and fires were kindled on their altars during religious rituals.

[12] lit. "all the embers"

[13] Word used here is Madhhab, meaning "school of thought" or "way of thinking" as it pertains to Islam.

[14] i.e. Allah

[15] i.e. Istanbul and the sultan's command.

[16] lit. "marriage"

[17] lit. "belching."